Centerville Library
Washington-Centerville Public Library
DISCARD
Centerville, Ohio

THE THEATRE OF TENNESSEE WILLIAMS

Volume III

By TENNESSEE WILLIAMS

THE THEATRE OF
TENNESSEE WILLIAMS

Volume III

Cat on a Hot Tin Roof

Orpheus Descending

Suddenly Last Summer

A NEW DIRECTIONS BOOK

Copyright © 1971 by Tennessee Williams

All rights reserved. Except for brief passages quoted in a newspaper, magazine, radio, or television review, no part of this book may be reproduced in any form or by any means, electronic or mechanical, including photocopying and recording, or by any information storage and retrieval system, without permission in writing from the Publisher.

Inquiries concerning the amateur acting rights of these plays should be directed to The Dramatists' Play Service, Inc., 440 Park Avenue South, New York, New York 10016, without whose permission in writing no amateur performance may be given.

CAUTION: Professionals and amateurs are hereby warned that THE GLASS MENAGERIE, being fully protected under the copyright laws of the United States of America, the British Empire including the Dominion of Canada, and all other countries of the Copyright Union, is subject to royalty. All rights, including professional, amateur, motion picture, recitation, lecturing, public reading, radio-broadcasting, and the rights of translation into foreign languages, are strictly reserved. Particular emphasis is laid on the question of readings, permission for which must be secured from the author's agent in writing. All inquiries should be addressed to the author's agent, Tom Erhardt, Casarotto Ramsay Ltd., National House, 60-66 Wardour Street, London W1V 311P, England.

Contents

CAT ON A HOT TIN ROOF

And you, my father, there on the sad height,
Curse, bless, me now with your fierce tears, I pray.
Do not go gentle into that good night.
Rage, rage against the dying of the light!

DYLAN THOMAS

TO AUDREY WOOD

Copyright © 1954, 1955 by Tennessee Williams

The quotation from Dylan Thomas is from "Do Not Go Gentle Into That Good Night" in *The Collected Poems of Dylan Thomas*, Copyright 1952 by Dylan Thomas, published by New Directions.

Grateful acknowledgement is made to *The New York Times Sunday Drama Section* in which the article "Person-to-Person" first appeared.

PERSON—TO—PERSON

Of course it is a pity that so much of all creative work is so closely related to the personality of the one who does it.

It is sad and embarrassing and unattractive that those emotions that stir him deeply enough to demand expression, and to charge their expression with some measure of light and power, are nearly all rooted, however changed in their surface, in the particular and sometimes peculiar concerns of the artist himself, that special world, the passions and images of it that each of us weaves about him from birth to death, a web of monstrous complexity, spun forth at a speed that is incalculable to a length beyond measure, from the spider mouth of his own singular perceptions.

It is a lonely idea, a lonely condition, so terrifying to think of that we usually don't. And so we talk to each other, write and wire each other, call each other short and long distance across land and sea, clasp hands with each other at meeting and at parting, fight each other and even destroy each other because of this always somewhat thwarted effort to break through walls to each other. As a character in a play once said, "We're all of us sentenced to solitary confinement inside our own skins."

Personal lyricism is the outcry of prisoner to prisoner from the cell in solitary where each is confined for the duration of his life.

I once saw a group of little girls on a Mississippi sidewalk all dolled up in their mothers' and sisters' castoff finery, ol raggedy ball gowns and plumed hats and high-heeled slippe enacting a meeting of ladies in a parlor with a perfect mimi of polite Southern gush and simper. But one child was not satisfied with the attention paid her enraptured performance by the others, they were too involved in their own performances to suit her, so she stretched out her skinny arms and threw back her skinny neck and shrieked to the deaf heavens and her equally oblivious playmates, "Look at me, look at me, look at me!"

And then her mother's high-heeled slippers threw her off balance and she fell to the sidewalk in a great howling tangle of soiled white satin and torn pink net, and still nobody looked at her.

I wonder if she is not, now, a Southern writer.

Of course it is not only Southern writers, of lyrical bent, who engage in such histrionics and shout, "Look at me!" Perhaps it is a parable of all artists. And not always do we topple over and land in a tangle of trappings that don't fit us. However, it is well to be aware of that peril, and not to content yourself with a demand for attention, to know that out of your personal lyricism, your sidewalk histrionics, something has to be created that will not only attract observers but participants in the performance.

I try very hard to do that.

The fact that I want you to observe what I do for your possible pleasure and to give you knowledge of things that I feel I may know better than you, because my world is different from yours, as different as every man's world is from the world of others, is not enough excuse for a personal lyricism that has not yet mastered its necessary trick of rising above the singular to the plural concern, from personal to general import. But for years and years now, which may have passed like a dream because of this obsession, I have been trying to learn how to

4

perform this trick and make it truthful, and sometimes I feel that I am able to do it. Sometimes, when the enraptured street-corner performer in me cries out "Look at me!," I feel that my hazardous footwear and fantastic regalia may not quite throw me off balance. Then, suddenly, you fellow performers in the sidewalk show may turn to give me your attention and allow me to hold it, at least for the interval between 8:40 and 11 something P.M.

Eleven years ago this month of March, when I was far closer than I knew, only nine months away from that long-delayed, but always expected, something that I lived for, the time when I would first catch and hold an audience's attention, I wrote my first preface to a long play. The final paragraph went like this:

"There is too much to say and not enough time to say it. Nor is there power enough. I am not a good writer. Sometimes I am a very bad writer indeed. There is hardly a successful writer in the field who cannot write circles around me . . . but I think of writing as something more organic than words, something closer to being and action. I want to work more and more with a more plastic theatre than the one I have (worked with) before. I have never for one moment doubted that there are people—millions!—to say things to. We come to each other, gradually, but with love. It is the short reach of my arms that hinders, not the length and multiplicity of theirs. With love and with honesty, the embrace is inevitable."

This characteristically emotional, if not rhetorical, statement of mine at that time seems to suggest that I thought of myself as having a highly personal, even intimate relationship with people who go to see plays. I did and I still do. A morbid shyness once prevented me from having much direct communication with people, and possibly that is why I began to write

5

to them plays and stories. But even now when that tongue-locking, face-flushing, silent and crouching timidity has worn off with the passage of the troublesome youth that it sprang from, I still find it somehow easier to "level with" crowds of strangers in the hushed twilight of orchestra and balcony sections of theatres than with individuals across a table from me. Their being strangers somehow makes them more familiar and more approachable, easier to talk to.

Of course I know that I have sometimes presumed too much upon corresponding sympathies and interest in those to whom I talk boldly, and this has led to rejections that were painful and costly enough to inspire more prudence. But when I weigh one thing against another, an easy liking against a hard respect, the balance always tips the same way, and whatever the risk of being turned a cold shoulder, I still don't want to talk to people only about the surface aspects of their lives, the sort of things that acquaintances laugh and chatter about on ordinary social occasions.

I feel that they get plenty of that, and heaven knows so do I, before and after the little interval of time in which I have their attention and say what I have to say to them. The discretion of social conversation, even among friends, is exceeded only by the discretion of "the deep six," that grave wherein nothing is mentioned at all. Emily Dickinson, that lyrical spinster of Amherst, Massachusetts, who wore a strict and savage heart on a taffeta sleeve, commented wryly on that kind of posthumous discourse among friends in these lines:

> *I died for beauty, but was scarce*
> *Adjusted in the tomb,*
> *When one who died for truth was lain*
> *In an adjoining room.*

He questioned softly why I failed?
"For beauty," I replied.
"And I for truth,—the two are one;
We brethren are," he said.

And so, as kinsmen met a night,
We talked between the rooms,
Until the moss had reached our lips,
And covered up our names.

Meanwhile!—I want to go on talking to you as freely and intimately about what we live and die for as if I knew you better than anyone else whom you know.

Tennessee Williams
1955

CHARACTERS OF THE PLAY

MARGARET

BRICK

MAE, sometimes called Sister Woman

BIG MAMA

DIXIE, a little girl

BIG DADDY

REVEREND TOOKER

GOOPER, sometimes called Brother Man

DOCTOR BAUGH, pronounced "Baw"

LACEY, a Negro servant

SOOKEY, another

Another little girl and two small boys

(The playing script of Act III also includes TRIXIE, another little girl, also DAISY, BRIGHTIE and SMALL, servants.)

Cat on a Hot Tin Roof was presented at the Morosco Theatre in New York on March 24, 1955, by The Playwrights' Company. It was directed by Elia Kazan; the stage sets were designed by Jo Mielziner, and the costumes by Lucinda Ballard. The cast was as follows:

LACEY	MAXWELL GLANVILLE
SOOKEY	MUSA WILLIAMS
MARGARET	BARBARA BEL GEDDES
BRICK	BEN GAZZARA
MAE	MADELEINE SHERWOOD
GOOPER	PAT HINGLE
BIG MAMA	MILDRED DUNNOCK
DIXIE	PAULINE HAHN
BUSTER	DARRYL RICHARD
SONNY	SETH EDWARDS
TRIXIE	JANICE DUNN
BIG DADDY	BURL IVES
REVEREND TOOKER	FRED STEWART
DOCTOR BAUGH	R. G. ARMSTRONG
DAISY	EVA VAUGHAN SMITH
BRIGHTIE	BROWNIE McGHEE
SMALL	SONNY TERRY

SKETCH OF STAGE SETTING FOR THE NEW YORK PRODUCTION BY JO MIELZINER

NOTES FOR THE DESIGNER

The set is the bed-sitting-room of a plantation home in the Mississippi Delta. It is along an upstairs gallery which probably runs around the entire house; it has two pairs of very wide doors opening onto the gallery, showing white balustrades against a fair summer sky that fades into dusk and night during the course of the play, which occupies precisely the time of its performance, excepting, of course, the fifteen minutes of intermission.

Perhaps the style of the room is not what you would expect in the home of the Delta's biggest cotton-planter. It is Victorian with a touch of the Far East. It hasn't changed much since it was occupied by the original owners of the place, Jack Straw and Peter Ochello, a pair of old bachelors who shared this room all their lives together. In other words, the room must evoke some ghosts; it is gently and poetically haunted by a relationship that must have involved a tenderness which was uncommon. This may be irrelevant or unnecessary, but I once saw a reproduction of a faded photograph of the verandah of Robert Louis Stevenson's home on that Samoan Island where he spent his last years, and there was a quality of tender light on weathered wood, such as porch furniture made of bamboo and wicker, exposed to tropical suns and tropical rains, which came to mind when I thought about the set for this play, bringing also to mind the grace and comfort of light, the reassurance it gives, on a late and fair afternoon in summer, the way that no matter what, even dread of death, is gently touched and soothed by it. For the set is the background for a play that deals with human extremities of emotion, and it needs that softness behind it.

15

The bathroom door, showing only pale-blue tile and silver towel racks, is in one side wall; the hall door in the opposite wall. Two articles of furniture need mention: a big double bed which staging should make a functional part of the set as often as suitable, the surface of which should be slightly raked to make figures on it seen more easily; and against the wall space between the two huge double doors upstage: a monumental monstrosity peculiar to our times, a *huge* console combination of radio-phonograph (hi-fi with three speakers) TV set *and* liquor cabinet, bearing and containing many glasses and bottles, all in one piece, which is a composition of muted silver tones, and the opalescent tones of reflecting glass, a chromatic link, this thing, between the sepia (tawny gold) tones of the interior and the cool (white and blue) tones of the gallery and sky. This piece of furniture (?!), this monument, is a very complete and compact little shrine to virtually all the comforts and illusions behind which we hide from such things as the characters in the play are faced with. . . .

The set should be far less realistic than I have so far implied in this description of it. I think the walls below the ceiling should dissolve mysteriously into air; the set should be roofed by the sky; stars and moon suggested by traces of milky pallor, as if they were observed through a telescope lens out of focus.

Anything else I can think of? Oh, yes, fanlights (transoms shaped like an open glass fan) above all the doors in the set, with panes of blue and amber, and above all, the designer should take as many pains to give the actors room to move about freely (to show their restlessness, their passion for breaking out) as if it were a set for a ballet.

An evening in summer. The action is continuous, with two intermissions.

16

ACT ONE

At the rise of the curtain someone is taking a shower in the bathroom, the door of which is half open. A pretty young woman, with anxious lines in her face, enters the bedroom and crosses to the bathroom door.

MARGARET [*shouting above roar of water*]:
One of those no-neck monsters hit me with a hot buttered biscuit so I have t' change!

[*Margaret's voice is both rapid and drawling. In her long speeches she has the vocal tricks of a priest delivering a liturgical chant, the lines are almost sung, always continuing a little beyond her breath so she has to gasp for another. Sometimes she intersperses the lines with a little wordless singing, such as "Da-da-daaaa!"*]

[*Water turns off and Brick calls out to her, but is still unseen. A tone of politely feigned interest, masking indifference, or worse, is characteristic of his speech with Margaret.*]

BRICK:
Wha'd you say, Maggie? Water was on s' loud I couldn't hearya. . . .

MARGARET:
Well, I!—just remarked that!—one of th' no-neck monsters messed up m' lovely lace dress so I got t'—cha-a-ange. . . .

[*She opens and kicks shut drawers of the dresser.*]

BRICK:
Why d'ya call Gooper's kiddies no-neck monsters?

MARGARET:
Because they've got no necks! Isn't that a good enough reason?

17

BRICK:
Don't they have any necks?

MARGARET:
None visible. Their fat little heads are set on their fat little bodies without a bit of connection.

BRICK:
That's too bad.

MARGARET:
Yes, it's too bad because you can't wring their necks if they've got no necks to wring! Isn't that right, honey?

[*She steps out of her dress, stands in a slip of ivory satin and lace.*]

Yep, they're no-neck monsters, all no-neck people are monsters . . .

[*Children shriek downstairs.*]

Hear them? Hear them screaming? I don't know where their voice boxes are located since they don't have necks. I tell you I got so nervous at that table tonight I thought I would throw back my head and utter a scream you could hear across the Arkansas border an' parts of Louisiana an' Tennessee. I said to your charming sister-in-law, Mae, honey, couldn't you feed those precious little things at a separate table with an oilcloth cover? They make such a mess an' the lace cloth looks *so* pretty! She made enormous eyes at me and said, "Ohhh, noooooo! On Big Daddy's birthday? Why, he would never forgive me!" Well, I want you to know, Big Daddy hadn't been at the table two minutes with those five no-neck monsters slobbering and drooling over their food before he threw down his fork an' shouted, "Fo' God's sake, Gooper, why

18

don't you put them pigs at a trough in th' kitchen?"—Well, I swear, I simply could have di-ieed!

Think of it, Brick, they've got five of them and number six is coming. They've brought the whole bunch down here like animals to display at a county fair. Why, they have those children doin' tricks all the time! "Junior, show Big Daddy how you do this, show Big Daddy how you do that, say your little piece fo' Big Daddy, Sister. Show your dimples, Sugar. Brother, show Big Daddy how you stand on your head!"—It goes on all the time, along with constant little remarks and innuendos about the fact that you and I have not produced any children, are totally childless and therefore totally useless! —Of course it's comical but it's also disgusting since it's so obvious what they're up to!

BRICK [*without interest*]:
What are they up to, Maggie?

MARGARET:
Why, you know what they're up to!

BRICK [*appearing*]:
No, I don't know what they're up to.

[*He stands there in the bathroom doorway drying his hair with a towel and hanging onto the towel rack because one ankle is broken, plastered and bound. He is still slim and firm as a boy. His liquor hasn't started tearing him down outside. He has the additional charm of that cool air of detachment that people have who have given up the struggle. But now and then, when disturbed, something flashes behind it, like lightning in a fair sky, which shows that at some deeper level he is far from peaceful. Perhaps in a stronger light he would show some signs of deliques-*

19

cence, but the fading, still warm, light from the gallery treats him gently.]

MARGARET:
I'll tell you what they're up to, boy of mine!—They're up to cutting you out of your father's estate, and—

[*She freezes momentarily before her next remark. Her voice drops as if it were somehow a personally embarassing admission.*]

—Now we know that Big Daddy's dyin' of—*cancer.* . . .

[*There are voices on the lawn below: long-drawn calls across distance. Margaret raises her lovely bare arms and powders her armpits with a light sigh.*

[*She adjusts the angle of a magnifying mirror to straighten an eyelash, then rises fretfully saying:*]

There's so much light in the room it—

BRICK [*softly but sharply*]:
Do we?

MARGARET:
Do we what?

BRICK:
Know Big Daddy's dyin' of cancer?

MARGARET:
Got the report today.

BRICK:
Oh . . .

MARGARET [*letting down bamboo blinds which cast long, gold-fretted shadows over the room*]:

20

Yep, got th' report just now . . . it didn't surprise me, Baby.
. . .

[*Her voice has range, and music; sometimes it drops low as a boy's and you have a sudden image of her playing boy's games as a child.*]

I recognized the symptoms soon's we got here last spring and I'm willin' to bet you that Brother Man and his wife were pretty sure of it, too. That more than likely explains why their usual summer migration to the coolness of the Great Smokies was passed up this summer in favor of—hustlin' down here ev'ry whipstitch with their whole screamin' tribe! And why so many allusions have been made to Rainbow Hill lately. You know what Rainbow Hill is? Place that's famous for treatin' alcoholics an dope fiends in the movies!

BRICK:
I'm not in the movies.

MARGARET:
No, and you don't take dope. Otherwise you're a perfect candidate for Rainbow Hill, Baby, and that's where they aim to ship you—over my dead body! Yep, over my dead body they'll ship you there, but nothing would please them better. Then Brother Man could get a-hold of the purse strings and dole out remittances to us, maybe get power of attorney and sign checks for us and cut off our credit wherever, whenever he wanted! Son-of-a-bitch!—How'd you like that, Baby?— Well, you've been doin' just about ev'rything in your power to bring it about, you've just been doin' ev'rything you can think of to aid and abet them in this scheme of theirs! Quittin' work, devoting yourself to the occupation of drinkin'! —Breakin' your ankle last night on the high school athletic field: doin' what? Jumpin' hurdles? At two or three in the

21

morning? Just fantastic! Got in the paper. *Clarksdale Register* carried a nice little item about it, human interest story about a well-known former athlete stagin' a one-man track meet on the Glorious Hill High School athletic field last night, but was slightly out of condition and didn't clear the first hurdle! Brother Man Gooper claims he exercised his influence t' keep it from goin' out over AP or UP or every goddam "P."

But, Brick? You still have one big advantage!

[*During the above swift flood of words, Brick has reclined with contrapuntal leisure on the snowy surface of the bed and has rolled over carefully on his side or belly.*]

BRICK [*wryly*]:
Did you *say* something, Maggie?

MARGARET:
Big Daddy dotes on you, honey. And he can't stand Brother Man and Brother Man's wife, that monster of fertility, Mae; she's downright odious to him! Know how I know? By little expressions that flicker over his face when that woman is holding fo'th on one of her choice topics such as—how she refused twilight sleep!—when the twins were delivered! Because she feels motherhood's an experience that a woman ought to experience fully!—in order to fully appreciate the wonder and beauty of it! HAH!

[*This loud "HAH!" is accompanied by a violent action such as slamming a drawer shut.*]

—and how she made Brother Man come in an' stand beside her in the delivery room so he would not miss out on the "wonder and beauty" of it either!—producin' those no-neck monsters. . . .

[*A speech of this kind would be antipathetic from almost anybody but Margaret; she makes it oddly funny, because her eyes constantly twinkle and her voice shakes with laughter which is basically indulgent.]*

—Big Daddy shares my attitude toward those two! As for me, well—I give him a laugh now and then and he tolerates me. In fact!—I sometimes suspect that Big Daddy harbors a little unconscious "lech" fo' me. . . .

BRICK:

What makes you think that Big Daddy has a lech for you, Maggie?

MARGARET:

Way he always drops his eyes down my body when I'm talkin' to him, drops his eyes to my boobs an' licks his old chops! Ha ha!

BRICK:

That kind of talk is disgusting.

MARGARET:

Did anyone ever tell you that you're an ass-aching Puritan, Brick?

I think it's mighty fine that that ole fellow, on the doorstep of death, still takes in my shape with what I think is deserved appreciation!

And you wanta know something else? Big Daddy didn't know how many little Maes and Goopers had been produced! "How many kids have you got?" he asked at the table, just like Brother Man and his wife were new acquaintances to him! Big Mama said he was jokin', but that ole boy wasn't jokin', Lord, no!

And when they infawmed him that they had five already and were turning out number six!—the news seemed to come as a sort of unpleasant surprise . . .

23

[*Children yell below.*]

Scream, monsters!

[*Turns to Brick with a sudden, gay, charming smile which fades as she notices that he is not looking at her but into fading gold space with a troubled expression.*

[*It is constant rejection that makes her humor "bitchy."*]

Yes, you should of been at that supper-table, Baby.

[*Whenever she calls him "baby" the word is a soft caress.*]

Y'know, Big Daddy, bless his ole sweet soul, he's the dearest ole thing in the world, but he does hunch over his food as if he preferred not to notice anything else. Well, Mae an' Gooper were side by side at the table, direckly across from Big Daddy, watchin' his face like hawks while they jawed an' jabbered about the cuteness an' brillance of th' no-neck monsters!

[*She giggles with a hand fluttering at her throat and her breast and her long throat arched.*

[*She comes downstage and recreates the scene with voice and gesture.*]

And the no-neck monsters were ranged around the table, some in high chairs and some on th' *Books of Knowledge,* all in fancy little paper caps in honor of Big Daddy's birthday, and all through dinner, well, I want you to know that Brother Man an' his partner never once, for one moment, stopped exchanging pokes an' pinches an' kicks an' signs an' signals! —Why, they were like a couple of cardsharps fleecing a sucker.—Even Big Mama, bless her ole sweet soul, she isn't th' quickest an' brightest thing in the world, she finally noticed, at last, an' said to Gooper, "Gooper, what are you an'

Mae makin' all these signs at each other about?"—I swear t' goodness, I nearly choked on my chicken!

[*Margaret, back at the dressing table, still doesn't see Brick. He is watching her with a look that is not quite definable —Amused? shocked? contemptuous?—part of those and part of something else.*]

Y'know—your brother Gooper still cherishes the illusion he took a giant step up on the social ladder when he married Miss Mae Flynn of the Memphis Flynns.

[*Margaret moves about the room as she talks, stops before the mirror, moves on.*]

But I have a piece of Spanish news for Gooper. The Flynns never had a thing in this world but money and they lost that, they were nothing at all but fairly successful climbers. Of course, Mae Flynn came out in Memphis eight years before I made my debut in Nashville, but I had friends at Ward-Belmont who came from Memphis and they used to come to see me and I used to go to see them for Christmas and spring vacations, and so I know who rates an' who doesn't rate in Memphis society. Why, y'know ole Papa Flynn, he barely escaped doing time in the Federal pen for shady manipulations on th' stock market when his chain stores crashed, and as for Mae having been a cotton carnival queen, as they remind us so often, lest we forget, well, that's one honor that I don't envy her for!—Sit on a brass throne on a tacky float an' ride down Main Street, smilin', bowin', and blowin' kisses to all the trash on the street—

[*She picks out a pair of .jeweled sandals and rushes to the dressing table.*]

Why, year before last, when Susan McPheeters was singled

25

out fo' that honor, y' know what happened to her? Y'know what happened to poor little Susie McPheeters?

BRICK [*absently*]:
No. What happened to little Susie McPheeters?

MARGARET:
Somebody spit tobacco juice in her face.

BRICK [*dreamily*]:
Somebody spit tobacco juice in her face?

MARGARET:
That's right, some old drunk leaned out of a window in the Hotel Gayoso and yelled, "Hey, Queen, hey, hey, there, Queenie!" Poor Susie looked up and flashed him a radiant smile and he shot out a squirt of tobacco juice right in poor Susie's face.

BRICK:
Well, what d'you know about that.

MARGARET [*gaily*]:
What do I know about it? I was there, I saw it!

BRICK [*absently*]:
Must have been kind of funny.

MARGARET:
Susie didn't think so. Had hysterics. Screamed like a banshee. They had to stop th' parade an' remove her from her throne an' go on with—

[*She catches sight of him in the mirror, gasps slightly, wheels about to face him. Count ten.*]

—Why are you looking at me like that?

BRICK [*whistling softly, now*]:
Like what, Maggie?

MARGARET [*intensely, fearfully*]:
The way y' were lookin' at me just now, befo' I caught your
eye in the mirror and you started t' whistle! I don't know how
t' describe it but it froze my blood!—I've caught you lookin'
at me like that so often lately. What are you thinkin' of
when you look at me like that?

BRICK:
I wasn't conscious of lookin' at you, Maggie.

MARGARET:
Well, I was conscious of it! What were you thinkin'?

BRICK:
I don't remember thinking of anything, Maggie.

MARGARET:
Don't you think I know that—? Don't you—?—Think I
know that—?

BRICK [*coolly*]:
Know *what*, Maggie?

MARGARET [*struggling for expression*]:
That I've gone through this—*hideous!*—*transformation*, become—*hard! Frantic!*

[*Then she adds, almost tenderly:*]

—*cruel!!*

That's what you've been observing in me lately. How could
y' help but observe it? That's all right. I'm not—thin-skinned
any more, can't afford t' be thin-skinned any more.

[*She is now recovering her power.*]

—But Brick? Brick?

BRICK:
Did you say something?

27

MARGARET:

I was *goin'* t' say something: that I get—lonely. Very!

BRICK:

Ev'rybody gets that . . .

MARGARET:

Living with someone you love can be lonelier—than living entirely *alone!*—if the one that y' love doesn't love you. . . .

[*There is a pause. Brick hobbles downstage and asks, without looking at her:*]

BRICK:

Would you like to live alone, Maggie?

[*Another pause: then—after she has caught a quick, hurt breath:*]

MARGARET:

No!—God!—I wouldn't!

[*Another gasping breath. She forcibly controls what must have been an impulse to cry out. We see her deliberately, very forcibly, going all the way back to the world in which you can talk about ordinary matters.*]

Did you have a nice shower?

BRICK:

Uh-huh.

MARGARET:

Was the water cool?

BRICK:

No.

MARGARET:

But it made y' feel fresh, huh?

BRICK:
Fresher. . . .

MARGARET:
I know something would make y' feel *much* fresher!

BRICK:
What?

MARGARET:
An alcohol rub. Or cologne, a rub with cologne!

BRICK:
That's good after a workout but I haven't been workin' out,
Maggie.

MARGARET:
You've kept in good shape, though.

BRICK [*indifferently*]:
You think so, Maggie?

MARGARET:
I always thought drinkin' men lost their looks, but I was
plainly mistaken.

BRICK [*wryly*]:
Why, thanks, Maggie.

MARGARET:
You're the only drinkin' man I know that it never seems t'
put fat on.

BRICK:
I'm gettin' softer, Maggie.

MARGARET:
Well, sooner or later it's bound to soften you up. It was just
beginning to soften up Skipper when—

[*She stops short.*]

I'm sorry. I never could keep my fingers off a sore—I wish you *would* lose your looks. If you did it would make the martyrdom of Saint Maggie a little more bearable. But no such goddam luck. I actually believe you've gotten better looking since you've gone on the bottle. Yeah, a person who didn't know you would think you'd never had a tense nerve in your body or a strained muscle.

[*There are sounds of croquet on the lawn below: the click of mallets, light voices, near and distant.*]

Of course, you always had that detached quality as if you were playing a game without much concern over whether you won or lost, and now that you've lost the game, not lost but just quit playing, you have that rare sort of charm that usually only happens in very old or hopelessly sick people, the charm of the defeated.—You look so cool, so cool, so enviably cool.

[*Music is heard.*]

They're playing croquet. The moon has appeared and it's white, just beginning to turn a little bit yellow. . . .

You were a wonderful lover. . . .

Such a wonderful person to go to bed with, and I think mostly because you were really indifferent to it. Isn't that right? Never had any anxiety about it, did it naturally, easily, slowly, with absolute confidence and perfect calm, more like opening a door for a lady or seating her at a table than giving expression to any longing for her. Your indifference made you wonderful at lovemaking—*strange?*—but true. . . .

You know, if I thought you would never, never, *never* make love to me again—I would go downstairs to the kitchen and pick out the longest and sharpest knife I could find and stick it straight into my heart, I swear that I would!

But one thing I don't have is the charm of the defeated, my hat is still in the ring, and I am determined to win!

[*There is the sound of croquet mallets hitting croquet balls.*]

—What is the victory of a cat on a hot tin roof?—I wish I knew....

Just staying on it, I guess, as long as she can....

[*More croquet sounds.*]

Later tonight I'm going to tell you I love you an' maybe by that time you'll be drunk enough to believe me. Yes, they're playing croquet....

Big Daddy is dying of cancer....

What were you thinking of when I caught you looking at me like that? Were you thinking of Skipper?

[*Brick takes up his crutch, rises.*]

Oh, excuse me, forgive me, but laws of silence don't work! No, laws of silence don't work....

[*Brick crosses to the bar, takes a quick drink, and rubs his head with a towel.*]

Laws of silence don't work....

When something is festering in your memory or your imagination, laws of silence don't work, it's just like shutting a door and locking it on a house on fire in hope of forgetting that the house is burning. But not facing a fire doesn't put it out. Silence about a thing just magnifies it. It grows and festers in silence, becomes malignant....

31

Get dressed, Brick.

[*He drops his crutch.*]

BRICK:
I've dropped my crutch.

[*He has stopped rubbing his hair dry but still stands hanging onto the towel rack in a white towel-cloth robe.*]

MARGARET:
Lean on me.

BRICK:
No, just give me my crutch.

MARGARET:
Lean on my shoulder.

BRICK:
I don't want to lean on your shoulder, I want my crutch!

[*This is spoken like sudden lightning.*]

Are you going to give me my crutch or do I have to get down on my knees on the floor and—

MARGARET:
Here, here, take it, take it!

[*She has thrust the crutch at him.*]

BRICK [*hobbling out*]:
Thanks . . .

MARGARET:
We mustn't scream at each other, the walls in this house have ears. . . .

[*He hobbles directly to liquor cabinet to get a new drink.*]

—but that's the first time I've heard you raise your voice in a long time, Brick. A crack in the wall?—Of composure?

—I think that's a good sign. . . .

A sign of nerves in a player on the defensive!

[*Brick turns and smiles at her coolly over his fresh drink.*]

BRICK:
It just hasn't happened yet, Maggie.

MARGARET:
What?

BRICK:
The click I get in my head when I've had enough of this stuff to make me peaceful. . . .

Will you do me a favor?

MARGARET:
Maybe I will. What favor?

BRICK:
Just, just keep your voice down!

MARGARET [*in a hoarse whisper*]:
I'll do you that favor, I'll speak in a whisper, if not shut up completely, if *you* will do *me* a favor and make that drink your last one till after the party.

BRICK:
What party?

MARGARET:
Big Daddy's birthday party.

BRICK:
Is this Big Daddy's birthday?

MARGARET:

You know this is Big Daddy's birthday!

BRICK:

No, I don't, I forgot it.

MARGARET:

Well, I remembered it for you. . . .

[They are both speaking as breathlessly as a pair of kids after a fight, drawing deep exhausted breaths and looking at each other with faraway eyes, shaking and panting together as if they had broken apart from a violent struggle.]

BRICK:

Good for you, Maggie.

MARGARET:

You just have to scribble a few lines on this card.

BRICK:

You scribble something, Maggie.

MARGARET:

It's got to be your handwriting; it's your present, I've given him my present; it's got to be your handwriting!

[The tension between them is building again, the voices becoming shrill once more.]

BRICK:

I didn't get him a present.

MARGARET:

I got one for you.

BRICK:

All right. You write the card, then.

MARGARET:

And have him know you didn't remember his birthday?

BRICK:
I didn't remember his birthday.

MARGARET:
You don't have to prove you didn't!

BRICK:
I don't want to fool him about it.

MARGARET:
Just write "Love, Brick!" for God's—

BRICK:
No.

MARGARET:
You've *got* to!

BRICK:
I don't have to do anything I don't want to do. You keep forgetting the conditions on which I agreed to stay on living with you.

MARGARET [*out before she knows it*]:
I'm not living with you. We occupy the same cage.

BRICK:
You've got to remember the conditions agreed on.

MARGARET:
They're impossible conditions!

BRICK:
Then why don't you—?

MARGARET:
HUSH! Who is out there? Is somebody at the door?

[*There are footsteps in hall.*]

35

MAE [*outside*]:
May I enter a moment?

MARGARET:
Oh, *you!* Sure. Come in, Mae.

[*Mae enters bearing aloft the bow of a young lady's archery set.*]

MAE:
Brick, is this thing yours?

MARGARET:
Why, Sister Woman—that's my Diana Trophy. Won it at the intercollegiate archery contest on the Ole Miss campus.

MAE:
It's a mighty dangerous thing to leave exposed round a house full of nawmal rid-blooded children attracted t'weapons.

MARGARET:
"Nawmal rid-blooded children attracted t'weapons" ought t'be taught to keep their hands off things that don't belong to them.

MAE:
Maggie, honey, if you had children of your own you'd know how funny that is. Will you please lock this up and put the key out of reach?

MARGARET:
Sister Woman, nobody is plotting the destruction of your kiddies. —Brick and I still have our special archers' license. We're goin' deer-huntin' on Moon Lake as soon as the season starts. I love to run with dogs through chilly woods, run, run leap over obstructions—

36

[*She goes into the closet carrying the bow.*]

MAE:
How's the injured ankle, Brick?

BRICK:
Doesn't hurt. Just itches.

MAE:
Oh, my! Brick—Brick, you should've been downstairs after supper! Kiddies put on a show. Polly played the piano, Buster an' Sonny drums, an' then they turned out the lights an' Dixie an' Trixie puhfawmed a toe dance in fairy costume with *spahkluhs!* Big Daddy just beamed! He just beamed!

MARGARET [*from the closet with a sharp laugh*]:
Oh, I bet. It breaks my heart that we missed it!

[*She reenters.*]

But Mae? Why did y'give dawgs' names to all your kiddies?

MAE:
Dogs' names?

[*Margaret has made this observation as she goes to raise the bamboo blinds, since the sunset glare has diminished. In crossing she winks at Brick.*]

MARGARET [*sweetly*]:
Dixie, Trixie, Buster, Sonny, Polly!—Sounds like four dogs and a parrot . . . animal act in a circus!

MAE:
Maggie?

[*Margaret turns with a smile.*]

Why are you so catty?

MARGARET:

Cause I'm a cat! But why can't *you* take a joke, Sister Woman?

MAE:

Nothin' pleases me more than a joke that's funny. You know the real names of our kiddies. Buster's real name is Robert. Sonny's real name is Saunders. Trixie's real name is Marlene and Dixie's—

[*Someone downstairs calls for her. "Hey, Mae!"—She rushes to door, saying:*]

Intermission is over!

MARGARET [*as Mae closes door*]:
I wonder what Dixie's real name is?

BRICK:

Maggie, being catty doesn't help things any . . .

MARGARET:

I know! *WHY!*—Am I so catty?—Cause I'm consumed with envy an' eaten up with longing?—Brick, I've laid out your beautiful Shantung silk suit from Rome and one of your monogrammed silk shirts. I'll put your cuff links in it, those lovely star sapphires I get you to wear so rarely. . . .

BRICK:

I can't get trousers on over this plaster cast.

MARGARET:
Yes, you can, I'll help you.

BRICK:

I'm not going to get dressed, Maggie.

MARGARET:

Will you just put on a pair of white silk pajamas?

BRICK:
Yes, I'll do that, Maggie.

MARGARET:
Thank you, thank you so *much!*

BRICK:
Don't mention it.

MARGARET:
Oh, Brick! How long does it have t' go on? This punishment?
Haven't I done time enough, haven't I served my term, can't I
apply for a—pardon?

BRICK:
Maggie, you're spoiling my liquor. Lately your voice always
sounds like you'd been running upstairs to warn somebody
that the house was on fire!

MARGARET:
Well, no wonder, no wonder. Y'know what I feel like, Brick?

[*Children's and grownups' voices are blended, below, in a
loud but uncertain rendition of "My Wild Irish Rose."*]

I feel all the time like a cat on a hot tin roof!

BRICK:
Then jump off the roof, jump off it, cats can jump off roofs
and land on their four feet uninjured!

MARGARET:
Oh, yes!

BRICK:
Do it!—fo' God's sake, do it . . .

MARGARET:
Do what?

39

BRICK:
Take a lover!

MARGARET:
I can't see a man but you! Even with my eyes closed, I just see you! Why don't you get ugly, Brick, why don't you please get fat or ugly or something so I could stand it?

[*She rushes to hall door, opens it, listens.*]

The concert is still going on! Bravo, no-necks, bravo!

[*She slams and locks door fiercely.*]

BRICK:
What did you lock the door for?

MARGARET:
To give us a little privacy for a while.

BRICK:
You know better, Maggie.

MARGARET:
No, I don't know better. . . .

[*She rushes to gallery doors, draws the rose-silk drapes across them.*]

BRICK:
Don't make a fool of yourself.

MARGARET:
I don't mind makin' a fool of myself over you!

BRICK:
I mind, Maggie. I feel embarrassed for you.

MARGARET:
Feel embarrassed! But don't continue my torture. I can't live on and on under these circumstances.

BRICK:
You agreed to—

MARGARET:
I know but—

BRICK:
—Accept that condition!

MARGARET:
I CAN'T! CAN'T! CAN'T!

[*She seizes his shoulder.*]

BRICK:
Let go!

[*He breaks away from her and seizes the small boudoir chair and raises it like a lion-tamer facing a big circus cat.*

[*Count five. She stares at him with her fist pressed to her mouth, then bursts into shrill, almost hysterical laughter. He remains grave for a moment, then grins and puts the chair down.*

[*Big Mama calls through closed door.*]

BIG MAMA:
Son? Son? Son?

BRICK:
What is it, Big Mama?

BIG MAMA [*outside*]:
Oh, son! We got the most wonderful news about Big Daddy. I just had t' run up an' tell you right this—

[*She rattles the knob.*]

—What's this door doin', locked, faw? You all think there's robbers in the house?

41

MARGARET:

Big Mama, Brick is dressin', he's not dressed yet.

BIG MAMA:

That's all right, it won't be the first time I've seen Brick not dressed. Come on, open this door!

[*Margaret, with a grimace, goes to unlock and open the hall door, as Brick hobbles rapidly to the bathroom and kicks the door shut. Big Mama has disappeared from the hall.*]

MARGARET:

Big Mama?

[*Big Mama appears through the opposite gallery doors behind Margaret, huffing and puffing like an old bulldog. She is a short, stout woman; her sixty years and 170 pounds have left her somewhat breathless most of the time; she's always tensed like a boxer, or rather, a Japanese wrestler. Her "family" was maybe a little superior to Big Daddy's, but not much. She wears a black or silver lace dress and at least half a million in flashy gems. She is very sincere.*]

BIG MAMA [*loudly, startling Margaret*]:

Here—I come through Gooper's and Mae's gall'ry door. Where's Brick? *Brick*—Hurry on out of there, son, I just have a second and want to give you the news about Big Daddy.— I hate locked doors in a house. . . .

MARGARET [*with affected lightness*]:

I've noticed you do, Big Mama, but people have got to have *some* moments of privacy, don't they?

BIG MAMA:

No, ma'am, not in *my* house. [*without pause*] Whacha took off you' dress faw? I thought that little lace dress was so sweet on yuh, honey.

MARGARET:

I thought it looked sweet on me, too, but one of m' cute little table-partners used it for a napkin so—!

BIG MAMA [*picking up stockings on floor*]:
What?

MARGARET:

You know, Big Mama, Mae and Gooper's so touchy about those children—thanks, Big Mama . . .

[*Big Mama has thrust the picked-up stockings in Margaret's hand with a grunt.*]

—that you just don't dare to suggest there's any room for improvement in their—

BIG MAMA:

Brick, hurry out!—Shoot, Maggie, you just don't like children.

MARGARET:

I do SO like children! Adore them!—well brought up!

BIG MAMA [*gentle—loving*]:
Well, why don't you have some and bring them up well, then, instead of all ᵗhe time pickin' on Gooper's an' Mae's?

GOOPER [*shouting up the stairs*]:
Hey, hey, Big Mama, Betsy an' Hugh got to go, waitin' t' tell yuh g'by!

BIG MAMA:

Tell 'em to hold their hawses, I'll be right down in a jiffy!

[*She turns to the bathroom door and calls out.*]

Son? Can you hear me in there?

[*There is a muffled answer.*]

We just got the full report from the laboratory at the Ochsner Clinic, completely negative, son, ev'rything negative, right on down the line! Nothin' a-tall's wrong with him but some little functional thing called a spastic colon. Can you hear me, son?

MARGARET:

He can hear you, Big Mama.

BIG MAMA:

Then why don't he say something? God Almighty, a piece of news like that should make him shout. It made *me* shout, I can tell you. I shouted and sobbed and fell right down on my knees!—Look!

[*She pulls up her skirt.*]

See the bruises where I hit my kneecaps? Took both doctors to haul me back on my feet!

[*She laughs—she always laughs like hell at herself.*]

Big Daddy was furious with me! But ain't that wonderful news?

[*Facing bathroom again, she continues:*]

After all the anxiety we been through to git a report like that on Big Daddy's birthday? Big Daddy tried to hide how much of a load that news took off his mind, but didn't fool *me*. He was mighty close to crying about it *himself!*

[*Goodbyes are shouted downstairs, and she rushes to door.*]

Hold those people down there, don't let them go!—Now, git dressed, we're all comin' up to this room fo' Big Daddy's birthday party because of your ankle.—How's his ankle, Maggie?

MARGARET:
Well, he broke it, Big Mama.

BIG MAMA:
I know he broke it.

[*A phone is ringing in hall. A Negro voice answers: "Mistuh Polly's res'dence."*]

I mean does it hurt him much still.

MARGARET:
I'm afraid I can't give you that information, Big Mama.
You'll have to ask Brick if it hurts much still or not.

SOOKEY [*in the hall*]:
It's Memphis, Mizz Polly, it's Miss Sally in Memphis.

BIG MAMA:
Awright, Sookey.

[*Big Mama rushes into the hall and is heard shouting on the phone:*]

Hello, Miss Sally. How are you, Miss Sally?—Yes, well, I was just gonna call you about it. *Shoot!*—

[*She raises her voice to a bellow.*]

Miss Sally? Don't ever call me from the Gayoso Lobby, too much talk goes on in that hotel lobby, no wonder you can't hear me! Now listen, Miss Sally. They's nothin' serious wrong with Big Daddy. We got the report just now, they's nothin' wrong but a thing called a—spastic! *SPASTIC!*—colon . . .

[*She appears at the hall door and calls to Margaret.*]

—Maggie, come out here and talk to that fool on the phone.
I'm shouted breathless!

45

MARGARET [*goes out and is heard sweetly at phone*]:
Miss Sally? This is Brick's wife, Maggie. So nice to hear your voice. Can you hear *mine?* Well, *good!*—Big Mama just wanted you to know that they've got the report from the Ochsner Clinic and what Big Daddy has is a spastic colon. Yes. Spastic colon, Miss Sally. That's right, spastic colon. *G'bye, Miss Sally, hope I'll see you real soon!*

[*Hangs up a little before Miss Sally was probably ready to terminate the talk. She returns through the hall door.*]

She heard me perfectly. I've discovered with deaf people the thing to do is not shout at them but just enunciate clearly. My rich old Aunt Cornelia was deaf as the dead but I could make her hear me just by sayin' each word slowly, distinctly, close to her ear. I read her the *Commercial Appeal* ev'ry night, read her the classified ads in it, even, she never missed a word of it. But was she a mean ole thing! Know what I got when she died? Her unexpired subscriptions to five magazines and the Book-of-the-Month Club and a LIBRARY full of ev'ry dull book ever written! All else went to her hellcat of a sister . . . meaner than she was, even!

[*Big Mama has been straightening things up in the room during this speech.*]

BIG MAMA [*closing closet door on discarded clothes*]:
Miss Sally sure is a case! Big Daddy says she's always got her hand out fo' something. He's not mistaken. That poor ole thing always has her hand out fo' somethin'. I don't think Big Daddy gives her as much as he should.

[*Somebody shouts for her downstairs and she shouts:*]

I'm comin'!

[*She starts out. At the hall door, turns and jerks a fore-finger, first toward the bathroom door, then toward the liquor cabinet, meaning: "Has Brick been drinking?" Margaret pretends not to understand, cocks her head and raises her brows as if the pantomimic performance was completely mystifying to her.*

[*Big Mama rushes back to Margaret:*]

Shoot! Stop playin' so dumb!—I mean has he been drinkin' that stuff much yet?

MARGARET [*with a little laugh*]:
Oh! I think he had a highball after supper.

BIG MAMA:
Don't laugh about it!—Some single men stop drinkin' when they git married and others start! Brick never touched liquor before he—!

MARGARET [*crying out*]:
THAT'S NOT FAIR!

BIG MAMA:
Fair or not fair I want to ask you a question, one question: D'you make Brick happy in bed?

MARGARET:
Why don't you ask if he makes *me* happy in bed?

BIG MAMA:
Because I know that—

MARGARET:
It works both ways!

BIG MAMA:
Something's not right! You're childless and my son drinks!

[*Someone has called her downstairs and she has rushed to the door on the line above. She turns at the door and points at the bed.*]

47

—When a marriage goes on the rocks, the rocks are *there*,
right *there!*

MARGARET:
That's—

[*Big Mama has swept out of the room and slammed the
door.*]

—not—*fair* . . .

[*Margaret is alone, completely alone, and she feels it. She
draws in, hunches her shoulders, raises her arms with fists
clenched, shuts her eyes tight as a child about to be stabbed
with a vaccination needle. When she opens her eyes again,
what she sees is the long oval mirror and she rushes straight
to it, stares into it with a grimace and says: "Who are
you?"—Then she crouches a little and answers herself in a
different voice which is high, thin, mocking: "I am Maggie
the Cat!"—Straightens quickly as bathroom door opens a
little and Bricks calls out to her.*]

BRICK:
Has Big Mama gone?

MARGARET:
She's gone.

[*He opens the bathroom door and hobbles out, with his
liquor glass now empty, straight to the liquor cabinet. He
is whistling softly. Margaret's head pivots on her long,
slender throat to watch him.*

[*She raises a hand uncertainly to the base of her throat, as
if it was difficult for her to swallow, before she speaks:*]

You know, our sex life didn't just peter out in the usual way,
it was cut off short, long before the natural time for it to, and

it's going to revive again, just as sudden as that. I'm confident of it. That's what I'm keeping myself attractive for. For the time when you'll see me again like other men see me. Yes, like other men see me. They still see me, Brick, and they like what they see. Uh-huh. Some of them would give their—

Look, Brick!

[*She stands before the long oval mirror, touches her breast and then her hips with her two hands.*]

How high my body stays on me!—Nothing has fallen on me —not a fraction. . . .

[*Her voice is soft and trembling: a pleading child's. At this moment as he turns to glance at her—a look which is like a player passing a ball to another player, third down and goal to go—she has to capture the audience in a grip so tight that she can hold it till the first intermission without any lapse of attention.*]

Other men still want me. My face looks strained, sometimes, but I've kept my figure as well as you've kept yours, and men admire it. I still turn heads on the street. Why, last week in Memphis everywhere that I went men's eyes burned holes in my clothes, at the country club and in restaurants and department stores, there wasn't a man I met or walked by that didn't just eat me up with his eyes and turn around when I passed him and look back at me. Why, at Alice's party for her New York cousins, the best-lookin' man in the crowd—followed me upstairs and tried to force his way in the powder room with me, followed me to the door and tried to force his way in!

BRICK:
Why didn't you let him, Maggie?

49

MARGARET:

Because I'm not that common, for one thing. Not that I wasn't almost tempted to. You like to know who it was? It was Sonny Boy Maxwell, that's who!

BRICK:

Oh, yeah, Sonny Boy Maxwell, he was a good end-runner but had a little injury to his back and had to quit.

MARGARET:

He has no injury now and has no wife and still has a lech for me!

BRICK:

I see no reason to lock him out of a powder room in that case.

MARGARET:

And have someone catch me at it? I'm not that stupid. Oh, I might sometime cheat on you with someone, since you're so insultingly eager to have me do it!—But if I do, you can be damned sure it will be in a place and a time where no one but me and the man could possibly know. Because I'm not going to give you any excuse to divorce me for being unfaithful or anything else. . . .

BRICK:

Maggie, I wouldn't divorce you for being unfaithful or anything else. Don't you know that? Hell. I'd be relieved to know that you'd found yourself a lover.

MARGARET:

Well, I'm taking no chances. No, I'd rather stay on this hot tin roof.

BRICK:

A hot tin roof's 'n uncomfo'table place t' stay on. . . .

[*He starts to whistle softly.*]

MARGARET [*through his whistle*]:
Yeah, but I can stay on it just as long as I have to.

BRICK:
You could leave me, Maggie.

[*He resumes whistle. She wheels about to glare at him.*]

MARGARET:
Don't want to and will not! Besides if I did, you don't have a cent to pay for it but what you get from Big Daddy and he's dying of cancer!

[*For the first time a realization of Big Daddy's doom seems to penetrate to Brick's consciousness, visibly, and he looks at Margaret.*]

BRICK:
Big Mama just said he *wasn't,* that the report was okay.

MARGARET:
That's what she thinks because she got the same story that they gave Big Daddy. And was just as taken in by it as he was, poor ole things. . . .

But tonight they're going to tell her the truth about it. When Big Daddy goes to bed, they're going to tell her that he is dying of cancer.

[*She slams the dresser drawer.*]

—It's malignant and it's terminal.

BRICK:
Does Big Daddy know it?

MARGARET:
Hell, do they *ever* know it? Nobody says, "You're dying." You have to fool them. They have to fool *themselves.*

51

BRICK:
Why?

MARGARET:
Why? Because human beings dream of life everlasting, that's the reason! But most of them want it on earth and not in heaven.

[*He gives a short, hard laugh at her touch of humor.*]

Well. . . . [*She touches up her mascara.*] That's how it is, anyhow. . . . [*She looks about.*] Where did I put down my cigarette? Don't want to burn up the home-place, at least not with Mae and Gooper and their five monsters in it!

[*She has found it and sucks at it greedily. Blows out smoke and continues:*]

So this is Big Daddy's last birthday. And Mae and Gooper, they know it, oh, *they* know it, all right. They got the first information from the Ochsner Clinic. That's why they rushed down here with their no-neck monsters. Because. Do you know something? Big Daddy's made no will? Big Daddy's never made out any will in his life, and so this campaign's afoot to impress him, forcibly as possible, with the fact that you drink and I've borne no children!

[*He continues to stare at her a moment, then mutters something sharp but not audible and hobbles rather rapidly out onto the long gallery in the fading, much faded, gold light.*]

MARGARET [*continuing her liturgical chant*]:
Y'know, I'm *fond* of Big Daddy, I am genuinely fond of that old man, I really *am*, you know. . . .

BRICK [*faintly, vaguely*]:
Yes, I know you are. . . .

MARGARET:

I've always sort of admired him in spite of his coarseness, his four-letter words and so forth. Because Big Daddy *is* what he *is,* and he makes no bones about it. He hasn't turned gentleman farmer, he's still a Mississippi redneck, as much of a redneck as he must have been when he was just overseer here on the old Jack Straw and Peter Ochello place. But he got hold of it an' built it into th' biggest an' finest plantation in the Delta.—I've always *liked* Big Daddy. . . .

[*She crosses to the proscenium.*]

Well, this is Big Daddy's last birthday. I'm sorry about it. But I'm facing the facts. It takes money to take care of a drinker and that's the office that I've been elected to lately.

BRICK:

You don't have to take care of me.

MARGARET:

Yes, I do. Two people in the same boat have got to take care of each other. At least you want money to buy more Echo Spring when this supply is exhausted, or will you be satisfied with a ten-cent beer?

Mae an' Gooper are plannin' to freeze us out of Big Daddy's estate because you drink and I'm childless. But we can defeat that plan. We're *going* to defeat that plan!

Brick, y'know, I've been so God damn disgustingly poor all my life!—That's the *truth,* Brick!

BRICK:

I'm not sayin' it isn't.

MARGARET:

Always had to suck up to people I couldn't stand because they had money and I was poor as Job's turkey. You don't

53

know what that's like. Well, I'll tell you, it's like you would feel a thousand miles away from Echo Spring!—And had to get back to it on that broken ankle . . . without a crutch!

That's how it feels to be as poor as Job's turkey and have to suck up to relatives that you hated because they had money and all you had was a bunch of hand-me-down clothes and a few old moldly three-per-cent government bonds. My daddy loved his liquor, he fell in love with his liquor the way you've fallen in love with Echo Spring!—And my poor Mama, having to maintain some semblance of social position, to keep appearances up, on an income of one hundred and fifty dollars a month on those old government bonds!

When I came out, the year that I made my debut, I had just two evening dresses! One Mother made me from a pattern in *Vogue,* the other a hand-me-down from a snotty rich cousin I hated!

—The dress that I married you in was my grandmother's weddin' gown. . . .

So that's why I'm like a cat on a hot tin roof!

[*Brick is still on the gallery. Someone below calls up to him in a warm Negro voice, "Hiya, Mistuh Brick, how yuh feelin'?" Brick raises his liquor glass as if that answered the question.*]

MARGARET:
You can be young without money, but you can't be old without it. You've got to be old *with* money because to be old without it is just too awful, you've got to be one or the other, either *young* or *with money,* you can't be old and *without* it.—That's the *truth,* Brick. . . .

[*Brick whistles softly, vaguely.*]

Well, now I'm dressed, I'm all dressed, there's nothing else for me to do.

[*Forlornly, almost fearfully.*]

I'm dressed, all dressed, nothing else for me to do. . . .

[*She moves about restlessly, aimlessly, and speaks, as if to herself.*]

I know when I made my mistake.—What am I—? Oh!—my bracelets. . . .

[*She starts working a collection of bracelets over her hands onto her wrists, about six on each, as she talks.*]

I've thought a whole lot about it and now I know when I made my mistake. Yes, I made my mistake when I told you the truth about that thing with Skipper. Never should have confessed it, a fatal error, tellin' you about that thing with Skipper.

BRICK:
Maggie, shut up about Skipper. I mean it, Maggie; you got to shut up about Skipper.

MARGARET:
You ought to understand that Skipper and I—

BRICK:
You don't think I'm serious, Maggie? You're fooled by the fact that I am saying this quiet? Look, Maggie. What you're doing is a dangerous thing to do. You're—you're—you're— foolin' with something that—nobody ought to fool with.

MARGARET:
This time I'm going to finish what I have to say to you. Skipper and I made love, if love you could call it, because it made both of us feel a little bit closer to you. You see, you

55

son of a bitch, you asked too much of people, of me, of him, of all the unlucky poor damned sons of bitches that happen to love you, and there was a whole pack of them, yes, there was a pack of them besides me and Skipper, you asked too goddam much of people that loved you, you—superior creature!—you godlike being!—And so we made love to each other to dream it was you, both of us! Yes, yes, yes! Truth, truth! What's so awful about it? I like it, I think the truth is—yeah! I shouldn't have told you. . . .

BRICK [*holding his head unnaturally still and uptilted a bit*]:
It was Skipper that told me about it. Not you, Maggie.

MARGARET:
I told you!

BRICK:
After he told me!

MARGARET:
What does it matter who—?

[*Brick turns suddenly out upon the gallery and calls:*]

BRICK:
Little girl! Hey, little girl!

LITTLE GIRL [*at a distance*]:
What, Uncle Brick?

BRICK:
Tell the folks to come up!—Bring everybody upstairs!

MARGARET:
I can't stop myself! I'd go on telling you this in front of them all, if I had to!

BRICK:

Little girl! Go on, go on, will you? Do what I told you, call them!

MARGARET:

Because it's got to be told and you, you!—you never let me!

[*She sobs, then controls herself, and continues almost calmly.*]

It was one of those beautiful, ideal things they tell about in the Greek legends, it couldn't be anything else, you being you, and that's what made it so sad, that's what made it so awful, because it was love that never could be carried through to anything satisfying or even talked about plainly. Brick, I tell you, you got to believe me, Brick, I *do* understand all about it! I—I think it was—*noble!* Can't you tell I'm sincere when I say I respect it? My only point, the only point that I'm making, is life has got to be allowed to continue even after the *dream* of life is—all—over. . . .

[*Brick is without his crutch. Leaning on furniture, he crosses to pick it up as she continues as if possessed by a will outside herself:*]

Why I remember when we double-dated at college, Gladys Fitzgerald and I and you and Skipper, it was more like a date between you and Skipper. Gladys and I were just sort of tagging along as if it was necessary to chaperone you!—to make a good public impression—

BRICK [*turns to face her, half lifting his crutch*]:
Maggie, you want me to hit you with this crutch? Don't you know I could kill you with this crutch?

MARGARET:
Good Lord, man, d' you think I'd care if you did?

57

BRICK:

One man has one great good true thing in his life. One great good thing which is true!—I had friendship with Skipper.—You are naming it dirty!

MARGARET:

I'm not naming it dirty! I am naming it clean.

BRICK:

Not love with you, Maggie, but friendship with Skipper was that one great true thing, and you are naming it dirty!

MARGARET:

Then you haven't been listenin', not understood what I'm saying! I'm naming it so damn clean that it killed poor Skipper!—You two had something that had to be kept on ice, yes, incorruptible, yes!—and death was the only icebox where you could keep it. . . .

BRICK:

I married you, Maggie. Why would I marry you, Maggie, if I was—?

MARGARET:

Brick, don't brain me yet, let me finish!—I know, believe me I know, that it was only Skipper that harbored even any *unconscious* desire for anything not perfectly pure between you two!—Now let me skip a little. You married me early that summer we graduated out of Ole Miss, and we were happy, weren't we, we were blissful, yes, hit heaven together ev'ry time that we loved! But that fall you an' Skipper turned down wonderful offers of jobs in order to keep on bein' football heroes—pro-football heroes. You organized the Dixie Stars that fall, so you could keep on bein' teammates forever! But somethin' was not right with it!—*Me included!*—between you. Skipper began hittin' the bottle . . . you got a spinal injury—couldn't play the Thanksgivin' game in Chicago, watched it on TV from a traction bed in Toledo. I joined Skipper. The Dixie Stars lost because poor Skipper was drunk. We drank together that night all night in the bar of the Blackstone and when cold day was comin' up over the Lake an' we were comin' out drunk to take a dizzy look at it, I said, "SKIPPER! STOP LOVIN' MY HUSBAND OR TELL HIM HE'S GOT TO LET YOU ADMIT IT TO HIM!"—one way or another!

HE SLAPPED ME HARD ON THE MOUTH!—then turned and ran without stopping once, I am sure, all the way back into his room at the Blackstone....

—When I came to his room that night, with a little scratch like a shy little mouse at his door, he made that pitiful, ineffectual little attempt to prove that what I had said wasn't true....

[*Brick strikes at her with crutch, a blow that shatters the gemlike lamp on the table.*]

—In this way, I destroyed him, by telling him truth that he and his world which he was born and raised in, yours and his world, had told him could not be told?

—From then on Skipper was nothing at all but a receptacle for liquor and drugs....

—*Who shot cock robin? I with my*—

[*She throws back her head with tight shut eyes.*]

—*merciful arrow!*

[*Brick strikes at her; misses.*]

Missed me!—Sorry,—I'm not tryin' to whitewash my behavior, Christ, no! Brick, I'm not good. I don't know why

59

people have to pretend to be good, nobody's good. The rich or the well-to-do can afford to respect moral patterns, conventional moral patterns, but I could never afford to, yeah, but—I'm honest! Give me credit for just that, will you *please?*—Born poor, raised poor, expect to die poor unless I manage to get us something out of what Big Daddy leaves when he dies of cancer! But Brick?!—*Skipper is dead! I'm alive!* Maggie the cat is—

[*Brick hops awkwardly forward and strikes at her again with his crutch.*]

—*alive! I am alive, alive! I am . . .*

[*He hurls the crutch at her, across the bed she took refuge behind, and pitches forward on the floor as she completes her speech.*]

—*alive!*

[*A little girl, Dixie, bursts into the room, wearing an Indian war bonnet and firing a cap pistol at Margaret and shouting: "Bang, bang, bang!"*

[*Laughter downstairs floats through the open hall door. Margaret had crouched gasping to bed at child's entrance. She now rises and says with cool fury:*]

Little girl, your mother or someone should teach you—[*gasping*]—to knock at a door before you come into a room. Otherwise people might think that you—lack—good breeding. . . .

DIXIE:

Yanh, yanh, yanh, what is Uncle Brick doin' on th' floor?

BRICK:

I tried to kill your Aunt Maggie, but I failed—and I fell. Little girl, give me my crutch so I can get up off th' floor.

MARGARET:

Yes, give your uncle his crutch, he's a cripple, honey, he broke his ankle last night jumping hurdles on the high school athletic field!

DIXIE:

What were you jumping hurdles for, Uncle Brick?

BRICK:

Because I used to jump them, and people like to do what they used to do, even after they've stopped being able to do it. . . .

MARGARET:

That's right, that's your answer, now go away, little girl.

[Dixie fires cap pistol at Margaret three times.]

Stop, you stop that, monster! You little no-neck monster!

[She seizes the cap pistol and hurls it through gallery doors.]

DIXIE *[with a precocious instinct for the cruelest thing]*:

You're *jealous!*—You're just jealous because you can't have babies!

[She sticks out her tongue at Margaret as she sashays past her with her stomach stuck out, to the gallery. Margaret slams the gallery doors and leans panting against them. There is a pause. Brick has replaced his spilt drink and sits, faraway, on the great four-poster bed.]

MARGARET:

You see?—they gloat over us being childless, even in front of their five little no-neck monsters!

[Pause. Voices approach on the stairs.]

Brick?—I've been to a doctor in Memphis, a—a gynecologist. . . .

I've been completely examined, and there is no reason why we can't have a child whenever we want one. And this is my time by the calendar to conceive. Are you listening to me? Are you? Are you LISTENING TO ME!

BRICK:
Yes. I hear you, Maggie.

[*His attention returns to her inflamed face.*]

—But how in hell on earth do you imagine—that you're going to have a child by a man that can't stand you?

MARGARET:
That's a problem that I will have to work out.

[*She wheels about to face the hall door.*]

Here they come!

[*The lights dim.*]

CURTAIN

ACT TWO

There is no lapse of time. Margaret and Brick are in the same positions they held at the end of Act I.

MARGARET [*at door*]:
Here they come!

[*Big Daddy appears first, a tall man with a fierce, anxious look, moving carefully not to betray his weakness even, or especially, to himself.*]

BIG DADDY:
Well, Brick.

BRICK:
Hello, Big Daddy.—Congratulations!

BIG DADDY:
—Crap. . . .

[*Some of the people are approaching through the hall, others along the gallery: voices from both directions. Gooper and Reverend Tooker become visible outside gallery doors, and their voices come in clearly.*]

[*They pause outside as Gooper lights a cigar.*]

REVEREND TOOKER [*vivaciously*]:
Oh, but St. Paul's in Grenada has three memorial windows, and the latest one is a Tiffany stained-glass window that cost twenty-five hundred dollars, a picture of Christ the Good Shepherd with a Lamb in His arms.

GOOPER:
Who give that window, Preach?

REVEREND TOOKER:

Clyde Fletcher's widow. Also presented St. Paul's with a baptismal font.

GOOPER:

Y'know what somebody ought t' give your church is a *coolin'* system, Preach.

REVEREND TOOKER:

Yes, siree, Bob! And y'know what Gus Hamma's family gave in his memory to the church at Two Rivers? A complete new stone parish-house with a basketball court in the basement and a—

BIG DADDY [*uttering a loud barking laugh which is far from truly mirthful*]:

Hey, Preach! What's all this talk about memorials, Preach? Y' think somebody's about t' kick off around here? 'S that it?

[*Startled by this interjection, Reverend Tooker decides to laugh at the question almost as loud as he can.*

[*How he would answer the question we'll never know, as he's spared that embarrassment by the voice of Gooper's wife, Mae, rising high and clear as she appears with "Doc" Baugh, the family doctor, through the hall door.*]

MAE [*almost religiously*]:

—Let's see now, they've had their *tyyy*-phoid shots, and their tetanus shots, their diphtheria shots and their hepatitis shots and their polio shots, they got *those* shots every month from May through September, and—Gooper? Hey! Gooper!— What all have the kiddies been shot faw?

MARGARET [*overlapping a bit*]:

Turn on the hi-fi, Brick! Let's have some music t' start off th' party with!

64

[*The talk becomes so general that the room sounds like a great aviary of chattering birds. Only Brick remains unengaged, leaning upon the liquor cabinet with his faraway smile, an ice cube in a paper napkin with which he now and then rubs his forehead. He doesn't respond to Margaret's command. She bounds forward and stoops over the instrument panel of the console.*]

GOOPER:

We gave 'em that thing for a third anniversary present, got three speakers in it.

[*The room is suddenly blasted by the climax of a Wagnerian opera or a Beethoven symphony.*]

BIG DADDY:
Turn that dam thing off!

[*Almost instant silence, almost instantly broken by the shouting charge of Big Mama, entering through hall door like a charging rhino.*]

BIG MAMA:
Wha's my Brick, wha's mah precious baby!!

BIG DADDY:
Sorry! Turn it back on!

[*Everyone laughs very loud. Big Daddy is famous for his jokes at Big Mama's expense, and nobody laughs louder at these jokes than Big Mama herself, though sometimes they're pretty cruel and Big Mama has to pick up or fuss with something to cover the hurt that the loud laugh doesn't quite cover.*]

[*On this occasion, a happy occasion because the dread in her heart has also been lifted by the false report on Big Daddy's condition, she giggles, grotesquely, coyly, in Big*]

65

Daddy's direction and bears down upon Brick, all very quick and alive.]

BIG MAMA:

Here he is, here's my precious baby! What's that you've got in your hand? You put that liquor down, son, your hand was made fo' holdin' somethin' better than that!

GOOPER:

Look at Brick put it down!

[Brick has obeyed Big Mama by draining the glass and handing it to her. Again everyone laughs, some high, some low.]

BIG MAMA:

Oh, you bad boy, you, you're my bad little boy. Give Big Mama a kiss, you bad boy, you!—Look at him shy away, will you? Brick never liked bein' kissed or made a fuss over, I guess because he's always had too much of it!

Son, you turn that thing off!

[Brick has switched on the TV set.]

I can't stand TV, radio was bad enough but TV has gone it one better, I mean—*[plops wheezing in chair]*—one worse, ha ha! Now what'm I sittin' down here faw? I want t' sit next to my sweetheart on the sofa, hold hands with him and love him up a little!

[Big Mama has on a black and white figured chiffon. The large irregular patterns, like the markings of some massive animal, the luster of her great diamonds and many pearls, the brilliants set in the silver frames of her glasses, her riotous voice, booming laugh, have dominated the room since she entered. Big Daddy has been regarding her with a steady grimace of chronic annoyance.]

BIG MAMA [*still louder*]:

Preacher, Preacher, hey, Preach! Give me you' hand an' help me up from this chair!

REVEREND TOOKER:

None of your tricks, Big Mama!

BIG MAMA:

What tricks? You give me you' hand so I can get up an'—

[*Reverend Tooker extends her his hand. She grabs it and pulls him into her lap with a shrill laugh that spans an octave in two notes.*]

Ever seen a preacher in a fat lady's lap? Hey, hey, folks! Ever seen a preacher in a fat lady's lap?

[*Big Mama is notorious throughout the Delta for this sort of inelegant horseplay. Margaret looks on with indulgent humor, sipping Dubonnet "on the rocks" and watching Brick, but Mae and Gooper exchange signs of humorless anxiety over these antics, the sort of behavior which Mae thinks may account for their failure to quite get in with the smartest young married set in Memphis, despite all. One of the Negroes, Lacy or Sookey, peeks in, cackling. They are waiting for a sign to bring in the cake and champagne. But Big Daddy's not amused. He doesn't understand why, in spite of the infinite mental relief he's received from the doctor's report, he still has these same old fox teeth in his guts. "This spastic thing sure is something," he says to himself, but aloud he roars at Big Mama:*]

BIG DADDY:

BIG MAMA, WILL YOU QUIT HORSIN'?—You're too old an' too fat fo' that sort of crazy kid stuff an' besides a woman with your blood pressure—she had two hundred last spring! —is riskin' a stroke when you mess around like that. . . .

BIG MAMA:
Here comes Big Daddy's birthday!

[*Negroes in white jackets enter with an enormous birthday cake ablaze with candles and carrying buckets of champagne with satin ribbons about the bottle necks.*

[*Mae and Gooper strike up song, and everybody, including the Negroes and Children, joins in. Only Brick remains aloof.*]

EVERYONE:
Happy birthday to you.
Happy birthday to you.
Happy birthday, Big Daddy—

[*Some sing: "Dear, Big Daddy!"*]

Happy birthday to you.

[*Some sing: "How old are you?"*]

[*Mae has come down center and is organizing her children like a chorus. She gives them a barely audible: "One, two, three!" and they are off in the new tune.*]

CHILDREN:
Skinamarinka—dinka—dink
Skinamarinka—do
We love you.
Skinamarinka—dinka—dink
Skinamarinka—do.

[*All together, they turn to Big Daddy.*]

Big Daddy, you!

[*They turn back front, like a musical comedy chorus.*]

We love you in the morning;

We love you in the night.
We love you when we're with you,
And we love you out of sight.
Skinamarinka—dinka—dink
Skinamarinka—do.

[*Mae turns to Big Mama.*]

Big Mama, too!

[*Big Mama bursts into tears. The Negroes leave.*]

BIG DADDY:
Now Ida, what the hell is the matter with you?

MAE:
She's just so happy.

BIG MAMA:
I'm just so happy, Big Daddy, I have to cry or something.

[*Sudden and loud in the hush:*]

Brick, do you know the wonderful news that Doc Baugh got
from the clinic about Big Daddy? Big Daddy's one hundred
per cent!

MARGARET:
Isn't that wonderful?

BIG MAMA:
He's just one hundred per cent. Passed the examination with
flying colors. Now that we know there's nothing wrong with
Big Daddy but a spastic colon, I can tell you something. I
was worried sick, half out of my mind, for fear that Big
Daddy might have a thing like—

[*Margaret cuts through this speech, jumping up and exclaiming shrilly:*]

69

MARGARET:

Brick, honey, aren't you going to give Big Daddy his birthday present?

[Passing by him, she snatches his liquor glass from him.

[She picks up a fancily wrapped package.]

Here it is, Big Daddy, this is from Brick!

BIG MAMA:

This is the biggest birthday Big Daddy's ever had, a hundred presents and bushels of telegrams from—

MAE *[at same time]*:
What is it, Brick?

GOOPER:

I bet 500 to 50 that Brick don't *know* what it is.

BIG MAMA:

The fun of presents is not knowing what they are till you open the package. Open your present, Big Daddy.

BIG DADDY:

Open it you'self. I want to ask Brick somethin! Come here, Brick.

MARGARET:

Big Daddy's callin' you, Brick.

[She is opening the package.]

BRICK:

Tell Big Daddy I'm crippled.

BIG DADDY:

I see you're crippled. I want to know how you got crippled.

MARGARET *[making diversionary tactics]*:
Oh, look, oh, look, why, it's a cashmere robe!

[*She holds the robe up for all to see.*]

MAE:
You sound surprised, Maggie.

MARGARET:
I never saw one before.

MAE:
That's funny.—*Hah!*

MARGARET [*turning on her fiercely, with a brilliant smile*]:
Why is it funny? All my family ever had was family—and luxuries such as cashmere robes still surprise me!

BIG DADDY [*ominously*]:
Quiet!

MAE [*heedless in her fury*]:
I don't see how you could be so surprised when you bought it yourself at Loewenstein's in Memphis last Saturday. You know how I know?

BIG DADDY:
I said, Quiet!

MAE:
—I know because the salesgirl that sold it to you waited on me and said, Oh, Mrs. Pollitt, your sister-in-law just bought a cashmere robe for your husband's father!

MARGARET:
Sister Woman! Your talents are wasted as a housewife and mother, you really ought to be with the FBI or—

BIG DADDY:
QUIET!

[*Reverend Tooker's reflexes are slower than the others'. He finishes a sentence after the bellow.*]

REVEREND TOOKER [*to Doc Baugh*]:
—the Stork and the Reaper are running neck and neck!

[*He starts to laugh gaily when he notices the silence and Big Daddy's glare. His laugh dies falsely.*]

BIG DADDY:
Preacher, I hope I'm not butting in on more talk about memorial stained-glass windows, am I, Preacher?

[*Reverend Tooker laughs feebly, then coughs dryly in the embarrassed silence.*]

Preacher?

BIG MAMA:
Now, Big Daddy, don't you pick on Preacher!

BIG DADDY [*raising his voice*]:
You ever hear that expression all hawk and no spit? You bring that expression to mind with that little dry cough of yours, all hawk an' no spit. . . .

[*The pause is broken only by a short startled laugh from Margaret, the only one there who is conscious of and amused by the grotesque.*]

MAE [*raising her arms and jangling her bracelets*]:
I wonder if the mosquitoes are active tonight?

BIG DADDY:
What's that, Little Mama? Did you make some remark?

MAE:
Yes, I said I wondered if the mosquitoes would eat us alive if we went out on the gallery for a while.

BIG DADDY:
Well, if they do, I'll have your bones pulverized for fertilizer!

BIG MAMA [*quickly*]:
Last week we had an airplane spraying the place and I think
it done some good, at least I haven't had a—

BIG DADDY [*cutting her speech*]:
Brick, they tell me, if what they tell me is true, that you done
some jumping last night on the high school athletic field?

BIG MAMA:
Brick, Big Daddy is talking to you, son.

BRICK [*smiling vaguely over his drink*]:
What was that, Big Daddy?

BIG DADDY:
They said you done some jumping on the high school track
field last night.

BRICK:
That's what they told me, too.

BIG DADDY:
Was it jumping or humping that you were doing out there?
What were doing out there at three A.M., layin' a woman
on that cinder track?

BIG MAMA:
Big Daddy, you are off the sick-list, now, and I'm not going
to excuse you for talkin' so—

BIG DADDY:
Quiet!

BIG MAMA:
—*nasty* in front of Preacher and—

BIG DADDY:
QUIET!—I ast you, Brick, if you was cuttin' you'self a piece
o' poon-tang last night on that cinder track? I thought maybe

73

you were chasin' poon-tang on that track an' tripped over something in the heat of the chase—'sthat it?

[*Gooper laughs, loud and false, others nervously following suit. Big Mama stamps her foot, and purses her lips, crossing to Mae and whispering something to her as Brick meets his father's hard, intent, grinning stare with a slow, vague smile that he offers all situations from behind the screen of his liquor.*]

BRICK:
No, sir, I don't think so. . . .

MAE [*at the same time, sweetly*]:
Reverend Tooker, let's you and I take a stroll on the widow's walk.

[*She and the preacher go out on the gallery as Big Daddy says:*]

BIG DADDY:
Then what the hell were you doing out there at three o'clock in the morning?

BRICK:
Jumping the hurdles, Big Daddy, runnin' and jumpin' the hurdles, but those high hurdles have gotten too high for me, now.

BIG DADDY:
Cause you was drunk?

BRICK [*his vague smile fading a little*]:
Sober I wouldn't have tried to jump the *low* ones. . . .

BIG MAMA [*quickly*]:
Big Daddy, blow out the candles on your birthday cake!

MARGARET [*at the same time*]:
I want to propose a toast to Big Daddy Pollitt on his sixty-fifth birthday, the biggest cotton planter in—

BIG DADDY [*bellowing with fury and disgust*]:
I told you to stop it, now stop it, quit this—!

BIG MAMA [*coming in front of Big Daddy with the cake*]:
Big Daddy, I will not allow you to talk that way, not even on your birthday, I—

BIG DADDY:
I'll talk like I want to on my birthday, Ida, or any other goddam day of the year and anybody here that don't like it knows what they can do!

BIG MAMA:
You don't mean that!

BIG DADDY:
What makes you think I don't mean it?

[*Meanwhile various discreet signals have been exchanged and Gooper has also gone out on the gallery.*]

BIG MAMA:
I just know you don't mean it.

BIG DADDY:
You don't know a goddam thing and you never did!

BIG MAMA:
Big Daddy, you don't mean that.

BIG DADDY:
Oh, yes, I do, oh, yes, I do, I mean it! I put up with a whole

75

lot of crap around here because I thought I was dying. And you thought I was dying and you started taking over, well, you can stop taking over now, Ida, because I'm not gonna die, you can just stop now this business of taking over because you're not taking over because I'm not dying, I went through the laboratory and the goddam exploratory operation and there's nothing wrong with me but a spastic colon. And I'm not dying of cancer which you thought I was dying of. Ain't that so? Didn't you think that I was dying of cancer, Ida?

[*Almost everybody is out on the gallery but the two old people glaring at each other across the blazing cake.*

[*Big Mama's chest heaves and she presses a fat fist to her mouth.*

[*Big Daddy continues, hoarsely:*]

Ain't that so, Ida? Didn't you have an idea I was dying of cancer and now you could take control of this place and everything on it? I got that impression, I seemed to get that impression. Your loud voice everywhere, your fat old body butting in here and there!

BIG MAMA:
Hush! The Preacher!

BIG DADDY:
Rut the goddam preacher!

[*Big Mama gasps loudly and sits down on the sofa which is almost too small for her.*]

Did you hear what I said? I said rut the goddam preacher!

[*Somebody closes the gallery doors from outside just as there is a burst of fireworks and excited cries from the children.*]

76

BIG MAMA:

I never seen you act like this before and I can't think what's got in you!

BIG DADDY:

I went through all that laboratory and operation and all just so I would know if you or me was boss here! Well, now it turns out that I am and you ain't—and that's my birthday present—and my cake and champagne!—because for three years now you been gradually taking over. Bossing. Talking. Sashaying your fat old body around the place I made! I made this place! I was overseer on it! I was the overseer on the old Straw and Ochello plantation. I quit school at ten! I quit school at ten years old and went to work like a nigger in the fields. And I rose to be overseer of the Straw and Ochello plantation. And old Straw died and I was Ochello's partner and the place got bigger and bigger and bigger and bigger and bigger! I did all that myself with no goddam help from you, and now you think you're just about to take over. Well, I am just about to tell you that you are not just about to take over, you are not just about to take over a God damn thing. Is that clear to you, Ida? Is that very plain to you, now? Is that understood completely? I been through the laboratory from A to Z. I've had the goddam exploratory operation, and nothing is wrong with me but a spastic colon—made spastic, I guess, by *disgust!* By all the goddam lies and liars that I have had to put up with, and all the goddam hypocrisy that I lived with all these forty years that we been livin' together!

Hey! Ida!! Blow out the candles on the birthday cake! Purse up your lips and draw a deep breath and blow out the goddam candles on the cake!

BIG MAMA:
Oh, Big Daddy, oh, oh, oh, Big Daddy!

77

BIG DADDY:
What's the matter with you?

BIG MAMA:
In all these years you never believed that I loved you??

BIG DADDY:
Huh?

BIG MAMA:
And I did, I did so much, I did love you!—I even loved your hate and your hardness, Big Daddy!

[*She sobs and rushes awkwardly out onto the gallery.*]

BIG DADDY [*to himself*]:
Wouldn't it be funny if that was true....

[*A pause is followed by a burst of light in the sky from the fireworks.*]

BRICK! HEY, BRICK!

[*He stands over his blazing birthday cake.*

[*After some moments, Brick hobbles in on his crutch, holding his glass.*

[*Margaret follows him with a bright, anxious smile.*]

I didn't call you, Maggie. I called Brick.

MARGARET:
I'm just delivering him to you.

[*She kisses Brick on the mouth which he immediately wipes with the back of his hand. She flies girlishly back out. Brick and his father are alone.*]

BIG DADDY:
Why did you do that?

BRICK:
Do what, Big Daddy?

BIG DADDY:
Wipe her kiss off your mouth like she'd spit on you.

BRICK:
I don't know. I wasn't conscious of it.

BIG DADDY:
That woman of yours has a better shape on her than Gooper's but somehow or other they got the same look about them.

BRICK:
What sort of look is that, Big Daddy?

BIG DADDY:
I don't know how to describe it but it's the same look.

BRICK:
They don't look peaceful, do they?

BIG DADDY:
No, they sure in hell don't.

BRICK:
They look nervous as cats?

BIG DADDY:
That's right, they look nervous as cats.

BRICK:
Nervous as a couple of cats on a hot tin roof?

BIG DADDY:
That's right, boy, they look like a couple of cats on a hot tin roof. It's funny that you and Gooper being so different would pick out the same type of woman.

79

BRICK:

Both of us married into society, Big Daddy.

BIG DADDY:

Crap . . . I wonder what gives them both that look?

BRICK:

Well. They're sittin' in the middle of a big piece of land, Big Daddy, twenty-eight thousand acres is a pretty big piece of land and so they're squaring off on it, each determined to knock off a bigger piece of it than the other whenever you let it go.

BIG DADDY:

I got a surprise for those women. I'm not gonna let it go for a long time yet if that's what they're waiting for.

BRICK:

That's right, Big Daddy. You just sit tight and let them scratch each other's eyes out. . . .

BIG DADDY:

You bet your life I'm going to sit tight on it and let those sons of bitches scratch their eyes out, ha ha ha. . . .

But Gooper's wife's a good breeder, you got to admit she's fertile. Hell, at supper tonight she had them all at the table and they had to put a couple of extra leafs in the table to make room for them, she's got five head of them, now, and another one's comin'.

BRICK:
Yep, number six is comin'. . . .

BIG DADDY:

Brick, you know, I swear to God, I don't know the way it happens?

BRICK:
The way what happens, Big Daddy?

BIG DADDY:
You git you a piece of land, by hook or crook, an' things start growin' on it, things accumulate on it, and the first thing you know it's completely out of hand, completely out of hand!

BRICK:
Well, they say nature hates a vacuum, Big Daddy.

BIG DADDY:
That's what they say, but sometimes I think that a vacuum is a hell of a lot better than some of the stuff that nature replaces it with.

Is someone out there by that door?

BRICK:
Yep.

BIG DADDY:
Who?

[*He has lowered his voice.*]

BRICK:
Someone int'rested in what we say to each other.

BIG DADDY:
Gooper?——*GOOPER!*

[*After a discreet pause, Mae appears in the gallery door.*]

MAE:
Did you call Gooper, Big Daddy?

BIG DADDY:
Aw, it was you.

MAE:

Do you want Gooper, Big Daddy?

BIG DADDY:

No, and I don't want you. I want some privacy here, while I'm having a confidential talk with my son Brick. Now it's too hot in here to close them doors, but if I have to close those rutten doors in order to have a private talk with my son Brick, just let me know and I'll close 'em. Because I hate eavesdroppers, I don't like any kind of sneakin' an' spyin'.

MAE:

Why, Big Daddy—

BIG DADDY:

You stood on the wrong side of the moon, it threw your shadow!

MAE:

I was just—

BIG DADDY:

You was just nothing but *spyin'* an' you *know* it!

MAE [*begins to sniff and sob*]:

Oh, Big Daddy, you're so unkind for some reason to those that really love you!

BIG DADDY:

Shut up, shut up, shut up! I'm going to move you and Gooper out of that room next to this! It's none of your goddam business what goes on in here at night between Brick an' Maggie. You listen at night like a couple of rutten peekhole spies and go and give a report on what you hear to Big Mama an' she comes to me and says they say such and such and so and so about what they heard goin' on between Brick an' Maggie, and Jesus, it makes me sick. I'm goin' to move you an' Gooper out of that room, I can't stand sneakin' an' spyin', it makes me sick. . . .

[*Mae throws back her head and rolls her eyes heavenward and extends her arms as if invoking God's pity for this unjust martyrdom; then she presses a handkerchief to her nose and flies from the room with a loud swish of skirts.*]

BRICK [*now at the liquor cabinet*]:
They listen, do they?

BIG DADDY:
Yeah. They listen and give reports to Big Mama on what goes on in here between you and Maggie. They say that—

[*He stops as if embarrassed.*]

—You won't sleep with her, that you sleep on the sofa. Is that true or not true? If you don't like Maggie, get rid of Maggie!—What are you doin' there now?

BRICK:
Fresh'nin' up my drink.

BIG DADDY:
Son, you know you got a real liquor problem?

BRICK:
Yes, sir, yes, I know.

BIG DADDY:
Is that why you quit sports-announcing, because of this liquor problem?

BRICK:
Yes, sir, yes, sir, I guess so.

[*He smiles vaguely and amiably at his father across his replenished drink.*]

BIG DADDY:
Son, don't guess about it, it's too important.

BRICK [*vaguely*]:
Yes, sir.

BIG DADDY:
And listen to me, don't look at the damn chandelier. . . .

[*Pause. Big Daddy's voice is husky.*]

—Somethin' else we picked up at th' big fire sale in Europe.

[*Another pause.*]

Life is important. There's nothing else to hold onto. A man that drinks is throwing his life away. Don't do it, hold onto your life. There's nothing else to hold onto. . . .

Sit down over here so we don't have to raise our voices, the walls have ears in this place.

BRICK [*hobbling over to sit on the sofa beside him*]:
All right, Big Daddy.

BIG DADDY:
Quit!—how'd that come about? Some disappointment?

BRICK:
I don't know. Do you?

BIG DADDY:
I'm askin' you, God damn it! How in hell would I know if you don't?

BRICK:
I just got out there and found that I had a mouth full of cotton. I was always two or three beats behind what was goin' on on the field and so I—

BIG DADDY:
Quit!

BRICK [*amiably*]:
Yes, quit.

BIG DADDY:
Son?

BRICK:
Huh?

BIG DADDY [*inhales loudly and deeply from his cigar; then bends suddenly a little forward, exhaling loudly and raising a hand to his forehead*]:

—Whew!—ha ha!—I took in too much smoke, it made me a little lightheaded. . . .

[*The mantel clock chimes.*]

Why is it so damn hard for people to talk?

BRICK:
Yeah. . . .

[*The clock goes on sweetly chiming till it has completed the stroke of ten.*]

—Nice peaceful-soundin' clock, I like to hear it all night. . . .

[*He slides low and comfortable on the sofa; Big Daddy sits up straight and rigid with some unspoken anxiety. All his gestures are tense and jerky as he talks. He wheezes and pants and sniffs through his nervous speech, glancing quickly, shyly, from time to time, at his son.*]

BIG DADDY:
We got that clock the summer we wint to Europe, me an' Big Mama on that damn Cook's Tour, never had such an awful

time in my life, I'm tellin' you, son, those gooks over there, they gouge your eyeballs out in their grand hotels. And Big Mama bought more stuff than you could haul in a couple of boxcars, that's no crap. Everywhere she wint on this whirlwind tour, she bought, bought, bought. Why, half that stuff she bought is still crated up in the cellar, under water last spring!

[*He laughs.*]

That Europe is nothin' on earth but a great big auction, that's all it is, that bunch of old worn-out places, it's just a big firesale, the whole rutten thing, an' Big Mama wint wild in it, why, you couldn't hold that woman with a mule's harness! Bought, bought, bought!—lucky I'm a rich man, yes siree, Bob, an' half that stuff is mildewin' in th' basement. It's lucky I'm a rich man, it sure is lucky, well, I'm a rich man, Brick, yep, I'm a mighty rich man.

[*His eyes light up for a moment.*]

Y'know how much I'm worth? Guess, Brick! Guess how much I'm worth!

[*Brick smiles vaguely over his drink.*]

Close on ten million in cash an' blue-chip stocks, outside, mind you, of twenty-eight thousand acres of the richest land this side of the valley Nile!

[*A puff and crackle and the night sky blooms with an eerie greenish glow. Children shriek on the gallery.*]

But a man can't buy his life with it, he can't buy back his life with it when his life has been spent, that's one thing not offered in the Europe fire-sale or in the American markets or any markets on earth, a man can't buy his life with it, he can't buy back his life when his life is finished. . . .

That's a sobering thought, a very sobering thought, and that's a thought that I was turning over in my head, over and over and over—until today. . . .

I'm wiser and sadder, Brick, for this experience which I just gone through. They's one thing else that I remember in Europe.

BRICK:
What is that, Big Daddy?

BIG DADDY:
The hills around Barcelona in the country of Spain and the children running over those bare hills in their bare skins beggin' like starvin' dogs with howls and screeches, and how fat the priests are on the streets of Barcelona, so many of them and so fat and so pleasant, ha ha!—Y'know I could feed that country? I got money enough to feed that goddam country, but the human animal is a selfish beast and I don't reckon the money I passed out there to those howling children in the hills around Barcelona would more than upholster one of the chairs in this room, I mean pay to put a new cover on this chair!

Hell, I threw them money like you'd scatter feed corn for chickens, I threw money at them just to get rid of them long enough to climb back into th' car and—drive away. . . .

And then in Morocco, them Arabs, why, prostitution begins at four or five, that's no exaggeration, why, I remember one day in Marrakech, that old walled Arab city, I set on a broken-down wall to have a cigar, it was fearful hot there and this Arab woman stood in the road and looked at me till I was embarrassed, she stood stock still in the dusty hot road and looked at me till I was embarrassed. But listen to this. She had a naked child with her, a little naked girl with her, barely able to toddle, and after a while she set this child on the ground and give her a push and whispered something to her.

This child come toward me, barely able t' walk, come toddling up to me and—

Jesus, it makes you sick t' remember a thing like this!
It stuck out its hand and tried to unbutton my trousers!

That child was not yet five! Can you believe me? Or do you think that I am making this up? I wint back to the hotel and said to Big Mama, Git packed! We're clearing out of this country. . . .

BRICK:
Big Daddy, you're on a talkin' jag tonight.

BIG DADDY [*ignoring this remark*]:
Yes, sir, that's how it is, the human animal is a beast that dies but the fact that he's dying don't give him pity for others, no, sir, it—

—Did you say something?

BRICK:
Yes.

BIG DADDY:
What?

BRICK:
Hand me over that crutch so I can get up.

BIG DADDY:
Where you goin'?

BRICK:
I'm takin' a little short trip to Echo Spring.

BIG DADDY:
To where?

BRICK:
Liquor cabinet. . . .

BIG DADDY:
Yes, sir, boy—

[*He hands Brick the crutch.*]

—the human animal is a beast that dies and if he's got money he buys and buys and buys and I think the reason he buys everything he can buy is that in the back of his mind he has the crazy hope that one of his purchases will be life ever-lasting!—Which it never can be. . . . The human animal is a beast that—

BRICK [*at the liquor cabinet*]:
Big Daddy, you sure are shootin' th' breeze here tonight.

[*There is a pause and voices are heard outside.*]

BIG DADDY:
I been quiet here lately, spoke not a word, just sat and stared into space. I had something heavy weighing on my mind but tonight that load was took off me. That's why I'm talking.— The sky looks diff'rent to me. . . .

BRICK:
You know what I like to hear most?

BIG DADDY:
What?

BRICK:
Solid quiet. Perfect unbroken quiet.

89

BIG DADDY:
Why?

BRICK:
Because it's more peaceful.

BIG DADDY:
Man, you'll hear a lot of that in the grave.

[*He chuckles agreeably.*]

BRICK:
Are you through talkin' to me?

BIG DADDY:
Why are you so anxious to shut me up?

BRICK:
Well, sir, ever so often you say to me, Brick, I want to have a talk with you, but when we talk, it never materializes. Nothing is said. You sit in a chair and gas about this and that and I look like I listen. I try to look like I listen, but I don't listen, not much. Communication is—awful hard between people an'—somehow between you and me, it just don't—

BIG DADDY:
Have you ever been scared? I mean have you ever felt downright terror of something?

[*He gets up.*]

Just one moment. I'm going to close these doors. . . .

[*He closes doors on gallery as if he were going to tell an important secret.*]

BRICK:
What?

BIG DADDY:
Brick?

BRICK:
Huh?

BIG DADDY:
Son, I thought I had it!

BRICK:
Had what? Had what, Big Daddy?

BIG DADDY:
Cancer!

BRICK:
Oh . . .

BIG DADDY:
I thought the old man made out of bones had laid his cold and heavy hand on my shoulder!

BRICK:
Well, Big Daddy, you kept a tight mouth about it.

BIG DADDY:
A pig squeals. A man keeps a tight mouth about it, in spite of a man not having a pig's advantage.

BRICK:
What advantage is that?

BIG DADDY:
Ignorance—of mortality—is a comfort. A man don't have that comfort, he's the only living thing that conceives of death, that knows what it is. The others go without knowing which is the way that anything living should go, go without knowing, without any knowledge of it, and yet a pig squeals,

but a man sometimes, he can keep a tight mouth about it.
Sometimes he—

[*There is a deep, smoldering ferocity in the old man.*]

—can keep a tight mouth about it. I wonder if—

BRICK:
What, Big Daddy?

BIG DADDY:
A whiskey highball would injure this spastic condition?

BRICK:
No, sir, it might do it good.

BIG DADDY [*grins suddenly, wolfishly*]:
*Jesus, I can't tell you! The sky is open! Christ, it's open
again! It's open, boy, it's open!*

[*Brick looks down at his drink.*]

BRICK:
You feel better, Big Daddy?

BIG DADDY:
Better? Hell! I can breathe!—All of my life I been like a
doubled up fist. . . .

[*He pours a drink.*]

—Poundin', smashin', drivin'!—now I'm going to loosen
these doubled-up hands and touch things *easy* with them. . . .

[*He spreads his hands as if caressing the air.*]

You know what I'm contemplating?

BRICK [*vaguely*]:
No, sir. What are you contemplating?

BIG DADDY:

Ha ha!—*Pleasure!*—pleasure with *women!*

[*Brick's smile fades a little but lingers.*]

Brick, this stuff burns me!—

—Yes, boy. I'll tell you something that you might not guess. I still have desire for women and this is my sixty-fifth birthday.

BRICK:

I think that's mighty remarkable, Big Daddy.

BIG DADDY:

Remarkable?

BRICK:

Admirable, Big Daddy.

BIG DADDY:

You're damn right it is, remarkable and admirable both. I realize now that I never had me enough. I let many chances slip by because of scruples about it, scruples, convention— crap. . . . All that stuff is bull, bull, bull!—It took the shadow of death to make me see it. Now that shadow's lifted, I'm going to cut loose and have, what is it they call it, have me a—ball!

BRICK:

A ball, huh?

BIG DADDY:

That's right, a ball, a ball! Hell!—I slept with Big Mama till, let's see, five years ago, till I was sixty and she was fifty-eight, and never even liked her, never did!

[*The phone has been ringing down the hall. Big Mama enters, exclaiming:*]

93

BIG MAMA:

Don't you men hear that phone ring? I heard it way out on the gall'ry.

BIG DADDY:

There's five rooms off this front gall'ry that you could go through. Why do you go through this one?

[*Big Mama makes a playful face as she bustles out the hall door.*]

Hunh!—Why, when Big Mama goes out of a room, I can't remember what that woman looks like, but when Big Mama comes back into the room, boy, then I see what she looks like, and I wish I didn't!

[*Bends over laughing at this joke till it hurts his guts and he straightens with a grimace. The laugh subsides to a chuckle as he puts the liquor glass a little distrustfully down on the table.*

[*Brick has risen and hobbled to the gallery doors.*]

Hey! Where you goin'?

BRICK:

Out for a breather.

BIG DADDY:

Not yet you ain't. Stay here till this talk is finished, young fellow.

BRICK:

I thought it was finished, Big Daddy.

BIG DADDY:

It ain't even begun.

BRICK:

My mistake. Excuse me. I just wanted to feel that river breeze.

BIG DADDY:

Turn on the ceiling fan and set back down in that chair.

[*Big Mama's voice rises, carrying down the hall.*]

BIG MAMA:

Miss Sally, you're a case! You're a caution, Miss Sally. Why didn't you give me a chance to explain it to you?

BIG DADDY:

Jesus, she's talking to my old maid sister again.

BIG MAMA:

Well, goodbye, now, Miss Sally. You come down real soon, Big Daddy's dying to see you! Yaisss, goodbye, Miss Sally. . . .

[*She hangs up and bellows with mirth. Big Daddy groans and covers his ears as she approaches.*

[*Bursting in:*]

Big Daddy, that was Miss Sally callin' from Memphis again! You know what she done, Big Daddy? She called her doctor in Memphis to git him to tell her what that spastic thing is! Ha-*HAAAA!*—And called back to tell me how relieved she was that—Hey! Let me in!

[*Big Daddy has been holding the door half closed against her.*]

BIG DADDY:

Naw I ain't. I told you not to come and go through this room. You just back out and go through those five other rooms.

BIG MAMA:

Big Daddy? Big Daddy? Oh, big Daddy!—You didn't mean those things you said to me, did you?

[*He shuts door firmly against her but she still calls.*]

Sweetheart? Sweetheart? Big Daddy? You didn't mean those awful things you said to me?—I know you didn't. I know you didn't mean those things in your heart. . . .

[*The childlike voice fades with a sob and her heavy footsteps retreat down the hall. Brick has risen once more on his crutches and starts for the gallery again.*]

BIG DADDY:

All I ask of that woman is that she leave me alone. But she can't admit to herself that she makes me sick. That comes of having slept with her too many years. Should of quit much sooner but that old woman she never got enough of it— and I was good in bed . . . I never should of wasted so much of it on her. . . . They say you got just so many and each one is numbered. Well, I got a few left in me, a few, and I'm going to pick me a good one to spend 'em on! I'm going to pick me a choice one, I don't care how much she costs, I'll smother her in—minks! Ha ha! I'll strip her naked and smother her in minks and choke her with diamonds! Ha ha! I'll strip her naked and choke her with diamonds and smother her with minks and hump her from hell to breakfast. *Ha aha ha ha ha!*

MAE [*gaily at door*]:
Who's that laughin' in there?

GOOPER:
Is Big Daddy laughin' in there?

BIG DADDY:
Crap!—them two—*drips.* . . .

[*He goes over and touches Brick's shoulder.*]

Yes, son. Brick, boy.—I'm—*happy!* I'm happy, son, I'm happy!

[*He chokes a little and bites his under lip, pressing his head quickly, shyly against his son's head and then, coughing with embarrassment, goes uncertainly back to the table where he set down the glass. He drinks and makes a grimace as it burns his guts. Brick sighs and rises with effort.*]

What makes you so restless? Have you got ants in your britches?

BRICK:
Yes, sir . . .

BIG DADDY:
Why?

BRICK:
—Something—hasn't—happened. . . .

BIG DADDY:
Yeah? What is that!

BRICK [*sadly*]:
—the click. . . .

BIG DADDY:
Did you say click?

BRICK:
Yes, click.

BIG DADDY:
What click?

BRICK:
A click that I get in my head that makes me peaceful.

BIG DADDY:
I sure in hell don't know what you're talking about, but it disturbs me.

BRICK:

It's just a mechanical thing.

BIG DADDY:

What is a mechanical thing?

BRICK:

This click that I get in my head that makes me peaceful. I got to drink till I get it. It's just a mechanical thing, something like a—like a—like a—

BIG DADDY:

Like a—

BRICK:

Switch clicking off in my head, turning the hot light off and the cool night on and—

[*He looks up, smiling sadly.*]

—all of a sudden there's—peace!

BIG DADDY [*whistles long and soft with astonishment; he goes back to Brick and clasps his son's two shoulders*]:

Jesus! I didn't know it had gotten that bad with you. Why, boy, you're—*alcoholic!*

BRICK:

That's the truth, Big Daddy. I'm alcoholic.

BIG DADDY:

This shows how I—let things go!

BRICK:

I have to hear that little click in my head that makes me peaceful. Usually I hear it sooner than this, sometimes as early as—noon, but—

—Today it's—dilatory. . . .

—I just haven't got the right level of alcohol in my blood-stream yet!

[*This last statement is made with energy as he freshens his drink.*]

BIG DADDY:
Uh—huh. Expecting death made me blind. I didn't have no idea that a son of mine was turning into a drunkard under my nose.

BRICK [*gently*]:
Well, now you do, Big Daddy, the news has penetrated.

BIG DADDY:
UH-huh, yes, now I do, the news has—penetrated. . . .

BRICK:
And so if you'll excuse me—

BIG DADDY:
No, I won't excuse you.

BRICK:
—I'd better sit by myself till I hear that click in my head, it's just a mechanical thing but it don't happen except when I'm alone or talking to no one. . . .

BIG DADDY:
You got a long, long time to sit still, boy, and talk to no one, but now you're talkin' to me. At least I'm talking to you. And you set there and listen until I tell you the conversation is over!

BRICK:
But this talk is like all the others we've ever had together in our lives! It's nowhere, nowhere!—it's—it's *painful*, Big Daddy. . . .

99

BIG DADDY:

All right, then let it be painful, but don't you move from that chair!—I'm going to remove that crutch. . . .

[*He seizes the crutch and tosses it across room.*]

BRICK:

I can hop on one foot, and if I fall, I can crawl!

BIG DADDY:

If you ain't careful you're gonna crawl off this plantation and then, by Jesus, you'll have to hustle your drinks along Skid Row!

BRICK:

That'll come, Big Daddy.

BIG DADDY:

Naw, it won't. You're my son and I'm going to straighten you out; now that *I'm* straightened out, I'm going to straighten out you!

BRICK:
Yeah?

BIG DADDY:

Today the report come in from Ochsner Clinic. Y'know what they told me?

[*His face glows with triumph.*]

The only thing that they could detect with all the instruments of science in that great hospital is a little spastic condition of the colon! And nerves torn to pieces by all that worry about it.

[*A little girl bursts into room with a sparkler clutched in each fist, hops and shrieks like a monkey gone mad and rushes back out again as Big Daddy strikes at her.*

100

[*Silence. The two men stare at each other. A woman laughs gaily outside.*]

I want you to know I breathed a sigh of relief almost as powerful as the Vicksburg tornado!

BRICK:
You weren't ready to go?

BIG DADDY:
GO WHERE?—crap. . . .

—When you are gone from here, boy, you are long gone and no where! The human machine is not no different from the animal machine or the fish machine or the bird machine or the reptile machine or the insect machine! It's just a whole God damn lot more complicated and consequently more trouble to keep together. Yep. I thought I had it. The earth shook under my foot, the sky come down like the black lid of a kettle and I couldn't breathe!—Today!!—that lid was lifted, I drew my first free breath in—how many years?— *God!—three.* . . .

[*There is laughter outside, running footsteps, the soft, plushy sound and light of exploding rockets.*

[*Brick stares at him soberly for a long moment; then makes a sort of startled sound in his nostrils and springs up on one foot and hops across the room to grab his crutch, swinging on the furniture for support. He gets the crutch and flees as if in horror for the gallery. His father seizes him by the sleeve of his white silk pajamas.*]

Stay here, you son of a bitch!—till I say go!

BRICK:
I can't.

BIG DADDY:

You sure in hell will, God damn it.

BRICK:

No, I can't. We talk, you talk, in—circles! We get no where, no where! It's always the same, you say you want to talk to me and don't have a ruttin' thing to say to me!

BIG DADDY:

Nothin' to say when I'm tellin' you I'm going to live when I thought I was dying?!

BRICK:

Oh—*that!*—Is that what you have to say to me?

BIG DADDY:

Why, you son of a bitch! Ain't that, ain't that—*important?!*

BRICK:

Well, you said that, that's said, and now I—

BIG DADDY:

Now you set back down.

BRICK:

You're all balled up, you—

BIG DADDY:

I ain't balled up!

BRICK:

You are, you're all balled up!

BIG DADDY:

Don't tell me what I am, you drunken whelp! I'm going to tear this coat sleeve off if you don't set down!

BRICK:

Big Daddy—

BIG DADDY:

Do what I tell you! I'm the boss here, now! I want you to know I'm back in the driver's seat now!

[*Big Mama rushes in, clutching her great heaving bosom.*]

What in hell do you want in here, Big Mama?

BIG MAMA:

Oh, Big Daddy! Why are you shouting like that? I just cain't *stainnnnnnnd*—it. . . .

BIG DADDY [*raising the back of his hand above his head*]: *GIT!*—outa here.

[*She rushes back out, sobbing.*]

BRICK [*softly, sadly*]:
Christ. . . .

BIG DADDY [*fiercely*]:
Yeah! Christ!—is right . . .

[*Brick breaks loose and hobbles toward the gallery.*

[*Big Daddy jerks his crutch from under Brick so he steps with the injured ankle. He utters a hissing cry of anguish, clutches a chair and pulls it over on top of him on the floor.*]

Son of a—tub of—hog fat. . . .

BRICK:

Big Daddy! Give me my crutch.

[*Big Daddy throws the crutch out of reach.*]

Give me that crutch, Big Daddy.

BIG DADDY:
Why do you drink?

103

BRICK:

Don't know, give me my crutch!

BIG DADDY:

You better think why you drink or give up drinking!

BRICK:

Will you please give me my crutch so I can get up off this floor?

BIG DADDY:

First you answer my question. Why do you drink? Why are you throwing your life away, boy, like somethin' disgusting you picked up on the street?

BRICK [*getting onto his knees*]:

Big Daddy, I'm in pain, I stepped on that foot.

BIG DADDY:

Good! I'm glad you're not too numb with the liquor in you to feel some pain!

BRICK:

You—spilled my—drink ...

BIG DADDY:

I'll make a bargain with you. You tell me why you drink and I'll hand you one. I'll pour you the liquor myself and hand it to you.

BRICK:

Why do I drink?

BIG DADDY:

Yea! Why?

BRICK:

Give me a drink and I'll tell you.

BIG DADDY:
Tell me first!

BRICK:
I'll tell you in one word.

BIG DADDY:
What word?

BRICK:
DISGUST!

[*The clock chimes softly, sweetly. Big Daddy gives it a short, outraged glance.*]

Now how about that drink?

BIG DADDY:
What are you disgusted with? You got to tell me that, first. Otherwise being disgusted don't make no sense!

BRICK:
Give me my crutch.

BIG DADDY:
You heard me, you got to tell me what I asked you first.

BRICK:
I told you, I said to kill my disgust!

BIG DADDY:
DISGUST WITH WHAT!

BRICK:
You strike a hard bargain.

BIG DADDY:
What are you disgusted with?—an' I'll pass you the liquor.

105

BRICK:
I can hop on one foot, and if I fall, I can crawl.

BIG DADDY:
You want liquor that bad?

BRICK [*dragging himself up, clinging to bedstead*]:
Yeah, I want it that bad.

BIG DADDY:
If I give you a drink, will you tell me what it is you're disgusted with, Brick?

BRICK:
Yes, sir, I will try to.

[*The old man pours him a drink and solemnly passes it to him.*

[*There is silence as Brick drinks.*]

Have you ever heard the word "mendacity"?

BIG DADDY:
Sure. Mendacity is one of them five dollar words that cheap politicians throw back and forth at each other.

BRICK:
You know what it means?

BIG DADDY:
Don't it mean lying and liars?

BRICK:
Yes, sir, lying and liars.

BIG DADDY:
Has someone been lying to you?

CHILDREN [*chanting in chorus offstage*]:
We want Big Dad-dee!
We want Big Dad-dee!

[*Gooper appears in the gallery door.*]

GOOPER:
Big Daddy, the kiddies are shouting for you out there.

BIG DADDY [*fiercely*]:
Keep out, Gooper!

GOOPER:
'Scuse *me!*

[*Big Daddy slams the doors after Gooper.*]

BIG DADDY:
Who's been lying to you, has Margaret been lying to you, has
your wife been lying to you about something, Brick?

BRICK:
Not her. That wouldn't matter.

BIG DADDY:
Then who's been lying to you, and what about?

BRICK:
No one single person and no one lie. . . .

BIG DADDY:
Then what, what then, for Christ's sake?

BRICK:
—The whole, the whole—thing. . . .

BIG DADDY:
Why are you rubbing your head? You got a headache?

BRICK:
No, I'm tryin' to—

BIG DADDY:
—Concentrate, but you can't because your brain's all soaked with liquor, is that the trouble? Wet brain!

[*He snatches the glass from Brick's hand.*]

What do you know about this mendacity thing? Hell! I could write a book on it! Don't you know that? I could write a book on it and still not cover the subject? Well, I could, I could write a goddam book on it and still not cover the subject any-where near enough!!—Think of all the lies I got to put up with!—Pretenses! Ain't that mendacity? Having to pre-tend stuff you don't think or feel or have any idea of? Having for instance to act like I care for Big Mama!—I haven't been able to stand the sight, sound, or smell of that woman for forty years now!—even when I *laid* her!—regular as a piston. . . .

Pretend to love that son of a bitch of a Gooper and his wife Mae and those five same screechers out there like parrots in a jungle? Jesus! Can't stand to look at 'em!

Church!—it bores the bejesus out of me but I go!—I go an' sit there and listen to the fool preacher!

Clubs!—Elks! Masons! Rotary!—*crap!*

[*A spasm of pain makes him clutch his belly. He sinks into a chair and his voice is softer and hoarser.*]

You I *do* like for some reason, did always have some kind of real feeling for—affection—respect—yes, always. . . .

You and being a success as a planter is all I ever had any devotion to in my whole life!—and that's the truth. . . .

I don't know why, but it is!

I've lived with mendacity!—Why can't *you* live with it? Hell, you *got* to live with it, there's nothing *else* to *live* with except mendacity, is there?

BRICK:
Yes, sir. Yes, sir there is something else that you can live with!

BIG DADDY:
What?

BRICK [*lifting his glass*]:
This!—Liquor. . . .

BIG DADDY:
That's not living, that's dodging away from life.

BRICK:
I want to dodge away from it.

BIG DADDY:
Then why don't you kill yourself, man?

BRICK:
I like to drink. . . .

BIG DADDY:
Oh, God, I can't talk to you. . . .

BRICK:
I'm sorry, Big Daddy.

BIG DADDY:
Not as sorry as I am. I'll tell you something. A little while back when I thought my number was up—

[*This speech should have torrential pace and fury.*]

—before I found out it was just this—spastic—colon. I thought about you. Should I or should I not, if the jig was up, give you this place when I go—since I hate Gooper an' Mae an' know that they hate me, and since all five same monkeys are little Maes an' Goopers.—And I thought, No!—Then I thought, Yes!—I couldn't make up my mind. I hate Gooper and his five same monkeys and that bitch Mae! Why should I turn over twenty-eight thousand acres of the richest land this side of the valley Nile to not my kind?—But why in hell, on the other hand, Brick—should I subsidize a goddam fool on the bottle?—Liked or not liked, well, maybe even—*loved!* —Why should I do that?—Subsidize worthless behavior? Rot? Corruption?

BRICK [*smiling*]:
I understand.

BIG DADDY:
Well, if you do, you're smarter than I am, God damn it, because I don't understand. And this I will tell you frankly. I didn't make up my mind at all on that question and still to this day I ain't made out no will!—Well, now I don't *have* to. The pressure is gone. I can just wait and see if you pull yourself together or if you don't.

BRICK:
That's right, Big Daddy.

BIG DADDY:
You sound like you thought I was kidding.

BRICK [*rising*]:
No, sir, I know you're not kidding.

BIG DADDY:
But you don't care—?

110

BRICK [*hobbling toward the gallery door*]:
No, sir, I don't care. . . .

Now how about taking a look at your birthday fireworks and getting some of that cool breeze off the river?

[*He stands in the gallery doorway as the night sky turns pink and green and gold with successive flashes of light.*]

BIG DADDY:
WAIT!—Brick. . . .

[*His voice drops. Suddenly there is something shy, almost tender, in his restraining gesture.*]

Don't let's—leave it like this, like them other talks we've had, we've always—talked around things, we've—just talked around things for some rutten reason, I don't know what, it's always like something was left not spoken, something avoided because neither of us was honest enough with the—other. . . .

BRICK:
I never lied to you, Big Daddy.

BIG DADDY:
Did I ever to *you?*

BRICK:
No, sir. . . .

BIG DADDY:
Then there is at least two people that never lied to each other.

BRICK:
But we've never *talked* to each other.

BIG DADDY:
We can *now*.

BRICK:
Big Daddy, there don't seem to be anything much to say.

BIG DADDY:
You say that you drink to kill your disgust with lying.

BRICK:
You said to give you a reason.

BIG DADDY:
Is liquor the only thing that'll kill this disgust?

BRICK:
Now. Yes.

BIG DADDY:
But not once, huh?

BRICK:
Not when I was still young an' believing. A drinking man's someone who wants to forget he isn't still young an' believing.

BIG DADDY:
Believing what?

BRICK:
Believing. . . .

BIG DADDY:
Believing *what?*

BRICK [*stubbornly evasive*]:
Believing. . . .

BIG DADDY:
I don't know what the hell you mean by believing and I don't think you know what you mean by believing, but if you still got sports in your blood, go back to sports announcing and—

BRICK:

Sit in a glass box watching games I can't play? Describing what I can't do while players do it? Sweating out their disgust and confusion in contests I'm not fit for? Drinkin' a coke, half bourbon, so I can stand it? That's no goddam good any more, no help—time just outran me, Big Daddy—got there first . . .

BIG DADDY:

I think you're passing the buck.

BRICK:

You know many drinkin' men?

BIG DADDY [*with a slight, charming smile*]:

I have known a fair number of that species.

BRICK:

Could any of them tell you why he drank?

BIG DADDY:

Yep, you're passin' the buck to things like time and disgust with "mendacity" and—crap!—if you got to use that kind of language about a thing, it's ninety-proof bull, and I'm not buying any.

BRICK:

I had to give you a reason to get a drink!

BIG DADDY:

You started drinkin' when your friend Skipper died.

[*Silence for five beats. Then Brick makes a startled movement, reaching for his crutch.*]

BRICK:

What are you suggesting?

113

BIG DADDY:

I'm suggesting nothing.

[*The shuffle and clop of Brick's rapid hobble away from his father's steady, grave attention.*]

—But Gooper an' Mae suggested that there was something not right exactly in your—

BRICK [*stopping short downstage as if backed to a wall*]: "Not right"?

BIG DADDY:

Not, well, exactly *normal* in your friendship with—

BRICK:

They suggested that, too? I thought that was Maggie's suggestion.

[*Brick's detachment is at last broken through. His heart is accelerated; his forehead sweat-beaded; his breath becomes more rapid and his voice hoarse. The thing they're discussing, timidly and painfully on the side of Big Daddy, fiercely, violently on Brick's side, is the inadmissible thing that Skipper died to disavow between them. The fact that if it existed it had to be disavowed to "keep face" in the world they lived in, may be at the heart of the "mendacity" that Brick drinks to kill his disgust with. It may be the root of his collapse. Or maybe it is only a single manifestation of it, not even the most important. The bird that I hope to catch in the net of this play is not the solution of one man's psychological problem. I'm trying to catch the true quality of experience in a group of people, that cloudy, flickering, evanescent—fiercely charged!—interplay of live human beings in the thundercloud of a common crisis. Some mystery should be left in the revelation of character in a play, just as a great deal of mystery is always left in*

*the revelation of character in life, even in one's own char-
acter to himself. This does not absolve the playwright of his
duty to observe and probe as clearly and deeply as he legiti-
mately can: but it should steer him away from "pat" con-
clusions, facile definitions which make a play just a play,
not a snare for the truth of human experience.*

[*The following scene should be played with great concentration, with most of the power leashed but palpable in
what is left unspoken.*]

Who else's suggestion is it, is it *yours?* How many others
thought that Skipper and I were—

BIG DADDY [*gently*]:
Now, hold on, hold on a minute, son.—I knocked around in
my time.

BRICK:
What's that got to do with—

BIG DADDY:
I said "Hold on!"—I bummed, I bummed this country till I
was—

BRICK:
Whose suggestion, who else's suggestion is it?

BIG DADDY:
Slept in hobo jungles and railroad Y's and flophouses in all
cities before I—

BRICK:
Oh, *you* think so, too, you call me your son and a queer. Oh!
Maybe that's why you put Maggie and me in this room that
was Jack Straw's and Peter Ochello's, in which that pair of
old sisters slept in a double bed where both of 'em died!

115

BIG DADDY:
Now just don't go throwing rocks at—

[*Suddenly Reverend Tooker appears in the gallery doors, his head slightly, playfully, fatuously cocked, with a practised clergyman's smile, sincere as a bird call blown on a hunter's whistle, the living embodiment of the pious, conventional lie.*]

[*Big Daddy gasps a little at this perfectly timed, but incongruous, apparition.*]

—What're you lookin' for, Preacher?

REVEREND TOOKER:
The gentleman's lavatory, ha ha!—heh, heh . . .

BIG DADDY [*with strained courtesy*]:
—Go back out and walk down to the other end of the gallery, Reverend Tooker, and use the bathroom connected with my bedroom, and if you can't find it, ask them where it is!

REVEREND TOOKER:
Ah, thanks.

[*He goes out with a deprecatory chuckle.*]

BIG DADDY:
It's hard to talk in this place . . .

BRICK:
Son of a—!

BIG DADDY [*leaving a lot unspoken*]:
—I seen all things and understood a lot of them, till 1910. Christ, the year that—I had worn my shoes through, hocked my—I hopped off a yellow dog freight car half a mile down the road, slept in a wagon of cotton outside the gin—Jack Straw an' Peter Ochello took me in. Hired me to manage this

116

place which grew into this one.—When Jack Straw died—
why, old Peter Ochello quit eatin' like a dog does when its
master's dead, and died, too!

BRICK:
Christ!

BIG DADDY:
I'm just saying I understand such—

BRICK [*violently*]:
Skipper is dead. I have not quit eating!

BIG DADDY:
No, but you started drinking.

[*Brick wheels on his crutch and hurls his glass across the
room shouting.*]

BRICK:
YOU THINK SO, TOO?

BIG DADDY:
Shhh!

[*Footsteps run on the gallery. There are women's calls.*

[*Big Daddy goes toward the door.*]

Go way!—Just broke a glass. . . .

[*Brick is transformed, as if a quiet mountain blew suddenly
up in volcanic flame.*]

BRICK:
You think so, too? You think so, too? You think me an'
Skipper did, did, did!—*sodomy!*—together?

BIG DADDY:
Hold—!

117

BRICK:
That what you—

BIG DADDY:
—*ON*—a minute!

BRICK:
You think we did dirty things between us, Skipper an'—

BIG DADDY:
Why are you shouting like that? Why are you—

BRICK:
—Me, is that what you think of Skipper, is that—

BIG DADDY:
—so excited? I don't think nothing. I don't know nothing. I'm simply telling you what—

BRICK:
You think that Skipper and me were a pair of dirty old men?

BIG DADDY:
Now that's—

BRICK:
Straw? Ochello? A couple of—

BIG DADDY:
Now just—

BRICK:
—ducking sissies? Queers? Is that what you—

BIG DADDY:
Shhh.

BRICK:
—think?

[*He loses his balance and pitches to his knees without noticing the pain. He grabs the bed and drags himself up.*]

BIG DADDY:
Jesus!—Whew. . . . Grab my hand!

BRICK:
Naw, I don't want your hand. . . .

BIG DADDY:
Well, I want yours. Git up!

[*He draws him up, keeps an arm about him with concern and affection.*]

You broken out in a sweat! You're panting like you'd run a race with—

BRICK [*freeing himself from his father's hold*]:
Big Daddy, you shock me, Big Daddy, you, you—*shock* me! Talkin' so—

[*He turns away from his father.*]

—casually!—about a—thing like that . . .

—Don't you know how people *feel* about things like that? How, how *disgusted* they are by things like that? Why, at Ole Miss when it was discovered a pledge to our fraternity, Skipper's and mine, did a, *attempted* to do a, unnatural thing with—

We not only dropped him like a hot rock!—We told him to git off the campus, and he did, he got!—All the way to—

[*He halts, breathless.*]

BIG DADDY:
—Where?

119

BRICK:

—North Africa, last I heard!

BIG DADDY:

Well, I have come back from further away than that, I have just now returned from the other side of the moon, death's country, son, and I'm not easy to shock by anything here.

[*He comes downstage and faces out.*]

Always, anyhow, lived with too much space around me to be infected by ideas of other people. One thing you can grow on a big place more important than cotton!—is *tolerance!*—I grown it.

[*He returns toward Brick.*]

BRICK:

Why can't exceptional friendship, *real, real, deep, deep friend-ship!* between two men be respected as something clean and decent without being thought of as—

BIG DADDY:

It can, it is, for God's sake.

BRICK:

—*Fairies.* . . .

[*In his utterance of this word, we gauge the wide and pro-found reach of the conventional mores he got from the world that crowned him with early laurel.*]

BIG DADDY:

I told Mae an' Gooper—

BRICK:

Frig Mae and Gooper, frig all dirty lies and liars!—Skipper and me had a clean, true thing between us!—had a clean friendship, practically all our lives, till Maggie got the idea

120

you're talking about. Normal? No!—It was too rare to be normal, any true thing between two people is too rare to be normal. Oh, once in a while he put his hand on my shoulder or I'd put mine on his, oh, maybe even, when we were touring the country in pro-football an' shared hotel-rooms we'd reach across the space between the two beds and shake hands to say goodnight, yeah, one or two times we—

BIG DADDY:
Brick, nobody thinks that that's not normal!

BRICK:
Well, they're mistaken, it was! It was a pure an' true thing an' that's not normal.

[*They both stare straight at each other for a long moment. The tension breaks and both turn away as if tired.*]

BIG DADDY:
Yeah, it's—hard t'—talk. . . .

BRICK:
All right, then, let's—let it go. . . .

BIG DADDY:
Why did Skipper crack up? Why have you?

[*Brick looks back at his father again. He has already decided, without knowing that he has made this decision, that he is going to tell his father that he is dying of cancer. Only this could even the score between them: one inadmissible thing in return for another.*]

BRICK [*ominously*]:
All right. You're asking for it, Big Daddy. We're finally going to have that real true talk you wanted. It's too late to stop it, now, we got to carry it through and cover every subject.

121

[*He hobbles back to the liquor cabinet.*]

Uh-huh.

[*He opens the ice bucket and picks up the silver tongs with slow admiration of their frosty brightness.*]

Maggie declares that Skipper and I went into pro-football after we left "Ole Miss" because we were scared to grow up . . .

[*He moves downstage with the shuffle and clop of a cripple on a crutch. As Margaret did when her speech became "recitative," he looks out into the house, commanding its attention by his direct, concentrated gaze—a broken, "tragically elegant" figure telling simply as much as he knows of "the Truth":*]

—Wanted to—keep on tossing—those long, long!—high, high!—passes that—couldn't be intercepted except by time, the aerial attack that made us famous! And so we did, we did, we kept it up for one season, that aerial attack, we held it high!—Yeah, but—

—that summer, Maggie, she laid the law down to me, said, Now or never, and so I married Maggie. . . .

BIG DADDY:
How was Maggie in bed?

BRICK [*wryly*]:
Great! the greatest!

[*Big Daddy nods as if he thought so.*]

She went on the road that fall with the Dixie Stars. Oh, she made a great show of being the world's best sport. She wore a—wore a—tall bearskin cap! A shako, they call it, a dyed moleskin coat, a moleskin coat dyed red!—Cut up crazy!

122

Rented hotel ballrooms for victory celebrations, wouldn't cancel them when it—turned out—defeat. . . .

MAGGIE THE CAT! Ha ha!

[*Big Daddy nods.*]

—But Skipper, he had some fever which came back on him which doctors couldn't explain and I got that injury—turned out to be just a shadow on the X-ray plate—and a touch of bursitis. . . .

I lay in a hospital bed, watched our games on TV, saw Maggie on the bench next to Skipper when he was hauled out of a game for stumbles, fumbles!—Burned me up the way she hung on his arm!—Y'know, I think that Maggie had always felt sort of left out because she and me never got any closer together than two people just get in bed, which is not much closer than two cats on a—fence humping. . . .

So! She took this time to work on poor dumb Skipper. He was a less than average student at Ole Miss, you know that, don't you?!—Poured in his mind the dirty, false idea that what we were, him and me, was a frustrated case of that ole pair of sisters that lived in this room, Jack Straw and Peter Ochello!—He, poor Skipper, went to bed with Maggie to prove it wasn't true, and when it didn't work out, he thought it *was* true!—Skipper broke in two like a rotten stick—nobody ever turned so fast to a lush—or died of it so quick. . . .

—Now are you satisfied?

[*Big Daddy has listened to this story, dividing the grain from the chaff. Now he looks at his son.*]

BIG DADDY:
Are *you* satisfied?

BRICK:
With what?

BIG DADDY:
That half-ass story!

BRICK:
What's half-ass about it?

BIG DADDY:
Something's left out of that story. What did you leave out?

[*The phone has started ringing in the hall. As if it reminded him of something, Brick glances suddenly toward the sound and says:*]

BRICK:
Yes!—I left out a long-distance call which I had from Skipper, in which he made a drunken confession to me and on which I hung up!—last time we spoke to each other in our lives. . . .

[*Muted ring stops as someone answers phone in a soft, indistinct voice in hall.*]

BIG DADDY:
You hung up?

BRICK:
Hung up. Jesus! Well—

BIG DADDY:
Anyhow now!—we have tracked down the lie with which you're disgusted and which you are drinking to kill your disgust with, Brick. You been passing the buck. This disgust with mendacity is disgust with yourself.

You!—dug the grave of your friend and kicked him in it!— before you'd face truth with him!

BRICK:
His truth, not *mine!*

BIG DADDY:
His truth, okay! But you wouldn't face it with him!

BRICK:
Who *can* face truth? Can *you?*

BIG DADDY:
Now don't start passin' the rotten buck again, boy!

BRICK:
*How about these birthday congratulations, these many, many
happy returns of the day, when ev'rybody but you knows there
won't be any!*

[*Whoever has answered the hall phone lets out a high,
shrill laugh; the voice becomes audible saying: "No, no, you
got it all wrong! Upside down! Are you crazy?"*

[*Brick suddenly catches his breath as he realized that he
has made a shocking disclosure. He hobbles a few paces,
then freezes, and without looking at his father's shocked
face, says:*]

Let's, let's—go out, now, and—

[*Big Daddy moves suddenly forward and grabs hold of the
boy's crutch like it was a weapon for which they were
fighting for possession.*]

BIG DADDY:
Oh, no, no! No one's going out! What did you start to say?

BRICK:
I don't remember.

BIG DADDY:
"Many happy returns when they know there won't be any"?

125

BRICK:

Aw, hell, Big Daddy, forget it. Come on out on the gallery and look at the fireworks they're shooting off for your birthday. . . .

BIG DADDY:

First you finish that remark you were makin' before you cut off. "Many happy returns when they know there won't be any"?—Ain't that what you just said?

BRICK:

Look, now. I can get around without that crutch if I have to but it would be a lot easier on the furniture an' glassware if I didn' have to go swinging along like Tarzan of th'—

BIG DADDY:

FINISH! WHAT YOU WAS SAYIN'!

[*An eerie green glow shows in sky behind him.*]

BRICK [*sucking the ice in his glass, speech becoming thick*]:
Leave th' place to Gooper and Mae an' their five little same little monkeys. All I want is—

BIG DADDY:

"LEAVE TH' PLACE," did you say?

BRICK [*vaguely*]:

All twenty-eight thousand acres of the richest land this side of the valley Nile.

BIG DADDY:

Who said I was "leaving the place" to Gooper or anybody? This is my sixty-fifth birthday! I got fifteen years or twenty years left in me! I'll outlive *you!* I'll bury you an' have to pay for your coffin!

BRICK:

Sure. Many happy returns. Now let's go watch the fireworks, come on, let's—

126

BIG DADDY:
Lying, have they been lying? About the report from th'—clinic? Did they, did they—find something?—*Cancer.* Maybe?

BRICK:
Mendacity is a system that we live in. Liquor is one way out an' death's the other. . . .

[*He takes the crutch from Big Daddy's loose grip and swings out on the gallery leaving the doors open.*

[*A song, "Pick a Bale of Cotton," is heard.*]

MAE [*appearing in door*]:
Oh, Big Daddy, the field hands are singin' fo' you!

BIG DADDY [*shouting hoarsely*]:
BRICK! BRICK!

MAE:
He's outside drinkin', Big Daddy.

BIG DADDY:
BRICK!

[*Mae retreats, awed by the passion of his voice. Children call Brick in tones mocking Big Daddy. His face crumbles like broken yellow plaster about to fall into dust.*

[*There is a glow in the sky. Brick swings back through the doors, slowly, gravely, quite soberly.*]

BRICK:
I'm sorry, Big Daddy. My head don't work any more and it's hard for me to understand how anybody could care if he lived or died or was dying or cared about anything but whether or not there was liquor left in the bottle and so I said what I said without thinking. In some ways I'm no better than the others, in some ways worse because I'm less alive. Maybe it's

127

being alive that makes them lie, and being almost *not* alive makes me sort of accidentally truthful—I don't know but—anyway—we've been friends ...

—And being friends is telling each other the truth. ...

[*There is a pause.*]

You told *me!* I told *you!*

[*A child rushes into the room and grabs a fistful of fire-crackers and runs out again.*]

CHILD [*screaming*]:
Bang, bang, bang, bang, bang, bang, bang, bang, bang!

BIG DADDY [*slowly and passionately*]:
CHRIST—DAMN—ALL—LYING SONS OF—LYING BITCHES!

[*He straightens at last and crosses to the inside door. At the door he turns and looks back as if he had some desperate question he couldn't put into words. Then he nods reflectively and says in a hoarse voice:*]

Yes, all liars, all liars, all lying dying liars!

[*This is said slowly, slowly, with a fierce revulsion. He goes on out.*]

—Lying! Dying! Liars!

[*His voice dies out. There is the sound of a child being slapped. It rushes, hideously bawling, through room and out the hall door.*

[*Brick remains motionless as the lights dim out and the curtain falls.*]

CURTAIN

ACT THREE

There is no lapse of time.
Mae enters with Reverend Tooker.

MAE:
Where is Big Daddy! Big Daddy?

BIG MAMA [*entering*]:
Too much smell of burnt fireworks makes me feel a little bit sick at my stomach.—Where is Big Daddy?

MAE:
That's what I want to know, where has Big Daddy gone?

BIG MAMA:
He must have turned in, I reckon he went to baid. . . .

[*Gooper enters.*]

GOOPER:
Where is Big Daddy?

MAE:
We don't know where he is!

BIG MAMA:
I reckon he's gone to baid.

GOOPER:
Well, then, now we can talk.

BIG MAMA:
What *is* this talk, *what* talk?

[*Margaret appears on gallery, talking to Dr. Baugh.*]

MARGARET [*musically*]:
My family freed their slaves ten years before abolition, my

great-great-grandfather gave his slaves their freedom five years before the war between the States started!

MAE:

Oh, for God's sake! Maggie's climbed back up in her family tree!

MARGARET [*sweetly*]:

What, Mae?—Oh, where's Big Daddy?!

[*The pace must be very quick. Great Southern animation.*]

BIG MAMA [*addressing them all*]:

I think Big Daddy was just worn out. He loves his family, he loves to have them around him, but it's a strain on his nerves. He wasn't himself tonight, Big Daddy wasn't himself, I could tell he was all worked up.

REVEREND TOOKER:

I think he's remarkable.

BIG MAMA:

Yaisss! Just remarkable. Did you all notice the food he ate at that table? Did you all notice the supper he put away? Why, he ate like a hawss!

GOOPER:

I hope he doesn't regret it.

BIG MAMA:

Why, that man—ate a huge piece of cawn-bread with molasses on it! Helped himself twice to hoppin' john.

MARGARET:

Big Daddy loves hoppin' john.—We had a real country dinner.

BIG MAMA [*overlapping Margaret*]:

Yais, he simply adores it! An' candied yams? That man put away enough food at that table to stuff a nigger *field* hand!

130

GOOPER [*with grim relish*]:
I hope he don't have to pay for it later on. . . .

BIG MAMA [*fiercely*]:
What's *that*, Gooper?

MAE:
Gooper says he hopes Big Daddy doesn't suffer tonight.

BIG MAMA:
Oh, shoot, Gooper says, Gooper says! Why should Big Daddy suffer for satisfying a normal appetite? There's nothin' wrong with that man but nerves, he's sound as a dollar! And now he knows he is an' that's why he ate such a supper. He had a big load off his mind, knowin' he wasn't doomed t'—what he thought he was doomed to. . . .

MARGARET [*sadly and sweetly*]:
Bless his old sweet soul. . . .

BIG MAMA [*vaguely*]:
Yais, bless his heart, where's Brick?

MAE:
Outside.

GOOPER:
—Drinkin' . . .

BIG MAMA:
I know he's drinkin'. You all don't have to keep tellin' *me* Brick is drinkin'. Cain't I see he's drinkin' without you continually tellin' me that boy's drinkin'?

MARGARET:
Good for you, Big Mama!

[*She applauds.*]

131

BIG MAMA:

Other people *drink* and *have* drunk an' will *drink,* as long as they make that stuff an' put it in bottles.

MARGARET:

That's the truth. I never trusted a man that didn't drink.

MAE:

Gooper never drinks. Don't you trust Gooper?

MARGARET:

Why, Gooper don't you drink? If I'd known you didn't drink, I wouldn't of made that remark—

BIG MAMA:

Brick?

MARGARET:

—at least not in your presence.

[*She laughs sweetly.*]

BIG MAMA:

Brick!

MARGARET:

He's still on the gall'ry. I'll go bring him in so we can talk.

BIG MAMA [*worriedly*]:

I don't know what this mysterious family conference is about.

[*Awkward silence. Big Mama looks from face to face, then belches slightly and mutters, "Excuse me. . . ." She opens an ornamental fan suspended about her throat, a black lace fan to go with her black lace gown and fans her wilting corsage, sniffing nervously and looking from face to face in the uncomfortable silence as Margaret calls "Brick?" and Brick sings to the moon on the gallery.*]

132

I don't know what's wrong here, you all have such long faces!
Open that door on the hall and let some air circulate through
here, will you please, Gooper?

MAE:
I think we'd better leave that door closed, Big Mama, till
after the talk.

BIG MAMA:
Reveren' Tooker, will *you* please open that door?!

REVEREND TOOKER:
I sure will, Big Mama.

MAE:
I just didn't think we ought t' take any chance of Big Daddy
hearin' a word of this discussion.

BIG MAMA:
I swan! Nothing's going to be said in Big Daddy's house that
he cain't hear if he wants to!

GOOPER:
Well, Big Mama, it's—

[*Mae gives him a quick, hard poke to shut him up. He
glares at her fiercely as she circles before him like a burlesque ballerina, raising her skinny bare arms over her
head, jangling her bracelets, exclaiming:*]

MAE:
A breeze! A breeze!

REVEREND TOOKER:
I think this house is the coolest house in the Delta.—Did you
all know that Halsey Banks' widow put air-conditioning units
in the church and rectory at Friar's Point in memory of
Halsey?

[*General conversation has resumed; everybody is chatting so that the stage sounds like a big bird-cage.*]

GOOPER:

Too bad nobody cools your church off for you. I bet you sweat in that pulpit these hot Sundays, Reverend Tooker.

REVEREND TOOKER:

Yes, my vestments are drenched.

MAE [*at the same time to Dr. Baugh*]:

You think those vitamin B_{12} injections are what they're cracked up t' be, Doc Baugh?

DOCTOR BAUGH:

Well, if you want to be stuck with something I guess they're as good to be stuck with as anything else.

BIG MAMA [*at gallery door*]:

Maggie, Maggie, aren't you comin' with Brick?

MAE [*suddenly and loudly, creating a silence*]:

I have a strange feeling, I have a peculiar feeling!

BIG MAMA [*turning from gallery*]:

What feeling?

MAE:

That Brick said somethin' he shouldn't of said t' Big Daddy.

BIG MAMA:

Now what on earth could Brick of said t' Big Daddy that he shouldn't say?

GOOPER:

Big Mama, there's somethin'—

MAE:

NOW, WAIT!

[*She rushes up to Big Mama and gives her a quick hug and kiss. Big Mama pushes her impatiently off as the Reverend Tooker's voice rises serenely in a little pocket of silence:*]

REVEREND TOOKER:
Yes, last Sunday the gold in my chasuble faded into th' purple. . . .

GOOPER:
Reveren' you must of been preachin' hell's fire last Sunday!

[*He guffaws at this witticism but the Reverend is not sincerely amused. At the same time Big Mama has crossed over to Dr. Baugh and is saying to him:*]

BIG MAMA [*her breathless voice rising high-pitched above the others*]:

In my day they had what they call the Keeley cure for heavy drinkers. But now I understand they just take some kind of tablets, they call them "Annie Bust" tablets. But *Brick* don't need to take *nothin'*.

[*Brick appears in gallery doors with Margaret behind him.*]

BIG MAMA [*unaware of his presence behind her*]:
That boy is just broken up over Skipper's death. You know how poor Skipper died. They gave him a big, big dose of that sodium amytal stuff at his home and then they called the ambulance and give him another big, big dose of it at the hospital and that and all of the alcohol in his system fo' months an' months an' months just proved too much for his heart. . . . I'm scared of needles! I'm more scared of a needle than the knife. . . . I think more people have been needled out of this world than—

[*She stops short and wheels about.*]

135

OH!—here's Brick! My precious baby—

[*She turns upon Brick with short, fat arms extended, at the same time uttering a loud, short sob, which is both comic and touching.*

[*Brick smiles and bows slightly, making a burlesque gesture of gallantry for Maggie to pass before him into the room. Then he hobbles on his crutch directly to the liquor cabinet and there is absolute silence, with everybody looking at Brick as everybody has always looked at Brick when he spoke or moved or appeared. One by one he drops ice cubes in his glass, then suddenly, but not quickly, looks back over his shoulder with a wry, charming smile, and says:*]

BRICK:
I'm sorry! Anyone else?

BIG MAMA [*sadly*]:
No, son. I *wish* you wouldn't!

BRICK:
I wish I didn't have to, Big Mama, but I'm still waiting for that click in my head which makes it all smooth out!

BIG MAMA:
Aw, Brick, you—BREAK MY HEART!

MARGARET [*at the same time*]:
Brick, go sit with Big Mama!

BIG MAMA:
I just cain't *staiiiiiiii-nnnnnd*—it. . . .

[*She sobs.*]

MAE:
Now that we're all assembled—

GOOPER:
We kin talk. . . .

BIG MAMA:
Breaks my heart. . . .

MARGARET:
Sit with Big Mama, Brick, and hold her hand.

[*Big Mama sniffs very loudly three times, almost like three drum beats in the pocket of silence.*]

BRICK:
You do that, Maggie. I'm a restless cripple. I got to stay on my crutch.

[*Brick hobbles to the gallery door; leans there as if waiting.*

[*Mae sits beside Big Mama, while Gooper moves in front and sits on the end of the couch, facing her. Reverend Tooker moves nervously into the space between them; on the other side, Dr. Baugh stands looking at nothing in particular and lights a cigar. Margaret turns away.*]

BIG MAMA:
Why're you all *surroundin'* me—like this? Why're you all starin' at me like this an' makin' signs at each other?

[*Reverend Tooker steps back startled.*]

MAE:
Calm yourself, Big Mama.

BIG MAMA:
Calm you'self, *you'self,* Sister Woman. How could I calm myself with everyone starin' at me as if big drops of blood had broken out on m'face? What's this all about, annh! What?

[*Gooper coughs and takes a center position.*]

137

GOOPER:
Now, Doc Baugh.

MAE:
Doc Baugh?

BRICK [*suddenly*]:
SHHH!—

[*Then he grins and chuckles and shakes his head regret-fully.*]

—Naw!—that wasn't th' click.

GOOPER:
Brick, shut up or stay out there on the gallery with your liquor! We got to talk about a serious matter. Big Mama wants to know the complete truth about the report we got today from the Ochsner Clinic.

MAE [*eagerly*]:
—on Big Daddy's condition!

GOOPER:
Yais, on Big Daddy's condition, we got to face it.

DOCTOR BAUGH:
Well. . . .

BIG MAMA [*terrified, rising*]:
Is there? Something? Something that I? Don't—Know?

[*In these few words, this startled, very soft, question, Big Mama reviews the history of her forty-five years with Big Daddy, her great, almost embarrassingly true-hearted and simple-minded devotion to Big Daddy, who must have had something Brick has, who made himself loved so much by the "simple expedient" of not loving enough to disturb his*]

138

charming detachment, also once coupled, like Brick's, with virile beauty.

[*Big Mama has a dignity at this moment: she almost stops being fat.*]

DOCTOR BAUGH [*after a pause, uncomfortably*]:
Yes?—Well—

BIG MAMA:
I!!!—want to—knowwwwwww. . . .

[*Immediately she thrusts her fist to her mouth as if to deny that statement.*

[*Then, for some curious reason, she snatches the withered corsage from her breast and hurls it on the floor and steps on it with her short, fat feet.*]

—Somebody must be lyin'!—I want to know!

MAE:
Sit down, Big Mama, sit down on this sofa.

MARGARET [*quickly*]:
Brick, go sit with Big Mama.

BIG MAMA:
What is it, what is it?

DOCTOR BAUGH:
I never have seen a more thorough examination than Big Daddy Pollitt was given in all my experience with the Ochsner Clinic.

GOOPER:
It's one of the best in the country.

MAE:
It's *THE* best in the country—bar *none!*

139

[*For some reason she gives Gooper a violent poke as she goes past him. He slaps at her hand without removing his eyes from his mother's face.*]

DOCTOR BAUGH:
Of course they were ninety-nine and nine-tenths percent sure before they even started.

BIG MAMA:
Sure of what, sure of what, sure of—*what?—what!*

[*She catches her breath in a startled sob. Mae kisses her quickly. She thrusts Mae fiercely away from her, staring at the doctor.*]

MAE:
Mommy, be a brave girl!

BRICK [*in the doorway, softly*]:
"By the light, by the light,
Of the sil-ve-ry mo-ooo-n . . ."

GOOPER:
Shut up!—Brick.

BRICK:
—Sorry. . . .

[*He wanders out on the gallery.*]

DOCTOR BAUGH:
But now, you see, Big Mama, they cut a piece off this growth, a specimen of the tissue and—

BIG MAMA:
Growth? You told Big Daddy—

DOCTOR BAUGH:
Now wait.

BIG MAMA [*fiercely*]:
You told me and Big Daddy there wasn't a thing wrong with him but—

MAE:
Big Mama, they always—

GOOPER:
Let Doc Baugh talk, will yuh?

BIG MAMA:
—little spastic condition of—

[*Her breath gives out in a sob.*]

DOCTOR BAUGH:
Yes, that's what we told Big Daddy. But we had this bit of tissue run through the laboratory and I'm sorry to say the test was positive on it. It's—well—malignant. . . .

[*Pause.*]

BIG MAMA:
—Cancer?! Cancer?!

[*Dr. Baugh nods gravely.*]

[*Big Mama gives a long gasping cry.*]

MAE and GOOPER:
Now, now, now, Big Mama, you had to know. . . .

BIG MAMA:
WHY DIDN'T THEY CUT IT OUT OF HIM? HANH? HANH?

DOCTOR BAUGH:
Involved too much, Big Mama, too many organs affected.

141

MAE:

Big Mama, the liver's affected and so's the kidneys, both! It's gone way past what they call a—

GOOPER:

A surgical risk.

MAE:

—Uh-huh. . . .

[*Big Mama draws a breath like a dying gasp.*]

REVEREND TOOKER:

Tch, tch, tch, tch, tch!

DOCTOR BAUGH:

Yes, it's gone past the knife.

MAE:

That's why he's turned yellow, Mommy!

BIG MAMA:

Git away from me, git away from me, Mae!

[*She rises abruptly.*]

I want Brick! Where's Brick? Where is my only son?

MAE:

Mama! Did she say "*only* son"?

GOOPER:

What does that make *me?*

MAE:

A sober responsible man with five precious children!—*Six!*

BIG MAMA:

I want Brick to tell me! Brick! Brick!

MARGARET [*rising from her reflections in a corner*]:
Brick was so upset he went back out.

BIG MAMA:
Brick!

MARGARET:
Mama, let *me* tell you!

BIG MAMA:
No, no, leave me alone, you're not my blood!

GOOPER:
Mama, I'm your son! Listen to *me!*

MAE:
Gooper's your son, Mama, he's your first-born!

BIG MAMA:
Gooper never liked Daddy.

MAE [*as if terribly shocked*]:
That's not TRUE!

[*There is a pause. The minister coughs and rises.*]

REVEREND TOOKER [*to Mae*]:
I think I'd better slip away at this point.

MAE [*sweetly and sadly*]:
Yes, Doctor Tooker, you go.

REVEREND TOOKER [*discreetly*]:
Goodnight, goodnight, everybody, and God bless you all . . .
on this place. . . .

[*He slips out.*]

DOCTOR BAUGH:
That man is a good man but lacking in tact. Talking about
people giving memorial windows—if he mentioned one
memorial window, he must have spoke of a dozen, and say-

143

ing how awful it was when somebody died intestate, the legal wrangles, and so forth.

[*Mae coughs, and points at Big Mama.*]

DOCTOR BAUGH:
Well, Big Mama. . . .

[*He sighs.*]

BIG MAMA:
It's all a mistake, I know it's just a bad dream.

DOCTOR BAUGH:
We're gonna keep Big Daddy as comfortable as we can.

BIG MAMA:
Yes, it's just a bad dream, that's all it is, it's just an awful dream.

GOOPER:
In my opinion Big Daddy is having some pain but won't admit that he has it.

BIG MAMA:
Just a dream, a bad dream.

DOCTOR BAUGH:
That's what lots of them do, they think if they don't admit they're having the pain they can sort of escape the fact of it.

GOOPER [*with relish*]:
Yes, they get sly about it, they get real sly about it.

MAE:
Gooper and I think—

GOOPER:
Shut up, Mae!—Big Daddy ought to be started on morphine.

BIG MAMA:
Nobody's going to give Big Daddy morphine.

DOCTOR BAUGH:
Now, Big Mama, when that pain strikes it's going to strike mighty hard and Big Daddy's going to need the needle to bear it.

BIG MAMA:
I tell you, nobody's going to give him morphine.

MAE:
Big Mama, you don't want to see Big Daddy suffer, you know you—

[*Gooper standing beside her gives her a savage poke.*]

DOCTOR BAUGH [*placing a package on the table*]:
I'm leaving this stuff here, so if there's a sudden attack you all won't have to send out for it.

MAE:
I know how to give a hypo.

GOOPER:
Mae took a course in nursing during the war.

MARGARET:
Somehow I don't think Big Daddy would want Mae to give him a hypo.

MAE:
You think he'd want *you* to do it?

[*Dr. Baugh rises.*]

GOOPER:
Doctor Baugh is goin'.

DOCTOR BAUGH:
Yes, I got to be goin'. Well, keep your chin up, Big Mama.

GOOPER [*with jocularity*]:
She's gonna keep *both* chins up, aren't you Big Mama?

[*Big Mama sobs.*]

Now stop that, Big Mama.

MAE:
Sit down with me, Big Mama.

GOOPER [*at door with Dr. Baugh*]:
Well, Doc, we sure do appreciate all you done. I'm telling you, we're surely obligated to you for—

[*Dr. Baugh has gone out without a glance at him.*]

GOOPER:
—I guess that doctor has got a lot on his mind but it wouldn't hurt him to act a little more human. . . .

[*Big Mama sobs.*]

Now be a brave girl, Mommy.

BIG MAMA:
It's not true, I know that it's just not true!

GOOPER:
Mama, those tests are infallible!

BIG MAMA:
Why are you so determined to see your father daid?

MAE:
Big Mama!

MARGARET [*gently*]:
I know what Big Mama means.

146

MAE [*fiercely*]:
Oh, do you?

MARGARET [*quietly and very sadly*]:
Yes, I think I do.

MAE:
For a newcomer in the family you sure do show a lot of understanding.

MARGARET:
Understanding is needed on this place.

MAE:
I guess you must have needed a lot of it in your family, Maggie, with your father's liquor problem and now you've got Brick with his!

MARGARET:
Brick does not have a liquor problem at all. Brick is devoted to Big Daddy. This thing is a terrible strain on him.

BIG MAMA:
Brick is Big Daddy's boy, but he drinks too much and it worries me and Big Daddy, and, Margaret, you've got to cooperate with us, you've got to cooperate with Big Daddy and me in getting Brick straightened out. Because it will break Big Daddy's heart if Brick don't pull himself together and take hold of things.

MAE:
Take hold of *what* things, Big Mama?

BIG MAMA:
The place.

[*There is a quick violent look between Mae and Gooper.*]

GOOPER:
Big Mama, you've had a shock.

MAE:
Yais, we've all had a shock, but . . .

GOOPER:
Let's be realistic—

MAE:
—Big Daddy would never, would *never,* be foolish enough to—

GOOPER:
—put this place in irresponsible hands!

BIG MAMA:
Big Daddy ain't going to leave the place in anybody's hands; Big Daddy is *not* going to die. I want you to get that in your heads, all of you!

MAE:
Mommy, Mommy, Big Mama, we're just as hopeful an' optimistic as you are about Big Daddy's prospects, we have faith in *prayer*—but nevertheless there are certain matters that have to be discussed an' dealt with, because otherwise—

GOOPER:
Eventualities have to be considered and now's the time. . . . Mae, will you please get my briefcase out of our room?

MAE:
Yes, honey.

[*She rises and goes out through the hall door.*]

GOOPER [*standing over Big Mama*]:
Now Big Mom. What you said just now was not at all true and you know it. I've always loved Big Daddy in my own

148

quiet way. I never made a show of it, and I know that Big
Daddy has always been fond of me in a quiet way, too, and
he never made a show of it neither.

[*Mae returns with Gooper's briefcase.*]

MAE:
Here's your briefcase, Gooper, honey.

GOOPER [*handing the briefcase back to her*]:
Thank you. . . . Of ca'use, my relationship with Big Daddy is
different from Brick's.

MAE:
You're eight years older'n Brick an' always had t'carry a
bigger load of th' responsibilities than Brick ever had t'carry.
He never carried a thing in his life but a football or a
highball.

GOOPER:
Mae, will y' let me talk, please?

MAE:
Yes, honey.

GOOPER:
Now, a twenty-eight thousand acre plantation's a mighty big
thing t'run.

MAE:
Almost singlehanded.

[*Margaret has gone out onto the gallery, and can be heard
calling softly to Brick.*]

BIG MAMA:
You never had to run this place! What are you talking about?
As if Big Daddy was dead and in his grave, you had to run it?

149

Why, you just helped him out with a few business details and had your law practice at the same time in Memphis!

MAE:

Oh, Mommy, Mommy, Big Mommy! Let's be fair! Why, Gooper has given himself body and soul to keeping this place up for the past five years since Big Daddy's health started failing. Gooper won't say it, Gooper never thought of it as a duty, he just did it. And what did Brick do? Brick kept living in his past glory at college! Still a football player at twenty-seven!

MARGARET [*returning alone*]:

Who are you talking about, now? Brick? A football player? He isn't a football player and you know it. Brick is a sport's announcer on TV and one of the best-known ones in the country!

MAE:

I'm talking about what he was.

MARGARET:

Well, I wish you would just stop talking about my husband.

GOOPER:

I've got a right to discuss my brother with other members of MY OWN family which don't include *you.* Why don't you go out there and drink with Brick?

MARGARET:

I've never seen such malice toward a brother.

GOOPER:

How about his for me? Why, he can't stand to be in the same room with me!

MARGARET:

This is a deliberate campaign of vilification for the most dis-

150

gusting and sordid reason on earth, and I know what it is! It's *avarice, avarice, greed, greed!*

BIG MAMA:
Oh, I'll scream! I will scream in a moment unless this stops!

[*Gooper has stalked up to Margaret with clenched fists at his sides as if he would strike her. Mae distorts her face again into a hideous grimace behind Margaret's back.*]

MARGARET:
We only remain on the place because of Big Mom and Big Daddy. If it is true what they say about Big Daddy we are going to leave here just as soon as it's over. Not a moment later.

BIG MAMA [*sobs*]:
Margaret. Child. Come here. Sit next to Big Mama.

MARGARET:
Precious Mommy. I'm sorry, I'm so sorry, I—!

[*She bends her long graceful neck to press her forehead to Big Mama's bulging shoulder under its black chiffon.*]

GOOPER:
How beautiful, how touching, this display of devotion!

MAE:
Do you know why she's childless? She's childless because that big beautiful athlete husband of hers won't go to bed with her!

GOOPER:
You jest won't let me do this in a nice way, will yah? Aw right—Mae and I have five kids with another one coming! I don't give a goddam if Big Daddy likes me or don't like me or did or never did or will or will never! I'm just appealing

151

to a sense of common decency and fair play. I'll tell you the truth. I've resented Big Daddy's partiality to Brick ever since Brick was born, and the way I've been treated like I was just barely good enough to spit on and sometimes not even good enough for that. Big Daddy is dying of cancer, and it's spread all through him and it's attacked all his vital organs including the kidneys and right now he is sinking into uremia, and you all know what uremia is, it's poisoning of the whole system due to the failure of the body to eliminate its poisons.

MARGARET [*to herself, downstage, hissingly*]:
Poisons, poisons! Venomous thoughts and words! In hearts and minds!—That's poisons!

GOOPER [*overlapping her*]:
I am asking for a square deal, and I expect to get one. But if I don't get one, if there's any peculiar shenanigans going on around here behind my back, or before me, well, I'm not a corporation lawyer for nothing, I know how to protect my own interests.—*OH! A late arrival!*

[*Brick enters from the gallery with a tranquil, blurred smile, carrying an empty glass with him.*]

MAE:
Behold the conquering hero comes!

GOOPER:
The fabulous Brick Pollitt! Remember him?—Who could forget him!

MAE:
He looks like he's been injured in a game!

GOOPER:
Yep, I'm afraid you'll have to warm the bench at the Sugar Bowl this year, Brick!

[*Mae laughs shrilly.*]

Or was it the Rose Bowl that he made that famous run in?

MAE:
The punch bowl, honey. It was in the punch bowl, the cut-glass punch bowl!

GOOPER:
Oh, that's right, I'm getting the bowls mixed up!

MARGARET:
Why don't you stop venting your malice and envy on a sick boy?

BIG MAMA:
Now you two hush, I mean it, hush, all of you, hush!

GOOPER:
All right, Big Mama. A family crisis brings out the best and the worst in every member of it.

MAE:
That's the truth.

MARGARET:
Amen!

BIG MAMA:
I said, hush! I won't tolerate any more catty talk in my house.

[*Mae gives Gooper a sign indicating briefcase.*

[*Brick's smile has grown both brighter and vaguer. As he prepares a drink, he sings softly:*]

BRICK:
Show me the way to go home,

153

I'm tired and I wanta go to bed,
I had a little drink about an hour ago—

GOOPER [*at the same time*]:
Big Mama, you know it's necessary for me t'go back to Memphis in th' mornin' t'represent the Parker estate in a lawsuit.

[*Mae sits on the bed and arranges papers she has taken from the briefcase.*]

BRICK [*continuing the song*]:
Wherever I may roam,
On land or sea or foam.

BIG MAMA:
Is it, Gooper?

MAE:
Yaiss.

GOOPER:
That's why I'm forced to—to bring up a problem that—

MAE:
Somethin' that's too important t' be put off!

GOOPER:
If Brick was sober, he ought to be in on this.

MARGARET:
Brick is present; we're here.

GOOPER:
Well, good. I will now give you this outline my partner, Tom Bullitt, an' me have drawn up—a sort of dummy—trusteeship.

MARGARET:
Oh, that's it! You'll be in charge an' dole out remittances, will you?

GOOPER:

This we did as soon as we got the report on Big Daddy from th' Ochsner Laboratories. We did this thing, I mean we drew up this dummy outline with the advice and assistance of the Chairman of the Boa'd of Directors of th' Southern Plantahs Bank and Trust Company in Memphis, C. C. Bellowes, a man who handles estates for all th' prominent fam'lies in West Tennessee and th' Delta.

BIG MAMA:

Gooper?

GOOPER [*crouching in front of Big Mama*]:

Now this is not—not final, or anything like it. This is just a preliminary outline. But it does provide a basis—a design—a —possible, feasible—*plan!*

MARGARET:

Yes, I'll bet.

MAE:

It's a plan to protect the biggest estate in the Delta from irresponsibility an'—

BIG MAMA:

Now you listen to me, all of you, you listen here! They's not goin' to be any more catty talk in my house! And Gooper, you put that away before I grab it out of our hand and tear it right up! I don't know what the hell's in it, and I don't want to know what the hell's in it. I'm talkin' in Big Daddy's language now; I'm his *wife*, not his *widow*, I'm still his *wife!* And I'm talkin' to you in his language an'—

GOOPER:

Big Mama, what I have here is—

MAE:

Gooper explained that it's just a plan. . . .

155

BIG MAMA:

I don't care what you got there. Just put it back where it came from, an' don't let me see it again, not even the outside of the envelope of it! Is that understood? Basis! Plan! Preliminary! Design! I say—what is it Big Daddy always says when he's disgusted?

BRICK [*from the bar*]:
Big Daddy says "crap" when he's disgusted.

BIG MAMA [*rising*]:
That's right—*CRAP!* I say *CRAP* too, like Big Daddy!

MAE:
Coarse language doesn't seem called for in this—

GOOPER:
Somethin' in me is *deeply outraged* by hearin' you talk like this.

BIG MAMA:
Nobody's goin' to take nothin'!—till Big Daddy lets go of it, and maybe, just possibly, not—not even then! No, not even then!

BRICK:
You can always hear me singin' this song,
Show me the way to go home.

BIG MAMA:
Tonight Brick looks like he used to look when he was a little boy, just like he did when he played wild games and used to come home all sweaty and pink-cheeked and sleepy, with his —red curls shining. . . .

[*She comes over to him and runs her fat shaky hand through his hair. He draws aside as he does from all physical contact and continues the song in a whisper, opening the*

156

ice bucket and dropping in the ice cubes one by one as if he were mixing some important chemical formula.]

BIG MAMA [*continuing*]:
Time goes by so fast. Nothin' can outrun it. Death commences too early—almost before you're half acquainted with life— you meet with the other. . . .

Oh, you know we just got to love each other an' stay together, all of us, just as close as we can, especially now that such a *black* thing has come and moved into this place without invitation.

[*Awkwardly embracing Brick, she presses her head to his shoulder.*

[*Gooper has been returning papers to Mae who has restored them to briefcase with an air of severely tried patience.]*

GOOPER:
Big Mama? Big Mama?

[*He stands behind her, tense with sibling envy.]*

BIG MAMA [*oblivious of Gooper*]:
Brick, you hear me, don't you?

MARGARET:
Brick hears you, Big Mama, he understands what you're saying.

BIG MAMA:
Oh, Brick, son of Big Daddy! Big Daddy does so love you! Y'know what would be his fondest dream come true? If before he passed on, if Big Daddy has to pass on, you gave him a child of yours, a grandson as much like his son as his son is like Big Daddy!

157

MAE [*zipping briefcase shut: an incongruous sound*]:
Such a pity that Maggie an' Brick can't oblige!

MARGARET [*suddenly and quietly but forcefully*]:
Everybody listen.

[*She crosses to the center of the room, holding her hands rigidly together.*]

MAE:
Listen to what, Maggie?

MARGARET:
I have an announcement to make.

GOOPER:
A sports announcement, Maggie?

MARGARET:
Brick and I are going to—*have a child!*

[*Big Mama catches her breath in a loud gasp.*]

[*Pause. Big Mama rises.*]

BIG MAMA:
Maggie! Brick! This is too good to believe!

MAE:
That's right, too good to believe.

BIG MAMA:
Oh, my, my! This is Big Daddy's dream, his dream come true!
I'm going to tell him right now before he—

MARGARET:
We'll tell him in the morning. Don't disturb him now.

BIG MAMA:
I want to tell him before he goes to sleep, I'm going to tell

him his dream's come true this minute! And Brick! A child will make you pull yourself together and quit this drinking!

[*She seizes the glass from his hand.*]

The responsibilities of a father will—

[*Her face contorts and she makes an excited gesture; bursting into sobs, she rushes out, crying.*]

I'm going to tell Big Daddy right this minute!

[*Her voice fades out down the hall.*

[*Brick shrugs slightly and drops an ice cube into another glass. Margaret crosses quickly to his side, saying something under her breath, and she pours the liquor for him, staring up almost fiercely into his face.*]

BRICK [*coolly*]:
Thank you, Maggie, that's a nice big shot.

[*Mae has joined Gooper and she gives him a fierce poke, making a low hissing sound and a grimace of fury.*]

GOOPER [*pushing her aside*]:
Brick, could you possibly spare me one small shot of that liquor?

BRICK:
Why, help yourself, Gooper boy.

GOOPER:
I will.

MAE [*shrilly*]:
Of course we know that this is—

GOOPER:
Be still, Mae!

MAE:
I won't be still! I know she's made this up!

GOOPER:
God damn it, I said to shut up!

MARGARET:
Gracious! I didn't know that my little announcement was going to provoke such a storm!

MAE:
That woman isn't *pregnant!*

GOOPER:
Who said she was?

MAE:
She did.

GOOPER:
The doctor didn't. Doc Baugh didn't.

MARGARET:
I haven't gone to Doc Baugh.

GOOPER:
Then who'd you go to, Maggie?

MARGARET:
One of the best gynecologists in the South.

GOOPER:
Uh huh, uh huh!—I see. . . .

[*He takes out pencil and notebook.*]

—May we have his name, please?

MARGARET:
No, you may not, Mister Prosecuting Attorney!

160

MAE:
He doesn't have any name, he doesn't exist!

MARGARET:
Oh, he exists all right, and so does my child, Brick's baby!

MAE:
You can't conceive a child by a man that won't sleep with you unless you think you're—

[*Brick has turned on the phonograph. A scat song cuts Mae's speech.*]

GOOPER:
Turn that off!

MAE:
We know it's a lie because we hear you in here; he won't sleep with you, we hear you! So don't imagine you're going to put a trick over on us, to fool a dying man with a—

[*A long drawn cry of agony and rage fills the house. Margaret turns phonograph down to a whisper.*

[*The cry is repeated.*]

MAE [*awed*]:
Did you hear that, Gooper, did you hear that?

GOOPER:
Sounds like the pain has struck.

MAE:
Go see, Gooper!

GOOPER:
Come along and leave these lovebirds together in their nest!

[*He goes out first. Mae follows but turns at the door, contorting her face and hissing at Margaret.*]

161

MAE:
Liar!

[*She slams the door.*

[*Margaret exhales with relief and moves a little unsteadily to catch hold of Brick's arm.*]

MARGARET:
Thank you for—keeping still . . .

BRICK:
OK, Maggie.

MARGARET:
It was gallant of you to save my face!

BRICK:
—It hasn't happened yet.

MARGARET:
What?

BRICK:
The click. . . .

MARGARET:
—the click in your head that makes you peaceful, honey?

BRICK:
Uh-huh. It hasn't happened. . . . I've got to make it happen before I can sleep. . . .

MARGARET:
—I—know what you—mean. . . .

BRICK:
Give me that pillow in the big chair, Maggie.

MARGARET:
I'll put it on the bed for you.

BRICK:

No, put it on the sofa, where I sleep.

MARGARET:

Not tonight, Brick.

BRICK:

I want it on the sofa. That's where I sleep.

[*He has hobbled to the liquor cabinet. He now pours down three shots in quick succession and stands waiting, silent. All at once he turns with a smile and says:*]

There!

MARGARET:

What?

BRICK:

The *click.* . . .

[*His gratitude seems almost infinite as he hobbles out on the gallery with a drink. We hear his crutch as he swings out of sight. Then, at some distance, he begins singing to himself a peaceful song.*

[*Margaret holds the big pillow forlornly as if it were her only companion, for a few moments, then throws it on the bed. She rushes to the liquor cabinet, gathers all the bottles in her arms, turns about undecidedly, then runs out of the room with them, leaving the door ajar on the dim yellow hall. Brick is heard hobbling back along the gallery, singing his peaceful song. He comes back in, sees the pillow on the bed, laughs lightly, sadly, picks it up. He has it under his arm as Margaret returns to the room. Margaret softly shuts the door and leans against it, smiling softly at Brick.*]

MARGARET:

Brick, I used to think that you were stronger than me and I

163

didn't want to be overpowered by you. But now, since you've taken to liquor—you know what?—I guess it's bad, but now I'm stronger than you and I can love you more truly!

Don't move that pillow. I'll move it right back if you do!

—Brick?

[*She turns out all the lamps but a single rose-silk-shaded one by the bed.*]

I really have been to a doctor and I know what to do and— Brick?—this is my time by the calendar to conceive!

BRICK:
Yes, I understand, Maggie. But how are you going to conceive a child by a man in love with his liquor?

MARGARET:
By locking his liquor up and making him satisfy my desire before I unlock it!

BRICK:
Is that what you've done, Maggie?

MARGARET:
Look and see. That cabinet's mighty empty compared to before!

BRICK:
Well, I'll be a son of a—

[*He reaches for his crutch but she beats him to it and rushes out on the gallery, hurls the crutch over the rail and comes back in, panting.*

[*There are running footsteps. Big Mama bursts into the room, her face all awry, gasping, stammering.*]

164

BIG MAMA:
Oh, my God, oh, my God, oh, my God, where is it?

MARGARET:
Is this what you want, Big Mama?

[*Margaret hands her the package left by the doctor.*]

BIG MAMA:
I can't bear it, oh, God! Oh, Brick! Brick, baby!

[*She rushes at him. He averts his face from her sobbing kisses. Margaret watches with a tight smile.*]

My son, Big Daddy's boy! Little Father!

[*The groaning cry is heard again. She runs out, sobbing.*]

MARGARET:
And so tonight we're going to make the lie true, and when that's done, I'll bring the liquor back here and we'll get drunk together, here, tonight, in this place that death has come into. . . .

—What do you say?

BRICK:
I don't say anything. I guess there's nothing to say.

MARGARET:
Oh, you weak people, you weak, beautiful people!—who give up.—What you want is someone to—

[*She turns out the rose-silk lamp.*]

—take hold of you.—Gently, gently, with love! And—

[*The curtain begins to fall slowly.*]

165

I *do* love you, Brick, I *do!*

BRICK [*smiling with charming sadness*]:
Wouldn't it be funny if that was true?

THE CURTAIN COMES DOWN

THE END

NOTE OF EXPLANATION

Some day when time permits I would like to write a piece about the influence, its dangers and its values, of a powerful and highly imaginative director upon the development of a play, before and during production. It does have dangers, but it has them only if the playwright is excessively malleable or submissive, or the director is excessively insistent on ideas or interpretations of his own. Elia Kazan and I have enjoyed the advantages and avoided the dangers of this highly explosive relationship because of the deepest mutual respect for each other's creative function: we have worked together three times with a phenomenal absence of friction between us and each occasion has increased the trust.

If you don't want a director's influence on your play, there are two ways to avoid it, and neither is good. One way is to arrive at an absolutely final draft of your play before you let your director see it, then hand it to him saying, Here it is, take it or leave it! The other way is to select a director who is content to put your play on the stage precisely as you conceived it with no ideas of his own. I said neither is a good way, and I meant it. No living playwright, that I can think of, hasn't something valuable to learn about his own work from a director so keenly perceptive as Elia Kazan. It so happened that in the case of *Streetcar*, Kazan was given a script that was completely finished. In the case of *Cat*, he was shown the first typed version of the play, and he was excited by it, but he had definite reservations about it which were concentrated in the third act. The gist of his reservations can be listed as three points: one, he felt that Big Daddy was too vivid and important a character to disappear from the play except as an offstage cry after the second act curtain; two, he felt that the character of Brick should undergo some apparent mutation as a result of the virtual vivisection that he undergoes in his interview with his father in Act Two. Three, he felt that the character of Margaret, while he understood that I sympathized with her and liked her myself, should be, if possible, more clearly sympathetic to an audience.

It was only the third of these suggestions that I embraced wholeheartedly from the outset, because it so happened that Maggie the Cat had become steadily more charming to me as I worked on her characterization. I didn't want Big Daddy to reappear in Act Three and I felt that the moral paralysis of Brick was a root thing in his tragedy, and to show a dramatic progression would obscure the meaning of that tragedy in him and because I don't believe that a conversation, however revelatory, ever effects so immediate a change in the heart or even conduct of a person in Brick's state of spiritual disrepair.

However, I wanted Kazan to direct the play, and though these suggestions were not made in the form of an ultimatum, I was fearful that I would lose his interest if I didn't re-examine the script from his point of view. I did. And you will find included in this published script the new third act that resulted from his creative influence on the play. The reception of the playing-script has more than justified, in my opinion, the adjustments made to that influence. A failure reaches fewer people, and touches fewer, than does a play that succeeds.

It may be that *Cat* number one would have done just as well, or nearly, as *Cat* number two; it's an interesting question. At any rate, with the publication of both third acts in this volume, the reader can, if he wishes, make up his own mind about it.

TENNESSEE WILLIAMS

EDITOR'S NOTE

Unlike the other dramatic material in this volume, the Broadway version of Act Three of *Cat on a Hot Tin Roof* includes directions for the stage, adapted from the production script. The positions and movements of the actors, their entrances and exits, are noted in abbreviated form, and always from a view *opposite* the audience. Thus a direction reading *"Brick XDSR on gallery"* might be rendered *"Brick, on the gallery, crosses downstage to the right—*"downstage" meaning *toward* the audience, and "right" referring to the part of the stage on the audience's *left*. The other common abbreviations used here in combination are: *C* (center, centerstage), *L* (left, stage left), *D* (downstage), *U* or *US* (upstage).

ACT THREE
AS PLAYED IN NEW YORK PRODUCTION

Big Daddy is seen leaving as at the end of Act II.

BIG DADDY [*shouts, as he goes out DR on gallery*]:
ALL—LYIN'—DYIN'—LIARS! LIARS! LIARS!

[*After Big Daddy has gone, Margaret enters from DR on gallery, into room through DS door. She X to Brick at LC.*]

MARGARET:
Brick, what in the name of God was goin' on in this room?

[*Dixie and Trixie rush through the room from the hall, L to gallery R, brandishing cap pistols, which they fire repeatedly, as they shout: "Bang! Bang! Bang!"*]

[*Mae appears from DR gallery entrance, and turns the children back UL, along gallery. At the same moment, Gooper, Reverend Tooker and Dr. Baugh enter from L in the hall.*]

MAE:
Dixie! You quit that! Gooper, will y'please git these kiddies t'baid? Right now?

[*Gooper and Reverend Tooker X along upper gallery. Dr. Baugh holds, UC, near hall door. Reverend Tooker X to Mae near section of gallery just outside doors, R.*]

GOOPER [*urging the children along*]:
Mae—you seen Big Mama?

MAE:
Not yet.

[*Dixie and Trixie vanish through hall, L.*]

REVEREND TOOKER [*to Mae*]:

Those kiddies are so full of vitality. I think I'll have to be startin' back to town.

[*Margaret turns to watch and listen.*]

MAE:

Not yet, Preacher. You know we regard you as a member of this fam'ly, one of our closest an' dearest, so you just got t'be with us when Doc Baugh gives Big Mama th' actual truth about th' report from th' clinic.

[*Calls through door:*]

Has Big Daddy gone to bed, Brick?

[*Gooper has gone out DR at the beginning of the exchange between Mae and Reverend Tooker.*]

MARGARET [*replying to Mae*]:
Yes, he's gone to bed.

[*To Brick:*]

Why'd Big Daddy shout "liars"?

GOOPER [*off DR*]:
Mae!

[*Mae exits DR. Reverend Tooker drifts along upper gallery.*]

BRICK:

I didn't lie to Big Daddy. I've lied to nobody, nobody but myself, just lied to myself. The time has come to put me in Rainbow Hill, put me in Rainbow Hill, Maggie, I ought to go there.

MARGARET:
Over my dead body!

[*Brick starts R. She holds him.*]

Where do you think you're goin'?

[*Mae enters from DR on gallery, X to Reverend Tooker, who comes to meet her.*]

BRICK [*X below to C*]:
Out for some air, I want air—

GOOPER [*entering from DR to Mae, on gallery*]:
Now, where is that old lady?

MAE:
Cantcha find her, Gooper?

[*Reverend Tooker goes out DR.*]

GOOPER [*X to Doc above hall door*]:
She's avoidin' this talk.

MAE:
I think she senses somethin'.

GOOPER [*calls off L*]:
Sookey! Go find Big Mama an' tell her Doc Baugh an' the Preacher've got tò go soon.

MAE:
Don't let Big Daddy hear yuh!

[*Brings Dr. Baugh to R on gallery.*]

REVEREND TOOKER [*off DR, calls*]:
Big Mama.

SOOKEY and DAISY [*running from L to R in lawn, calling*]:
Miss Ida! Miss Ida!

[*They go out UR.*]

GOOPER [*calling off upper gallery*]:
Lacey, you look downstairs for Big Mama!

MARGARET:
Brick, they're going to tell Big Mama the truth now, an' she needs you!

[*Reverend Tooker appears in lawn area, UR, X C.*]

DOCTOR BAUGH [*to Mae, on R gallery*]:
This is going to be painful.

MAE:
Painful things can't always be avoided.

DOCTOR BAUGH:
That's what I've noticed about 'em, Sister Woman.

REVEREND TOOKER [*on lawn, points off R*]:
I see Big Mama!

[*Hurries off L. and reappears shortly in hall.*]

GOOPER [*hurrying into hall*]:
She's gone round the gall'ry to Big Daddy's room. Hey, Mama!

[*Off:*]

Hey, Big Mama! Come here!

MAE [*calls*]:
Hush, Gooper! Don't holler, go to her!

[*Gooper and Reverend Tooker now appear together in hall. Big Mama runs in from DR, carrying a glass of milk. She X past Dr. Baugh to Mae, on R gallery. Dr. Baugh turns away.*]

BIG MAMA:
Here I am! What d'you all want with me?

174

GOOPER [*steps toward Big Mama*]:
Big Mama, I told you we got to have this talk.

BIG MAMA:
What talk you talkin' about? I saw the light go on in Big
Daddy's bedroom an' took him his glass of milk, an' he just
shut the shutters right in my face.

[*Steps into room through R door.*]

When old couples have been together as long as me an' Big
Daddy, they, they get irritable with each other just from too
much—devotion! Isn't that so?

[*X below wicker seat to RC area.*]

MARGARET [*X to Big Mama, embracing her*]:
Yes, of course it's so.

[*Brick starts out UC through hall, but sees Gooper and
Reverend Tooker entering, so he hobbles through C out DS
door and onto gallery.*]

BIG MAMA:
I think Big Daddy was just worn out. He loves his fam'ly. He
loves to have 'em around him, but it's a strain on his nerves.
He wasn't himself tonight, Brick—

[*XC toward Brick. Brick passes her on his way out, DS.*]

Big Daddy wasn't himself, I could tell he was all worked up.

REVEREND TOOKER [*USC*]:
I think he's remarkable.

BIG MAMA:
Yaiss! Just remarkable.

[*Faces US, turns, X to bar, puts down glass of milk.*]

175

Did you notice all the food he ate at that table?

[*XR a bit.*]

Why he ate like a hawss!

GOOPER [*USC*]:
I hope he don't regret it.

BIG MAMA [*turns US toward Gooper*]:
What! Why that man ate a huge piece of cawn bread with molassess on it! Helped himself twice to hoppin' john!

MARGARET [*X to Big Mama*]:
Bid Daddy loves hoppin' john. We had a real country dinner.

BIG MAMA:
Yais, he simply adores it! An' candied yams. Son—

[*X to DS door, looking out at Brick. Margaret X above Big Mama to her L.*]

That man put away enough food at that table to stuff a field hand.

GOOPER:
I hope he don't have to pay for it later on.

BIG MAMA [*turns US*]:
What's that, Gooper?

MAE:
Gooper says he hopes Big Daddy doesn't suffer tonight.

BIG MAMA [*turns to Margaret, DC*]:
Oh, shoot, Gooper says, Gooper says! Why should Big Daddy suffer for satisfyin' a nawmal appetite? There's nothin' wrong with that man but nerves; he's sound as a dollar! An' now he knows he is, an' that's why he ate such a supper. He had a big

load off his mind, knowin' he wasn't doomed to—what—he thought he was—doomed t'—

[*She wavers.*]

[*Margaret puts her arms around Big Mama.*]

GOOPER [*urging Mae forward*]:
MAE!

[*Mae runs forward below wicker seat. She stands below Big Mama, Margaret above Big Mama. They help her to the wicker seat. Big Mama sits. Margaret sits above her. Mae stands behind her.*]

MARGARET:
Bless his ole sweet soul.

BIG MAMA:
Yes—bless his heart.

BRICK [*DS on gallery, looking out front*]:
Hello, moon, I envy you, you cool son of a bitch.

BIG MAMA:
I want Brick!

MARGARET:
He just stepped out for some fresh air.

BIG MAMA:
Honey! I want Brick!

MAE:
Bring li'l Brother in here so we cin talk.

[*Margaret rises, X through DS door to Brick on gallery.*]

BRICK [*to the moon*]:
I envy you—you cool son of a bitch.

177

MARGARET:

Brick, what're you doin' out here on the gall'ry, baby?

BRICK:

Admirin' an' complimentin' th' man in the moon.

[*Mae X to Dr. Baugh on R gallery. Reverend Tooker and Gooper move R UC, looking at Big Mama.*]

MARGARET [*to Brick*]:

Come in, baby. They're gettin' ready to tell Big Mama the truth.

BRICK:

I can't witness that thing in there.

MAE:

Doc Baugh, d'you think those vitamin B_{12} injections are all they're cracked up t'be?

[*Enters room to upper side, behind wicker seat.*]

DOCTOR BAUGH [*X to below wicker seat*]:

Well, I guess they're as good t'be stuck with as anything else.

[*Looks at watch; X through to LC.*]

MARGARET [*to Brick*]:

Big Mama needs you!

BRICK:

I can't witness that thing in there!

BIG MAMA:

What's wrong here? You all have such long faces, you sit here waitin' for somethin' like a bomb—to go off.

GOOPER:

We're waitin' for Brick an' Maggie to come in for this talk.

MARGARET [*X above Brick, to his R*]:
Brother Man an' Mae have got a trick up their sleeves, an' if
you don't go in there t'help Big Mama, y'know what I'm
goin' to do—?

BIG MAMA:
Talk. Whispers! Whispers!

[*Looks out DR.*]

Brick! . . .

MARGARET [*answering Big Mama's call*]:
Comin', Big Mama!

[*To Brick.*]

I'm going' to take every dam' bottle on this place an' pitch
it off th' levee into th' river!

BIG MAMA:
Never had this sort of atmosphere here before.

MAE [*sits above Big Mama on wicker seat*]:
Before what, Big Mama?

BIG MAMA:
This occasion. What's Brick an' Maggie doin' out there now?

GOOPER [*X DC, looks out*]:
They seem to be havin' some little altercation.

[*Brick X toward DS step. Maggie moves R above him to
portal DR. Reverend Tooker joins Dr. Baugh, LC.*]

BIG MAMA [*taking a pill from pill box on chain at her
wrist*]:

Give me a little somethin' to wash this tablet down with.
Smell of burnt fireworks always makes me sick.

179

[*Mae X to bar to pour glass of water. Dr. Baugh joins her. Gooper X to Reverend Tooker, LC.*]

BRICK [*to Maggie*]:
You're a live cat, aren't you?

MARGARET:
You're dam' right I am!

BIG MAMA:
Gooper, will y'please open that hall door—an' let some air circulate in this stiflin' room?

[*Gooper starts US, but is restrained by Mae who X through C with glass of water. Gooper turns to men DLC.*]

MAE [*X to Big Mama with water, sits above her*]:
Big Mama, I think we ought to keep that door closed till after we talk.

BIG MAMA:
I swan!

[*Drinks water. Washes down pill.*]

MAE:
I just don't think we ought to take any chance of Big Daddy hearin' a word of this discussion.

BIG MAMA [*hands glass to Mae*]:
What discussion of what? Maggie! Brick! Nothin' is goin' to be said in th' house of Big Daddy Pollitt that he can't hear if he wants to!

[*Mae rises, X to bar, puts down glass, joins Gooper and the two men, LC.*]

BRICK:
How long are you goin' to stand behind me, Maggie?

MARGARET:
Forever, if necessary.

[*Brick X US to R gallery door.*]

BIG MAMA:
Brick!

[*Mae rises, looks out DS, sits.*]

GOOPER:
That boy's gone t'pieces—he's just gone t'pieces.

DOCTOR BAUGH:
Y'know, in my day they used to have somethin' they called the Keeley cure for drinkers.

BIG MAMA:
Shoot!

DOCTOR BAUGH:
But nowadays, I understand they take some kind of tablets that kill their taste for the stuff.

GOOPER [*turns to Dr. Baugh*]:
Call 'em antibust pills.

BIG MAMA:
Brick don't need to take nothin'. That boy is just broken up over Skipper's death. You know how poor Skipper died. They gave him a big, big dose of that sodium amytal stuff at his home an' then they called the ambulance an' give him another big, big dose of it at th' hospital an' that an' all the alcohol in his system fo' months an' months just proved too much for his heart an' his heart quit beatin'. I'm scared of needles! I'm more scared of a needle than th' knife—

[*Brick has entered the room to behind the wicker seat. He*

181

CAT ON A HOT TIN ROOF

rests his hand on Big Mama's head. Gooper has moved a
bit URC, facing Big Mama.]

BIG MAMA:
Oh! Here's Brick! My precious baby!

[Dr. Baugh X to bar, puts down drink. Brick X below Big
Mama through C to bar.]

BRICK:
Take it, Gooper!

MAE [rising]:
What?

BRICK:
Gooper knows what. Take it, Gooper!

[Mae turns to Gooper URC. Dr. Baugh X to Reverend
Tooker. Margaret, who has followed Brick US on R gallery
before he entered the room, now enters room, to behind
wicker seat.]

BIG MAMA [to Brick]:
You just break my heart.

BRICK [at bar]:
Sorry—anyone else?

MARGARET:
Brick, sit with Big Mama an' hold her hand while we talk.

BRICK:
You do that, Maggie. I'm a restless cripple. I got to stay on
my crutch.

[Mae sits above Big Mama. Gooper moves in front, below,
and sits on couch, facing Big Mama. Reverend Tooker
closes in to RC. Dr. Baugh XDC, faces upstage, smoking
cigar. Margaret turns away to R doors.]

BIG MAMA:

Why're you all *surroundin'* me?—like this? Why're you all starin' at me like this an' makin' signs at each other?

[*Brick hobbles out hall door and X along R gallery.*]

I don't need nobody to hold my hand. Are you all crazy? Since when did Big Daddy or me need anybody—?

[*Reverend Tooker moves behind wicker seat.*]

MAE:

Calm yourself, Big Mama.

BIG MAMA:

Calm you'self *you'self,* Sister Woman! How could I calm myself with everyone starin' at me as if big drops of blood had broken out on m'face? What's all this about annh! What?

GOOPER:

Doc Baugh—

[*Mae rises.*]

Sit down, Mae—

[*Mae sits.*]

—Big Mama wants to know the complete truth about th' report we got today from the Ochsner Clinic!

[*Dr. Baugh buttons his coat, faces group at RC.*]

BIG MAMA:

Is there somethin'—somethin' that I don't know?

DOCTOR BAUGH:

Yes—well . . .

BIG MAMA [*rises*]:

I—want to—*knowwwww!*

[*X to Dr. Baugh.*]

Somebody must be lyin'! *I want to know!*

[*Mae, Gooper, Reverend Tooker surround Big Mama.*]

MAE:
Sit down, Big Mama, sit down on this sofa!

[*Brick has passed Margaret Xing DR on gallery.*]

MARGARET:
Brick! Brick!

BIG MAMA:
What is it, what is it?

[*Big Mama drives Dr. Baugh a bit DLC. Others follow, surrounding Big Mama.*]

DOCTOR BAUGH:
I never have seen a more thorough examination than Big Daddy Pollitt was given in all my experience at the Ochsner Clinic.

GOOPER:
It's one of th' best in th' country.

MAE:
It's *THE* best in th' country—bar none!

DOCTOR BAUGH:
Of course they were ninety-nine and nine-tenths per cent certain before they even started.

BIG MAMA:
Sure of what, sure of what, sure of what—*what!?*

MAE:
Now, Mommy, be a brave girl!

BRICK [*on DR gallery, covers his ears, sings*]:
"By the light, by the light, of the silvery moon!"

GOOPER [*breaks DR. Calls out to Brick*]:
Shut up, Brick!

[*Returns to group LC.*]

BRICK:
Sorry . . .

[*Continues singing.*]

DOCTOR BAUGH:
But now, you see, Big Mama, they cut a piece off this growth,
a specimen of the tissue, an'—

BIG MAMA:
Growth? You told Big Daddy—

DOCTOR BAUGH:
Now, wait—

BIG MAMA:
You told me an' Big Daddy there wasn't a thing wrong with
him but—

MAE:
Big Mama, they always—

GOOPER:
Let Doc Baugh talk, will yuh?

BIG MAMA:
—little spastic condition of—

REVEREND TOOKER [*throughout all this*]:
Shh! Shh! Shh!

[*Big Mama breaks UC, they all follow.*]

185

DOCTOR BAUGH:
Yes, that's what we told Big Daddy. But we had this bit of tissue run through the laboratory an' I'm sorry t'say the test was positive on it. It's malignant.

[*Pause.*]

BIG MAMA:
Cancer! Cancer!

MAE:
Now now, Mommy—

GOOPER [*at the same time*]:
You had to know, Big Mama.

BIG MAMA:
Why didn't they cut it out of him? Hanh? Hannh?

DOCTOR BAUGH:
Involved too much, Big Mama, too many organs affected.

MAE:
Big Mama, the liver's affected, an' so's the kidneys, both. It's gone way past what they call a—

GOOPER:
—a surgical risk.

[*Big Mama gasps.*]

REVEREND TOOKER:
Tch, tch, tch.

DOCTOR BAUGH:
Yes, it's gone past the knife.

MAE:
That's why he's turned yellow!

[*Brick stops singing, turns away UR on gallery.*]

BIG MAMA [*pushes Mae DS*]:
Git away from me, git away from me, Mae!

[*XDSR.*]

I want Brick! Where's Brick! *Where's my only son?*

MAE [*a step after Big Mama*]:
Mama! Did she say "only" son?

GOOPER [*following Big Mama*]:
What does that make me?

MAE [*above Gooper*]:
A sober responsible man with five precious children—*six!*

BIG MAMA:
I want Brick! Brick! Brick!

MARGARET [*a step to Big Mama above couch*]:
Mama, let *me* tell you.

BIG MAMA [*pushing her aside*]:
No, no, leave me alone, you're not my blood!

[*She rushes onto the DS gallery.*]

GOOPER [*X to Big Mama on gallery*]:
Mama! I'm your son! Listen to me!

MAE:
Gooper's your son, Mama, he's your first-born!

BIG MAMA:
Gooper never liked Daddy!

MAE:
That's not true!

187

REVEREND TOOKER [*UC*]:
I think I'd better slip away at this point. Good night, good night everybody, and God bless you all—on this place.

[*Goes out through hall.*]

DOCTOR BAUGH [*XDR to above DS door*]:
Well, Big Mama—

BIG MAMA [*leaning against Gooper, on lower gallery*]:
It's all a mistake, I know it's just a bad dream.

DOCTOR BAUGH:
We're gonna keep Big Daddy as comfortable as we can.

BIG MAMA:
Yes, it's just a bad dream, that's all it is, it's just an awful dream.

GOOPER:
In my opinion Big Daddy is havin' some pain but won't admit that he has it.

BIG MAMA:
Just a dream, a bad dream.

DOCTOR BAUGH:
That's what lots of 'em do, they think if they don't admit they're havin' the pain they can sort of escape th' fact of it.

[*Brick X US on R gallery. Margaret watches him from R doors.*]

GOOPER:
Yes, they get sly about it, get real sly about it.

MAE [*X to R of Dr. Baugh*]:
Gooper an' I think—

188

GOOPER:

Shut up, Mae!—Big Mama, I really do think Big Daddy should be started on morphine.

BIG MAMA [*pulling away from Gooper*]:
Nobody's goin't to give Big Daddy morphine!

DOCTOR BAUGH:
Now, Big Mama, when that pain strikes it's goin' to strike mighty hard an' Big Daddy's goin' t'need the needle to bear it.

BIG MAMA [*X to Dr. Baugh*]:
I tell you, nobody's goin' to give him morphine!

MAE:
Big Mama, you don't want to see Big Daddy suffer, y'know y'—

DOCTOR BAUGH [*X to bar*]:
Well, I'm leavin' this stuff here

[*Puts packet of morphine, etc., on bar.*]

so if there's a sudden attack you won't have to send out for it.

[*Big Mama hurries to L side bar.*]

MAE [*X C, below Dr. Baugh*]:
I know how to give a hypo.

BIG MAMA:
Nobody's goin' to give Big Daddy morphine!

GOOPER [*X C*]:
Mae took a course in nursin' durin' th' war.

MARGARET:
Somehow I don't think Big Daddy would want Mae t'give him a hypo.

189

MAE [*to Margaret*]:
You think he'd want *you* to do it?

DOCTOR BAUGH:
Well—

GOOPER:
Well, Doc Baugh is goin'—

DOCTOR BAUGH:
Yes, I got to be goin'. Well, keep your chin up, Big Mama.

[*X to hall.*]

GOOPER [*as he and Mae follow Dr. Baugh into the hall*]:
She's goin' to keep her ole chin up, aren't you, Big Mama?

[*They go out L.*]

Well, Doc, we sure do appreciate all you've done. I'm telling
you, we're obligated—

BIG MAMA:
Margaret!

[*XRC.*]

MARGARET [*meeting Big Mama in front of wicker seat*]:
I'm right here, Big Mama.

BIG MAMA:
Margaret, you've got to cooperate with me an' Big Daddy to
straighten Brick out now—

GOOPER [*off L, returning with Mae*]:
I guess that Doctor has got a lot on his mind, but it wouldn't
hurt him to act a little more human—

BIG MAMA:
—because it'll break Big Daddy's heart if Brick don't pull
himself together an' take hold of things here.

190

[*Brick XDSR on gallery.*]

MAE [*UC, overhearing*]:
Take hold of what things, Big Mama?

BIG MAMA [*sits in wicker chair, Margaret standing behind chair*]:
The place.

GOOPER [*UC*]:
Big Mama, you've had a shock.

MAE [*X with Gooper to Big Mama*]:
Yais, we've all had a shock, but—

GOOPER:
Let's be realistic—

MAE:
Big Daddy would not, would *never*, be foolish enough to—

GOOPER:
—put this place in irresponsible hands!

BIG MAMA:
Big Daddy ain't goin' t'put th' place in anybody's hands, Big Daddy is *not* goin' t'die! I want you to git that into your haids, all of you!

[*Mae sits above Big Mama, Margaret turns R to door, Gooper X L C a bit.*]

▄MAE:
Mommy, Mommy, Big Mama, we're just as hopeful an' optimistic as you are about Big Daddy's prospects, we have faith in prayer—but nevertheless there are certain matters that have to be discussed an' dealt with, because otherwise—

GOOPER:
Mae, will y'please get my briefcase out of our room?

191

MAE:
Yes, honey.

[*Rises, goes out through hall L.*]

MARGARET [*X to Brick on DS gallery*]:
Hear them in there?

[*X back to R gallery door.*]

GOOPER [*stands above Big Mama. Leaning over her*]:
Big Mama, what you said just now was not at all true, an' you
know it. I've always loved Big Daddy in my own quiet way.
I never made a show of it. I know that Big Daddy has always
been fond of me in a quiet way, too.

[*Margaret drifts UR on gallery. Mae returns, X to Gooper's
L with briefcase.*]

MAE:
Here's your briefcase, Gooper, honey.

[*Hands it to him.*]

GOOPER [*hands briefcase back to Mae*]:
Thank you. Of ca'use, my relationship with Big Daddy is
different from Brick's.

MAE:
You're eight years older'n Brick an' always had t'carry a bigger
load of th' responsibilities than Brick ever had t'carry; he
never carried a thing in his life but a football or a highball.

GOOPER:
Mae, will y'let me talk, please?

MAE:
Yes, honey.

GOOPER:

Now, a twenty-eight thousand acre plantation's a mighty big thing t'run.

MAE:

Almost single-handed!

BIG MAMA:

You never had t'run this place, Brother Man, what're you talkin' about, as if Big Daddy was dead an' in his grave, you had to run it? Why, you just had t'help him out with a few business details an' had your law practice at the same time in Memphis.

MAE:

Oh, Mommy, Mommy, Mommy! Let's be fair! Why, Gooper has given himself body and soul t'keepin' this place up fo' the past five years since Big Daddy's health started fallin'. Gooper won't say it, Gooper never thought of it as a duty, he just did it. An' what did Brick do? Brick kep' livin' in his past glory at college!

[*Gooper places a restraining hand on Mae's leg; Margaret drifts DS in gallery.*]

GOOPER:
Still a football player at twenty-seven!

MARGARET [*bursts into UR door*]:
Who are you talkin' about now? Brick? A football player? He isn't a football player an' you know it! Brick is a sports announcer on TV an' one of the best-known ones in the country!

MAE [*breaks UC*]:
I'm talkin' about what he was!

193

MARGARET [X *to above lower gallery door*]:
Well, I wish you would just stop talkin' about my husband!

GOOPER [X *to above Margaret*]:
Listen, Margaret, I've got a right to discuss my own brother with other members of my own fam'ly, which don't include *you!*

[*Pokes finger at her; she slaps his finger away.*]

Now, why don't you go on out there an' drink with Brick?

MARGARET:
I've never seen such malice toward a brother.

GOOPER:
How about his for me? Why can't he stand to be in the same room with me!

BRICK [*on lower gallery*]:
That's the truth!

MARGARET:
This is a deliberate campaign of vilification for the most disgusting and sordid reason on earth, and I know what it is! *It's avarice, avarice, greed, greed!*

BIG MAMA:
Oh, I'll scream, I will scream in a moment unless this stops! Margaret, child, come here, sit next to Big Mama.

MARGARET [X *to Big Mama, sits above her*]:
Precious Mommy.

[*Gooper X to bar.*]

MAE:
How beautiful, how touchin' this display of devotion! Do you know why she's childless? She's childless because that big,

beautiful athlete husband of hers won't go to bed with her, that's why!

[*X to L of bed, looks at Gooper.*]

GOOPER:

You jest won't let me do this the nice way, will yuh? Aw right—

[*X to above wicker seat.*]

I don't give a goddam if Big Daddy likes me or don't like me or did or never did or will or will never! I'm just appealin' to a sense of common decency an' fair play! I'm tellin' you th' truth—

[*X DS through lower door to Brick on DR gallery.*]

I've resented Big Daddy's partiality to Brick ever since th' goddam day you were born, son, an' th' way I've been treated, like I was just barely good enough to spit on, an' sometimes not even good enough for that.

[*X back through room to above wicker seat.*]

Big Daddy is dyin' of cancer an' it's spread all through him an' it's attacked all his vital organs includin' the kidneys an' right now he is sinkin' into uremia, an' you all know what uremia is, it's poisonin' of the whole system due to th' failure of th' body to eliminate its poisons.

MARGARET:

Poisons, poisons, venomous thoughts and words! In hearts and minds! That's poisons!

GOOPER:

I'm askin' for a square deal an' by God I expect to get one. But if I don't get one, if there's any peculiar shenanigans

195

goin' on around here behind my back, well I'm not a corporation lawyer for nothin!

[XDS *toward lower gallery door, on apex.*]

I know how to protect my own interests.

[*Rumble of distant thunder.*]

BRICK [*entering the room through DS door*]:
Storm comin' up.

GOOPER:
Oh, a late arrival!

MAE [X *through C to below bar, LCO*]:
Behold, the conquerin' hero comes!

GOOPER [X *through C to bar, following Brick, imitating
his limp*]:
The fabulous Brick Pollitt! Remember him? Who could forget him?

MAE:
He looks like he's been injured in a game!

GOOPER:
Yep, I'm afraid you'll have to warm th' bench at the Sugar
Bowl this year, Brick! Or was it the Rose Bowl that he made
his famous run in.

[*Another rumble of thunder, sound of wind rising.*]

MAE [X *to L of Brick, who has reached the bar*]:
The punch bowl, honey, it was the punch bowl, the cut-glass
punch bowl!

GOOPER:
That's right! I'm always gettin' the boy's *bowls* mixed up!

[*Pats Brick on the butt.*]

196

MARGARET [*rushes at Gooper, striking him*]:

Stop that! You stop that!

[*Thunder.*]

[*Mae X toward Margaret from L of Gooper, flails at Margaret; Gooper keeps the women apart. Lacey runs through the US lawn area in a raincoat.*]

DAISY and SOOKEY [*off UL*]:
Storm! Storm comin! Storm! Storm!

LACEY [*running out UR*]:
Brightie, close them shutters!

GOOPER [*X onto R gallery, calls after Lacey*]:
Lacey, put the top up on my Cadillac, will yuh?

LACEY [*off R*]:
Yes, sur, Mistah Pollit!

GOOPER [*X to above Big Mama*]:
Big Mama, you know it's goin' to be necessary for me t'go back to Memphis in th' mornin' t'represent the Parker estate in a lawsuit.

[*Mae sits on L side bed, arranges papers she removes from briefcase.*]

BIG MAMA:
Is it, Gooper?

MAE:
Yaiss.

GOOPER:
That's why I'm forced to—to bring up a problem that—

197

MAE:
Somethin' that's too important t' be put off!

GOOPER:
If Brick was sober, he ought to be in on this. I think he ought
to be present when I present this plan.

MARGARET [*UC*]:
Brick is present, we're present!

GOOPER:
Well, good. I will now give you this outline my partner, Tom
Bullit, an' me have drawn up—a sort of dummy—trustee-
ship!

MARGARET:
Oh, that's it! You'll be in charge an' dole out remittances,
will you?

GOOPER:
This we did as soon as we got the report on Big Daddy from
th' Ochsner Laboratories. We did this thing, I mean we drew
up this dummy outline with the advice and assistance of the
Chairman of the Boa'd of Directors of th' Southern Plantuhs
Bank and Trust Company in Memphis, C. C. Bellowes, a man
who handles estates for all th' prominent fam'lies in West
Tennessee and th' Delta!

BIG MAMA:
Gooper?

GOOPER [*X behind seat to below Big Mama*]:
Now this is not—not final, or anything like it, this is just a
preliminary outline. But it does provide a—basis—a design—
a—possible, feasible—*plan!*

[*He waves papers Mae has thrust into his hand, US.*]

198

MARGARET [*XDL*]:
Yes, I'll bet it's a plan!

[*Thunder rolls. Interior lighting dims.*]

MAE:
It's a plan to protect the biggest estate in the Delta from irresponsibility an'—

BIG MAMA:
Now you listen to me, all of you, you listen here! They's not
goin' to be no more catty talk in my house! And Gooper,
you put that away before I grab it out of your hand and tear
it right up! I don't know what the hell's in it, and I don't want
to know what the hell's in it. I'm talkin' in Big Daddy's
language now, I'm his *wife,* not his *widow,* I'm still his *wife!*
And I'm talkin' to you in his language an'—

GOOPER:
Big Mama, what I have here is—

MAE:
Gooper explained that it's just a plan . . .

BIG MAMA:
I don't care what you got there, just put it back where it come
from an' don't let me see it again, not even the outside of the
envelope of it! Is that understood? Basis! Plan! Preliminary!
Design!—I say—what is it that Big Daddy always says when
he's disgusted?

[*Storm clouds race across sky.*]

BRICK [*from bar*]:
Big Daddy says "crap" when he is disgusted.

BIG MAMA [*rising*]:
That's right—*CRAPPPP!* I say *CRAP* too, like Big Daddy!

199

[*Thunder rolls.*]

MAE:
Coarse language don't seem called for in this—

GOOPER:
Somethin' in me is *deeply outraged* by this.

BIG MAMA:
Nobody's goin' to do nothin'! till Big Daddy lets go of it, and maybe just possibly not—not even then! No, not even then!

[*Thunder clap. Glass crash, off L.*

[*Off UR, children commence crying. Many storm sounds, L and R: barnyard animals in terror, papers crackling, shutters rattling. Sookey and Daisy hurry from L to R in lawn area. Inexplicably, Daisy hits together two leather pillows. They cry, "Storm! Storm!" Sookey waves a piece of wrapping paper to cover lawn furniture. Mae exits to hall and upper gallery. Strange man runs across lawn, R to L.*

[*Thunder rolls repeatedly.*]

MAE:
Sookey, hurry up an' git that po'ch fu'niture covahed; want th' paint to come off?

[*Starts DR on gallery.*

[*Gooper runs through hall to R gallery.*]

GOOPER [*yells to Lacey, who appears from R*]:
Lacey, put mah car away!

LACEY:
Cain't, Mistah Pollit, you got the kevs!

[*Exit US.*]

GOOPER:
Naw, you got 'em, man.

[*Exit DR. Reappears UR, calls to Mae:*]

Where th' keys to th' car, honey?

[*Runs C.*]

MAE [*DR on gallery*]:
You got 'em in your pocket!

[*Exit DR.*

[*Gooper exits UR. Dog howls. Daisy and Sookey sing off UR to comfort children. Mae is heard placating the children.*

[*Storm fades away.*

[*During the storm, Margaret X and sits on couch, DR. Big Mama X DC.*]

BIG MAMA:
BRICK! Come here, Brick, I need you.

[*Thunder distantly.*

[*Children whimper, off L Mae consoles them. Brick X to R of Big Mama.*]

BIG MAMA:
Tonight Brick looks like he used to look when he was a little boy just like he did when he played wild games in the orchard back of the house and used to come home when I hollered myself hoarse for him! all—sweaty—and pink-cheeked—an' sleepy with his curls shinin'—

[*Thunder distantly.*

201

[*Children whimper, off L Mae consoles them. Dog howls, off.*]

Time goes by so fast. Nothin' can outrun it. Death commences too early—almost before you're half-acquainted with life—you meet with the other. Oh, you know we just got to love each other, an' stay together all of us just as close as we can, specially now that such a *black* thing has come and moved into this place without invitation.

[*Dog howls, off.*]

Oh, Brick, son of Big Daddy, Big Daddy does so love you. Y'know what would be his fondest dream come true? If before he passed on, if Big Daddy has to pass on ...

[*Dog howls, off.*]

You give him a child of yours, a grandson as much like his son as his son is like Big Daddy. . . .

MARGARET:
I know that's Big Daddy's dream.

BIG MAMA:
That's his dream.

BIG DADDY [*off DR on gallery*]:
Looks like the wind was takin' liberties with this place.

[*Lacey appears UL, X to UC in lawn area; Brightie and Small appear UR on lawn. Big Daddy X onto the UR gallery.*]

LACEY:
Evenin', Mr. Pollitt.

BRIGHTIE and SMALL:
Evenin', Cap'n. Hello, Cap'n.

MARGARET [*X to R door*]:
Big Daddy's on the gall'ry.

BIG DADDY:
Stawm crossed th' river, Lacey?

LACEY:
Gone to Arkansas, Cap'n.

[*Big Mama has turned toward the hall door at the sound of Big Daddy's voice on the gallery. Now she X's DSR and out the DS door onto the gallery.*]

BIG MAMA:
I can't stay here. He'll see somethin' in my eyes.

BIG DADDY [*on upper gallery, to the boys*]:
Stawm done any damage around here?

BRIGHTIE:
Took the po'ch off ole Aunt Crawley's house.

BIG DADDY:
Ole Aunt Crawley should of been settin' on it. It's time fo' th' wind to blow that ole girl away!

[*Field hands laugh, exit, UR. Big Daddy enters room, UC, hall door.*]

Can I come in?

[*Puts his cigar in ash tray on bar.*

[*Mae and Gooper hurry along the upper gallery and stand behind Big Daddy in hall door.*]

MARGARET:
Did the storm wake you up, Big Daddy?

BIG DADDY:

Which stawm are you talkin' about—th' one outside or th' hullaballoo in here?

[*Gooper squeezes past Big Daddy.*]

GOOPER [*X toward bed, where legal papers are strewn*]: 'Scuse me, sir . . .

[*Mae tries to squeeze past Big Daddy to join Gooper, but Big Daddy puts his arm firmly around her.*]

BIG DADDY:

I heard some mighty loud talk. Sounded like somethin' important was bein' discussed. What was the powwow about?

MAE [*flustered*]:
Why—nothin', Big Daddy . . .

BIG DADDY [*XDLC, taking Mae with him*]:
What is that pregnant-lookin' envelope you're puttin' back in your briefcase, Gooper?

GOOPER [*at foot of bed, caught, as he stuffs papers into envelope*]:
That? Nothin', suh—nothin' much of anythin' at all . . .

BIG DADDY:
Nothin'? It looks like a whole lot of nothing!

[*Turns US to group:*]

You all know th' story about th' young married couple—

GOOPER:
Yes, sir!

BIG DADDY:
Hello, Brick—

BRICK:

Hello, Big Daddy.

[*The group is arranged in a semicircle above Big Daddy, Margaret at the extreme R, then Mae and Gooper, then Big Mama, with Brick at L.*]

BIG DADDY:

Young married couple took Junior out to th' zoo one Sunday, inspected all of God's creatures in their cages, with satisfaction.

GOOPER:

Satisfaction.

BIG DADDY [*XUSC, face front*]:

This afternoon was a warm afternoon in spring an' that ole elephant had somethin' else on his mind which was bigger'n peanuts. You know this story, Brick?

[*Gooper nods.*]

BRICK:

No, sir, I don't know it.

BIG DADDY:

Y'see, in th' cage adjoinin' they was a young female elephant in heat!

BIG MAMA [*at Big Daddy's shoulder*]:

Oh, Big Daddy!

BIG DADDY:

What's the matter, preacher's gone, ain't he? All right. That female elephant in the next cage was permeatin' the atmosphere about her with a powerful and excitin' odor of female fertility! Huh! Ain't that a nice way to put it, Brick?

205

BRICK:
Yes, sir, nothin' wrong with it.

BIG DADDY:
Brick says the's nothin' wrong with it!

BIG MAMA:
Oh, Big Daddy!

BIG DADDY [*XDSC*]:
So this ole bull elephant still had a couple of fornications left in him. He reared back his trunk an' got a whiff of that elephant lady next door!—began to paw at the dirt in his cage an' butt his head against the separatin' partition and, first thing y'know, there was a conspicuous change in his *profile*—very *conspicuous!* Ain't I tellin' this story in decent language, Brick?

BRICK:
Yes, sir, too ruttin' decent!

BIG DADDY:
So, the little boy pointed at it and said, "What's that?" His Mam said, "Oh, that's—nothin'!"—His Papa said, "She's spoiled!"

[*Field-hands sing off R, featuring Sookey: "I Just Can't Stay Here by Myself," through following scene.*

[*Big Daddy X to Brick at L.*]

BIG DADDY:
You didn't laugh at that story, Brick.

[*Big Mama X DRC crying. Margaret goes to her. Mae and Gooper hold URC.*]

BRICK:
No, sir, I didn't laugh at that story.

206

[*On the lower gallery, Big Mama sobs. Big Daddy looks toward her.*]

BIG DADDY:
What's wrong with that long, thin woman over there, loaded with diamonds? Hey, what's-your-name, what's the matter with you?

MARGARET [*X toward Big Daddy*]:
She had a slight dizzy spell, Big Daddy.

BIG DADDY [*ULC*]:
You better watch that, Big Mama. A stroke is a bad way to go.

MARGARET [*X to Big Daddy at C*]:
Oh, Brick, Big Daddy has on your birthday present to him, Brick, he has on your cashmere robe, the softest material I have ever felt.

BIG DADDY:
Yeah, this is my soft birthday, Maggie. . . .

Not my gold or my silver birthday, but my soft birthday, everything's got to be soft for Big Daddy on this soft birthday.

[*Maggie kneels before Big Daddy C. As Gooper and Mae speak, Big Mama X USRC in front of them, hushing them with a gesture.*]

GOOPER:
Maggie, I hate to make such a crude observation, but there is somethin' a little indecent about your—

MAE:
Like a slow-motion football tackle—

MARGARET:
Big Daddy's got on his Chinese slippers that I gave him, Brick. Big Daddy, I haven't given you my big present yet, but now

207

I will, now's the time for me to present it to you! I have an announcement to make!

MAE:
What? What kind of announcement?

GOOPER:
A sports announcement, Maggie?

MARGARET:
Announcement of life beginning! A child is coming, sired by Brick, and out of Maggie the Cat! I have Brick's child in my body, an' that's my birthday present to Big Daddy on this birthday!

[*Big Daddy looks at Brick who X behind Big Daddy to DS portal, L.*]

BIG DADDY:
Get up, girl, get up off your knees, girl.

[*Big Daddy helps Margaret rise. He X above her, to her R, bites off the end of a fresh cigar, taken from his bathrobe pocket, as he studies Margaret.*]

Uh-huh, this girl has life in her body, that's no lie!

BIG MAMA:
BIG DADDY'S DREAM COME TRUE!

BRICK:
JESUS!

BIG DADDY [*X R below wicker seat*]:
Gooper, I want my lawyer in the mornin'.

BRICK:
Where are you goin', Big Daddy?

BIG DADDY:

Son, I'm goin' up on the roof to the belvedere on th' roof to look over my kingdom before I give up my kingdom—twenty-eight thousand acres of th' richest land this side of the Valley Nile!

[*Exit through R doors, and DR on gallery.*]

BIG MAMA [*following*]:

Sweetheart, sweetheart, sweetheart—can I come with you?

[*Exits DR.*

[*Margaret is DSC in mirror area.*]

GOOPER [*X to bar*]:

Brick, could you possibly spare me one small shot of that liquor?

BRICK [*DLC*]:

Why, help yourself, Gooper boy.

GOOPER:

I will.

MAE [*X forward*]:

Of course we know that this is a lie!

GOOPER [*drinks*]:

Be still, Mae!

MAE [*X to Gooper at bar*]:

I won't be still! I know she's made this up!

GOOPER:

God damn it, I said to shut up!

MAE:

That woman isn't pregnant!

209

GOOPER:
Who said she was?

MAE:
She did!

GOOPER:
The doctor didn't. Doc Baugh didn't.

MARGARET [*X R to above couch*]:
I haven't gone to Doc Baugh.

GOOPER [*X through to L of Margaret*]:
Then who'd you go to, Maggie?

[*Offstage song finishes.*]

MARGARET:
One of the best gynecologists in the South.

GOOPER:
Uh-huh, I see—

[*Foot on end of couch, trapping Margaret:*]

May we have his name please?

MARGARET:
No, you may not, Mister—Prosecutin' Attorney!

MAE [*X to R of Margaret, above*]:
He doesn't have any name, he doesn't exist!

MARGARET:
He does so exist, and so does my baby, Brick's baby!

MAE:
You can't conceive a child by a man that won't sleep with you unless you think you're—

[*Forces Margaret onto couch, turns away C.*

[Brick starts C for Mae.]

He drinks all the time to be able to tolerate you! Sleeps on the sofa to keep out of contact with you!

GOOPER [*X above Margaret, who lies face down on couch*]:
Don't try to kid us, Margaret—

MAE [*X to bed, L side, rumpling pillows*]:
How can you conceive a child by a man that won't sleep with you? How can you conceive? How can you? How can you!

GOOPER [*sharply*]:
MAE!

BRICK [*X below Mae to her R, takes hold of her*]:
Mae, Sister Woman, how d'you know that I don't sleep with Maggie?

MAE:
We occupy the next room an' th' wall between isn't soundproof.

BRICK:
Oh . . .

MAE:
We hear the nightly pleadin' and the nightly refusal. So don't imagine you're goin' t'put a trick over on us, to fool a dyin' man with—a—

BRICK:
Mae, Sister Woman, not everybody makes much noise about love. Oh, I know some people are huffers an' puffers, but others are silent lovers.

GOOPER [*behind seat, R*]:
This talk is pointless, completely.

BRICK:

How d'y'know that we're not silent lovers?

Even if y'got a peep-hole drilled in the wall, how can y'tell if sometime when Gooper's got business in Memphis an' you're playin' scrabble at the country club with other ex-queens of cotton, Maggie and I don't come to some temporary agreement? How do you know that—?

[*He X above wicker seat to above R end couch.*]

MAE:

Brick, I never thought that you would stoop to her level, I just never dreamed that you would stoop to her level.

GOOPER:

I don't think Brick will stoop to her level.

BRICK [*sits R of Margaret on couch*]:

What is your level? Tell me your level so I can sink or rise to it.

[*Rises.*]

You heard what Big Daddy said. This girl has life in her body.

MAE:

That is a lie!

BRICK:

No, truth is something desperate, an' she's got it. Believe me, it's somethin' desperate, an' she's got it.

[*X below seat to below bar.*]

An' now if you will stop actin' as if Brick Pollitt was dead an' buried, invisible, not heard, an' go on back to your peephole in the wall—I'm drunk, and sleepy—not as alive as Maggie, but still alive. . . .

[*Pours drink, drinks.*]

GOOPER [*picks up briefcase from R foot of bed*]:
Come on, Mae. We'll leave these love birds together in their
nest.

MAE:
Yeah, nest of lice! Liars!

GOOPER:
Mae—Mae, you jes' go on back to our room—

MAE:
Liars!

[*Exits through hall.*]

GOOPER [*DR above Margaret*]:
We're jest goin' to wait an' see. Time will tell.

[*X to R of bar.*]

Yes, sir, little brother, we're just goin' to wait an' see!

[*Exit, hall.*

[*The clock strikes twelve.*

[*Maggie and Brick exchange a look. He drinks deeply, puts
his glass on the bar. Gradually, his expression changes. He
utters a sharp exhalation.*

[*The exhalation is echoed by the singers, off UR, who
commence vocalizing with "Gimme a Cool Drink of Water
Fo' I Die," and continue till end of act.*]

MARGARET [*as she hears Brick's exhalation*]:
The click?

[*Brick looks toward the singers, happily, almost gratefully.
He XR to bed, picks up his pillow, and starts toward head*

213

CAT ON A HOT TIN ROOF

*of couch, DR, Xing above wicker seat. Margaret seizes the
pillow from his grasp, rises, stands facing C, holding the
pillow close. Brick watches her with growing admiration.
She moves quickly USC, throwing pillow onto bed. She X
to bar. Brick counters below wicker seat, watching her.
Margaret grabs all the bottles from the bar. She goes into
hall, pitches the bottles, one after the other, off the platform
into the UL lawn area. Bottles break, off L. Margaret re-
enters the room, stands UC, facing Brick.]*

Echo Spring has gone dry, and no one but me could drive you
to town for more.

BRICK:
Lacey will get me—

MARGARET:
Lacey's been told not to!

BRICK:
I could drive—

MARGARET:
And you lost your driver's license! I'd phone ahead and have
you stopped on the highway before you got halfway to Ruby
Lightfoot's gin mill. I told a lie to Big Daddy, but we can
make that lie come true. And then I'll bring you liquor, and
we'll get drunk together, here, tonight, in this place that death
has come into! What do you say? What do you say, baby?

BRICK [*X to L side bed*]:
I admire you, Maggie.

*[Brick sits on edge of bed. He looks up at the overhead
light, then at Margaret. She reaches for the light, turns it
out; then she kneels quickly beside Brick at foot of bed.]*

214

MARGARET:

Oh, you weak, beautiful people who give up with such grace. What you need is someone to take hold of you—gently, with love, and hand your life back to you, like something gold you let go of—and I can! I'm determined to do it—and nothing's more determined than a cat on a tin roof—is there? Is there, baby?

[*She touches his cheek, gently.*]

CURTAIN

ORPHEUS DESCENDING

FOR MARION BLACK VACCARO

Copyright © 1955, 1958 by Tennessee Williams

Grateful acknowledgment is made to *The New York Times,* in which
the article, "The Past, the Present and the Perhaps" first appeared.

THE PAST, THE PRESENT
AND THE PERHAPS

One icy bright winter morning in the last week of 1940, my brave representative, Audrey Wood, and I were crossing the Common in Boston, from an undistinguished hotel on one side to the grandeur of the Ritz-Carlton on the other. We had just read in the morning notices of *Battles of Angels,** which had opened at the Wilbur the evening before. As we crossed the Common there was a series of loud reports like gunfire from the street that we were approaching, and one of us said, "My God, they're shooting at us!"

We were still laughing, a bit hysterically, as we entered the Ritz-Carlton suite in which the big brass of the Theatre Guild and director Margaret Webster were waiting for us with that special air of gentle gravity that hangs over the demise of a play so much like the atmosphere that hangs over a home from which a living soul has been snatched by the Reaper.

Not present was little Miriam Hopkins, who was understandably shattered and cloistered after the events of the evening before, in which a simulated on-stage fire had erupted clouds of smoke so realistically over both stage and auditorium that a lot of Theatre Guild first-nighters had fled choking from the Wilbur before the choking star took her bows, which were about the quickest and most distracted that I have seen in a theatre.

It was not that morning that I was informed that the show must close. That morning I was only told that the play must be cut to the bone. I came with a rewrite of the final scene and I remember saying, heroically, "I will crawl on my belly through brimstone if you will substitute this!" The response was gently evasive. It was a few mornings later that I received

* For the text of *Battle of Angels,* see Volume I of *The Theatre of Tennessee Williams.*

the *coup de grace,* the announcement that the play would close at the completion of its run in Boston. On that occasion I made an equally dramatic statement, on a note of anguish. "You don't seem to see that I put my heart into this play!"

It was Miss Webster who answered with a remark I have never forgotten and yet never heeded. She said, "You must not wear your heart on your sleeve for daws to peck at!" Someone else said, "At least you are not out of pocket." I don't think I had any answer for that one, any more than I had anything in my pocket to be out of.

Well, in the end, when the Boston run was finished, I was given a check for $200 and told to get off somewhere and rewrite the play. I squandered half of this subsidy on the first of four operations performed on a cataracted left eye, and the other half took me to Key West for the rewrite. It was a long rewrite. In fact, it is still going on, though the two hundred bucks are long gone.

Why have I stuck so stubbornly to this play? For seventeen years, in fact? Well, nothing is more precious to anybody than the emotional record of his youth, and you will find the trail of my sleeve-worn heart in this completed play that I now call *Orpheus Descending.* On its surface it was and still is the tale of a wild-spirited boy who wanders into a conventional community of the South and creates the commotion of a fox in a chicken coop.

But beneath that now familiar surface it is a play about unanswered questions that haunt the hearts of people and the difference between continuing to ask them, a difference represented by the four major protagonists of the play, and the acceptance of prescribed answers that are not answers at all, but expedient adaptations or surrender to a state of quandary.

Battle was actually my fifth long play, but the first to be given a professional production. Two of the others, *Candles to the Sun* and *Fugitive Kind,* were produced by a brilliant, but semiprofessional group called The Mummers of St. Louis. A third one, called *Spring Storm,* was written for the late Prof. E. C. Mabie's seminar in playwriting at the University of Iowa, and I read it aloud, appropriately in the spring.

When I had finished reading, the good professor's eyes had a glassy look as though he had drifted into a state of trance. There was a long and all but unendurable silence. Everyone seemed more or less embarrassed. At last the professor pushed back his chair, thus dismissing the seminar, and remarked casually and kindly, "Well, we all have to paint our nudes!" And this is the only reference that I can remember anyone making to the play. That is, in the playwriting class, but I do remember that the late Lemuel Ayers, who was a graduate student at Iowa that year, read it and gave me sufficient praise for its dialogue and atmosphere to reverse my decision to give up the theatre in favor of my other occupation of waiting on tables, or more precisely, handing out trays in the cafeteria of the State Hospital.

Then there was Chicago for a while and a desperate effort to get on the W. P. A. Writers' Project, which didn't succeed, for my work lacked "social content" or "protest" and I couldn't prove that my family was destitute and I still had, in those days, a touch of refinement in my social behavior which made me seem frivolous and decadent to the conscientiously rough-hewn pillars of the Chicago Project.

And so I drifted back to St. Louis, again, and wrote my fourth long play which was the best of the lot. It was called *Not About Nightingales* and it concerned prison life, and I have never written anything since then that could compete with it in violence and horror, for it was based on something that actually occurred along about that time, the literal roasting-alive of a group of intransigent convicts sent for correction to a hot room called "The Klondike."

I submitted it to The Mummers of St. Louis and they were

eager to perform it but they had come to the end of their economic tether and had to disband at this point.

Then there was New Orleans and another effort, while waiting on tables in a restaurant where meals cost only two-bits, to get on a Writers' Project or the Theatre Project, again unsuccessful.

And then there was a wild and wonderful trip to California with a young clarinet player. We ran out of gas in El Paso, also out of cash, and it seemed for days that we would never go farther, but my grandmother was an "easy touch" and I got a letter with a $10 bill stitched neatly to one of the pages, and we continued westward.

In the Los Angeles area, in the summer of 1939, I worked for a while at Clark's Bootery in Culver City, within sight of the M-G-M studio and I lived on a pigeon ranch, and I rode between the two, a distance of ten miles, on a secondhand bicycle that I bought for $5.

Then a most wonderful thing happened. While in New Orleans I had heard about a play contest being conducted by the Group Theatre of New York. I submitted all four of the long plays I have mentioned that preceded *Battle of Angels,* plus a group of one-acts called *American Blues.* One fine day I received, when I returned to the ranch on my bike, a telegram saying that I had won a special award of $100 for the one-acts, and it was signed by Harold Clurman, Molly Day Thacher, who is the present Mrs. Elia Kazan, and that fine writer, Irwin Shaw, the judges of the contest.

I retired from Clark's Bootery and from picking squabs at the pigeon ranch. And the clarinet player and I hopped on our bicycles and rode all the way down to Tiajuana and back as far as Laguna Beach, where we obtained, rent free, a small cabin on a small ranch in return for taking care of the poultry.

We lived all that summer on the $100 from the Group

Theatre and I think it was the happiest summer of my life. All the days were pure gold, the nights were starry, and I looked so young, or carefree, that they would sometimes refuse to sell me a drink because I did not appear to have reached 21. But toward the end of the summer, maybe only because it was the end of the summer as well as the end of the $100, the clarinet player became very moody and disappeared without warning into the San Bernardino Mountains to commune with his soul in solitude, and there was nothing left in the cabin in the canyon but a bag of dried peas.

I lived on stolen eggs and avocados and dried peas for a week, and also on a faint hope stirred by a letter from a lady in New York whose name was Audrey Wood, who had taken hold of all those plays that I had submitted to the Group Theatre contest, and told me that it might be possible to get me one of the Rockefeller Fellowships, or grants, of $1,000 which were being passed out to gifted young writers at that time. And I began to write *Battle of Angels,* a lyrical play about memories and the loneliness of them. Although my beloved grandmother was living on the pension of a retired minister (I believe it was only $85 a month in those days), and her meager earnings as a piano instructor, she once again stitched some bills to a page of a letter, and I took a bus to St. Louis. *Battle of Angels* was finished late that fall and sent to Miss Wood.

One day the phone rang and, in a terrified tone, my mother told me that it was long distance, for me. The voice was Audrey Wood's. Mother waited, shakily, in the doorway. When I hung up I said, quietly, "Rockefeller has given me a $1,000 grant and they want me to come to New York." For the first time since I had known her, my mother burst into tears. "I am so happy," she said. It was all she could say.

And so you see it is a very old play that *Orpheus Descending* has come out of, but a play is never an old one until you quit

223

working on it and I have never quit working on this one, not even now. It never went into the trunk, it always stayed on the work bench, and I am not presenting it now because I have run out of ideas or material for completely new work. I am offering it this season because I honestly believe that it is finally finished. About 75 per cent of it is new writing, but what is much more important, I believe that I have now finally managed to say in it what I wanted to say, and I feel that it now has in it a sort of emotional bridge between those early years described in this article and my present state of existence as a playwright.

So much for the past and present. The future is called "perhaps," which is the only possible thing to call the future. And the important thing is not to allow that to scare you.

Tennessee Williams

Orpheus Descending was presented at the Martin Beck Theatre in New York on March 21, 1957, by the Producers Theatre. It was directed by Harold Clurman; the stage set was designed by Boris Aronson, the costumes by Lucinda Ballard, and the lighting by Feder. The cast was as follows:

DOLLY HAMMA	ELIZABETH EUSTIS
BEULAH BINNINGS	JANE ROSE
PEE WEE BINNINGS	WARREN KEMMERLING
DOG HAMMA	DAVID CLARKE
CAROL CUTRERE	LOIS SMITH
EVA TEMPLE	NELL HARRISON
SISTER TEMPLE	MARY FARRELL
UNCLE PLEASANT	JOHN MARRIOTT
VAL XAVIER	CLIFF ROBERTSON
VEE TALBOT	JOANNA ROOS
LADY TORRANCE	MAUREEN STAPLETON
JABE TORRANCE	CRAHAN DENTON
SHERIFF TALBOTT	R. G. ARMSTRONG
MR. DUBINSKY	BEAU TILDEN
WOMAN	JANICE MARS
DAVID CUTRERE	ROBERT WEBBER
NURSE PORTER	VIRGILIA CHEW
FIRST MAN	ALBERT HENDERSON
SECOND MAN	CHARLES TYNER

Other characters: CONJURE MAN, CLOWN.

ACT ONE

SCENE: *The set represents in nonrealistic fashion a general dry-goods store and part of a connecting "confectionery" in a small Southern town. The ceiling is high and the upper walls are dark, as if streaked with moisture and cobwebbed. A great dusty window upstage offers a view of disturbing emptiness that fades into late dusk. The action of the play occurs during a rainy season, late winter and early spring, and sometimes the window turns opaque but glistening silver with sheets of rain. "TORRANCE MERCANTILE STORE" is lettered on the window in gilt of old-fashioned design.*

Merchandise is represented very sparsely and it is not realistic. Bolts of pepperel and percale stand upright on large spools, the black skeleton of a dressmaker's dummy stands meaninglessly against a thin white column, and there is a motionless ceiling fan with strips of flypaper hanging from it.

There are stairs that lead to a landing and disappear above it, and on the landing there is a sinister-looking artificial palm tree in a greenish-brown jardiniere.

But the confectionery, which is seen partly through a wide arched door, is shadowy and poetic as some inner dimension of the play.

Another, much smaller, playing area is a tiny bedroom alcove which is usually masked by an Oriental drapery which is worn dim but bears the formal design of a gold tree with scarlet fruit and fantastic birds.

At the rise of the curtain two youngish middle-aged women, DOLLY *and* BEULAH, *are laying out a buffet supper on a pair of pink-and-gray-veined marble-topped tables with gracefully curved black-iron legs, brought into the main area from the confectionery. They are wives of small planters and tastelessly overdressed in a somewhat bizarre fashion.*

227

A train whistles in the distance and dogs bark in response from various points and distances. The women pause in their occupations at the tables and rush to the archway, crying out harshly.

DOLLY: Pee Wee!

BEULAH: Dawg!

DOLLY: Cannonball is comin' into th' depot!

BEULAH: You all git down to th' depot an' meet that train!

[*Their husbands slouch through, heavy, red-faced men in clothes that are too tight for them or too loose, and mud-stained boots.*]

PEE WEE: I fed that one-armed bandit a hunnerd nickels an' it coughed up five.

DOG: Must have hed indigestion.

PEE WEE: I'm gonna speak to Jabe about them slots. [*They go out and a motor starts and pauses.*]

DOLLY: I guess Jabe Torrance has got more to worry about than the slot machines and pinball games in that confectionery.

BEULAH: You're not tellin' a lie. I wint to see Dr. Johnny about Dawg's condition. Dawg's got sugar in his urine again, an' as I was leavin' I ast him what was the facks about Jabe Torrance's operation in Mimphis. Well—

DOLLY: What'd he tell you, Beulah?

BEULAH: He said the worse thing a doctor ever can say.

DOLLY: What's that, Beulah?

BEULAH: Nothin' a-tall, not a spoken word did he utter! He just looked at me with those big dark eyes of his and shook his haid like this!

DOLLY [*with doleful satisfaction*]: I guess he signed Jabe Torrance's death warrant with just that single silent motion of his haid.

BEULAH: That's exactly what passed through my mind. I understand that they cut him open—[*Pauses to taste something on the table.*]

DOLLY:—An' sewed him right back up!—that's what I heard . . .

BEULAH: I didn't know these olives had seeds in them!

DOLLY: You thought they was stuffed?

BEULAH: Uh-huh. Where's the Temple sisters?

DOLLY: Where d'you think?

BEULAH: Snoopin' aroun' upstairs. If Lady catches 'em at it she'll give those two old maids a touch of her tongue! She's not a Dago for nothin'!

DOLLY: Ha, ha, no! You spoke a true word, honey . . . [*Looks out door as car passes.*] Well, I was surprised when I wint up myself!

BEULAH: You wint up you'self?

DOLLY: I did and so did you because I seen you, Beulah.

BEULAH: I never said that I didn't. Curiosity is a human instinct.

DOLLY: They got two separate bedrooms which are not even connectin'. At opposite ends of the hall, and everything is so dingy an' dark up there. Y'know what it seemed like to me? A county jail! I swear to goodness it didn't seem to me like a place for white people to live in!—that's the truth . . .

BEULAH [*darkly*]: Well, I wasn't surprised. Jabe Torrance bought that woman.

DOLLY: Bought her?

BEULAH: Yais, he bought ·her, when she was a girl of eighteen! He bought her and bought her cheap because she'd been thrown over and her heart was broken by that—[*Jerks head toward a passing car, then continues:*]—that Cutrere boy. . . . *Oh, what a—Mmmm, what a—beautiful* thing he was. . . . And those two met like you struck two stones together and made a fire!—yes—fire . . .

DOLLY: What?

BEULAH: *Fire!*—Ha . . . [*Strikes another match and lights one of the candelabra. Mandolin begins to fade in. The following monologue should be treated frankly as exposition, spoken to audience, almost directly, with a force that commands attention.* DOLLY *does not remain in the playing area, and after the first few sentences, there is no longer any pretense of a duologue.*]

—Well, that was a long time ago, before you and Dog moved into Two River County. Although you must have heard of it. Lady's father was a Wop from the old country and when he first come here with a mandolin and a monkey that wore a little green velvet suit, ha ha.

—He picked up dimes and quarters in the saloons—this was before Prohibition. . . .

—People just called him "The Wop," nobody knew his name, just called him "The Wop," ha ha ha. . . .

DOLLY [*Off, vaguely*]: Anh-hannnh. . . .

[BEULAH *switches in the chair and fixes the audience with her eyes, leaning slightly forward to compel their attention. Her voice is rich with nostalgia, and at a sign of restlessness, she rises and comes straight out to the proscenium, like a pitchman. This monologue should set the nonrealistic key for the whole production.*]

BEULAH: Oh, my law, well, that was Lady's daddy! Then come Prohibition an' first thing ennyone knew, The Wop had took to bootleggin' like a duck to water! He picked up a piece of land cheap, it was on the no'th shore of Moon Lake which used to be the old channel of the river and people thought some day the river might swing back that way, and so he got it cheap. . . . [*Moves her chair up closer to proscenium.*] He planted an orchard on it; he covered the whole no'th shore of the lake with grapevines and fruit trees, and then he built little arbors, little white wooden arbors with tables and benches to drink in and carry on in, ha ha! And in the spring and the summer, young couples would come out there, like me and Pee Wee, we used to go out there, an' court up a storm, ha ha, just court up a—storm! Ha ha!— The county was dry in those days, I don't mean dry like now, why, now you just walk a couple of feet off the highway and whistle three times like a jay bird and a nigger pops out of a bush with a bottle of corn!

DOLLY: Ain't that the truth? Ha ha.

BEULAH: But in those days the county was dry for true, I mean bone dry except for The Wop's wine garden. So we'd go out to The Wop's an' drink that Dago red wine an' cut up an' carry on an' raise such cane in those arbors! Why, I remember one Sunday old Doctor Tooker, Methodist minister then, he bust a blood vessel denouncing The Wop in the pulpit!

DOLLY: Lawd have mercy!

BEULAH: Yes, ma'am!—Each of those white wooden arbors had a lamp in it, and one by one, here and there, the lamps would go out as the couples begun to make love . . .

DOLLY: *Oh*—oh . . .

BEULAH: What strange noises you could hear if you listened, calls, cries, whispers, moans—giggles. . . . [*Her voice*

231

is soft with recollection]—And then, one by one, the lamps would be lighted again, and The Wop and his daughter would sing and play Dago songs. . . . [*Bring up mandolin: voice under "Dicitencello Vuoi."*] But sometimes The Wop would look around for his daughter, and all of a sudden Lady wouldn't be there!

DOLLY: Where would she be?

BEULAH: She'd be with David Cutrere.

DOLLY: Awwwwww—ha ha . . .

BEULAH:—Carol Cutrere's big brother, Lady and him would disappear in the orchard and old Papa Romano, The Wop, would holler, "Lady, Lady!"—no answer whatsoever, no matter how long he called and no matter how loud. . . .

DOLLY: Well, I guess it's hard to shout back, "Here I am, Papa," when where you are is in the arms of your lover!

BEULAH: Well, that spring, no, it was late that summer . . . [DOLLY *retires again from the playing area.*]—Papa Romano made a bad mistake. He sold liquor to niggers. The Mystic Crew took action. —They rode out there, one night, with gallons of coal oil—it was a real dry summer—and set that place on fire!—They burned the whole thing up, vines, arbors, fruit trees.—Pee Wee and me, we stood on the dance pavilion across the lake and watched that fire spring up. Inside of tin minutes the whole nawth shore of the lake was a mass of flames, a regular sea of flames, and all the way over the lake we could hear Lady's papa shouting, "Fire, fire, fire!"—as if it was necessary to let people know, and the whole sky lit up with it, as red as Guinea red wine! —Ha ha ha ha. . . . Not a fire engine, not a single engine pulled out of a station that night in Two River County!—The poor old fellow, The Wop, he took a blanket and run up into the orchard to fight the fire singlehanded—*and* burned *alive.* . . . Uh-huh! *burned alive.* . . .

[*Mandolin stops short.* DOLLY *has returned to the table to have her coffee.*]

You know what I sometimes wonder?

DOLLY: No. What do you wonder?

BEULAH: I wonder sometimes if Lady has any suspicion that her husband, Jabe Torrance, was the leader of the Mystic Crew the night they burned up her father in his wine garden on Moon Lake?

DOLLY: Beulah Binnings, you make my blood run cold with such a thought! How could she live in marriage twenty years with a man if she knew he'd burned her father up in his wine garden?

[*Dog bays in distance.*]

BEULAH: She could live with him in hate. People can live together in hate for a long time, Dolly. Notice their passion for money. I've always noticed when couples don't love each other they develop a passion for money. Haven't you seen that happen? Of course you have. Now there's not many couples that stay devoted forever. Why, some git so they just barely tolerate each other's existence. Isn't that true?

DOLLY: You couldn't of spoken a truer word if you read it out loud from the Bible!

BEULAH: Barely tolerate each other's existence, and some don't even do that. You know, Dolly Hamma, I don't think half as many married min have committed suicide in this county as the coroner says has done so!

DOLLY: [*with voluptuous appreciation of* BEULAH'S *wit*]: You think it's their wives that give them the deep six, honey?

BEULAH: I don't think so, I know so. Why there's couples that loathe and despise the sight, smell and sound of each other before that round-trip honeymoon ticket is punched at both ends, Dolly.

233

DOLLY: I hate to admit it but I can't deny it.

BEULAH: But they hang on together.

DOLLY: Yes, they hang on together.

BEULAH: Year after year after year, accumulating property and money, building up wealth and respect and position in the towns they live in and the counties and cities and the churches they go to, belonging to the clubs and so on and so forth and not a soul but them knowin' they have to go wash their hands after touching something the other one just put down! ha ha ha ha ha!—

DOLLY: Beulah, that's an evil laugh of yours, that laugh of yours is evil!

BEULAH [*louder*]: Ha ha ha ha ha!—But you know it's the truth.

DOLLY: Yes, she's tellin' the truth! [*Nods to audience.*]

BEULAH: Then one of them—gits—*cincer* or has a—*stroke* or somethin'?—The other one—

DOLLY:—Hauls in the loot?

BEULAH: That's right, hauls in the loot! Oh, my, then you should see how him or her blossoms out. New house, new car, new clothes. Some of 'em even change to a different church!—If it's a widow, she goes with a younger man, and if it's a widower, he starts courtin' some chick, ha ha ha ha ha!
And so I said, I said to Lady this morning before she left for Mamphis to bring Jabe home, I said, "Lady, I don't suppose you're going to reopen the confectionery till Jabe is completely recovered from his operation." She said, "It can't wait for anything that might take that much time." Those are her exact words. It can't wait for anything that might take that much time. Too much is invested in it. It's going to be done over, redecorated, and opened on schedule the Saturday

before Easter this spring!—Why?—Because—she knows Jabe is dying and she wants to clean up quick!

DOLLY: An awful thought. But a true one. Most awful thoughts are.

[*They are startled by sudden light laughter from the dim upstage area. The light changes on the stage to mark a division.*]

The women turn to see CAROL CUTRERE *in the archway
between the store and the confectionery. She is past thirty and,
lacking prettiness, she has an odd, fugitive beauty which is
stressed, almost to the point of fantasy, by a style of make-up
with which a dancer named Valli has lately made such an impression in the bohemian centers of France and Italy, the face
and lips powdered white and the eyes outlined and exaggerated
with black pencil and the lids tinted blue. Her family name is
the oldest and most distinguished in the country.*

BEULAH: Somebody don't seem to know that the store is
closed.

DOLLY: Beulah?

BEULAH: What?

DOLLY: Can you understand how anybody would deliberately make themselves look fantastic as that?

BEULAH: Some people have to show off, it's a passion with
them, anything on earth to get attention.

DOLLY: I sure wouldn't care for that kind of attention. Not
me. I wouldn't desire it. . . .

[*During these lines, just loud enough for her to hear them,*
CAROL *has crossed to the pay-phone and deposited a coin.*]

CAROL: I want Tulane 0370 in New Orleans. What? Oh.
Hold on a minute.

[EVA TEMPLE *is descending the stairs, slowly, as if awed by*
CAROL'S *appearance.* CAROL *rings open the cashbox and
removes some coins; returns to deposit coins in phone.*]

BEULAH: She helped herself to money out of the cashbox.

[EVA *passes* CAROL *like a timid child skirting a lion cage.*]

CAROL: Hello, Sister.

EVA: I'm Eva.

CAROL: Hello, Eva.

EVA: Hello . . . [*Then in a loud whisper to* BEULAH *and* DOLLY:] She took money out of the cashbox.

DOLLY: Oh, she can do as she pleases, she's a Cutrere!

BEULAH: Shoot . . .

EVA: What is she doin' barefooted?

BEULAH: The last time she was arrested on the highway, they say that she was naked under her coat.

CAROL [*to operator*]: I'm waiting. [*Then to women:*]—I caught the heel of my slipper in that rotten boardwalk out there and it broke right off. [*Raises slippers in hand.*] They say if you break the heel of your slipper in the morning it means you'll meet the love of your life before dark. But it was already dark when I broke the heel of my slipper. Maybe that means I'll meet the love of my life before daybreak. [*The quality of her voice is curiously clear and childlike.* SISTER TEMPLE *appears on stair landing bearing an old waffle iron.*]

SISTER: Wasn't that them?

EVA: No, it was Carol Cutrere!

CAROL [*at phone*]: Just keep on ringing, please, he's probably drunk.

[SISTER *crosses by her as* EVA *did.*]

Sometimes it takes quite a while to get through the living-room furniture. . . .

SISTER:—She a *sight?*

EVA: Uh-huh!

CAROL: Bertie?—Carol!—Hi, doll! Did you trip over something? I heard a crash. Well, I'm leaving right now, I'm already on the highway and everything's fixed, I've got my allowance back on condition that I remain forever away from Two River County! I had to blackmail them a little. I came to dinner with my eyes made up and my little black sequin jacket and Betsy Boo, my brother's wife, said, "Carol, you going out to a fancy dress ball?" I said, "Oh, no, I'm just going jooking tonight up and down the Dixie Highway between here and Memphis like I used to when I lived here." Why, honey, she flew so fast you couldn't see her passing and came back in with the ink still wet on the check! And this will be done once a month as long as I stay away from Two River County. . . . [*Laughs gaily.*]—How's Jackie? Bless his heart, give him a sweet kiss for me! Oh, honey, I'm driving straight through, not even stopping for pickups unless you need one! I'll meet you in the Starlite Lounge before it closes, or if I'm irresistibly delayed, I'll certainly join you for coffee at the Morning Call before the all-night places have closed for the day . . . —I—Bertie? Bertie? [*Laughs uncertainly and hangs up.*]—let's see, now. . . . [*Removes a revolver from her trench coat pocket and crosses to fill it with cartridges back of counter.*]

EVA: What she looking for?

SISTER: Ask her.

EVA [*advancing*]: What're you looking for, Carol?

CAROL: Cartridges for my revolver.

DOLLY: She don't have a license to carry a pistol.

BEULAH: She don't have a license to drive a car.

CAROL: When I stop for someone I want to be sure it's someone I want to stop for.

DOLLY: Sheriff Talbott ought to know about this when he gits back from the depot.

CAROL: Tell him, ladies. I've already given him notice that if he ever attempts to stop me again on the highway, I'll shoot it out with him. . . .

BEULAH: When anybody has trouble with the law—

[*Her sentence is interrupted by a panicky scream from* EVA, *immediately repeated by* SISTER. *The* TEMPLE SISTERS *scramble upstairs to the landing.* DOLLY *also cries out and turns, covering her face. A Negro* CONJURE MAN *has entered the store. His tattered garments are fantastically bedizened with many talismans and good-luck charms of shell and bone and feather. His blue-black skin is daubed with cryptic signs in white paint.*]

DOLLY: Git him out, git him out, he's going to mark my baby!

BEULAH: Oh, shoot, Dolly. . . .

[DOLLY *has now fled after the* TEMPLE SISTERS, *to the landing of the stairs. The* CONJURE MAN *advances with a soft, rapid, toothless mumble of words that sound like wind in dry grass. He is holding out something in his shaking hand.*]

It's just that old crazy conjure man from Blue Mountain. He cain't mark your baby.

[*Phrase of primitive music or percussion as* NEGRO *moves into light.* BEULAH *follows* DOLLY *to landing.*]

CAROL [*very high and clear voice*]: Come here, Uncle, and let me see what you've got there. Oh, it's a bone of some kind. No, I don't want to touch it, it isn't clean yet, there's still some flesh clinging to it.

239

[*Women make sounds of revulsion.*]

Yes, I know it's the breastbone of a bird but it's still tainted with corruption. Leave it a long time on a bare rock in the rain and the sun till every sign of corruption is burned and washed away from it, and then it will be a good charm, a white charm, but now it's a black charm, Uncle. So take it away and do what I told you with it. . . .

[*The* NEGRO *makes a ducking obeisance and shuffles slowly back to the door.*]

Hey, Uncle Pleasant, give us the Choctaw cry.

[NEGRO *stops in confectionery.*]

He's part Choctaw, he knows the Choctaw cry.

SISTER TEMPLE: Don't let him holler in *here!*

CAROL: Come on, Uncle Pleasant, *you* know it!

[*She takes off her coat, sits on right window sill. She starts the cry herself. The* NEGRO *throws back his head and completes it: a series of barking sounds that rise to a high sustained note of wild intensity. The women on the landing retreat further upstairs. Just then, as though the cry had brought him,* VAL *enters the store. He is a young man, about 30, who has a kind of wild beauty about him that the cry would suggest. He does not wear Levi's or a T-shirt, he has on a pair of dark serge pants, glazed from long wear and not excessively tight-fitting. His remarkable garment is a snakeskin jacket, mottled white, black and gray. He carries a guitar which is covered with inscriptions.*]

CAROL [*looking at the young man*]: Thanks, Uncle . . .

BEULAH: Hey, old man, you! *Choctaw! Conjure man! Nigguh! Will you go out-a this sto'? So we can come back downstairs?*

[CAROL *hands* NEGRO *a dollar; he goes out right cackling.*

VAL *holds the door open for* VEE TALBOTT, *a heavy, vague woman in her forties. She does primitive oil paintings and carries one into the store, saying:*]

VEE: I got m'skirt caught in th' door of the Chevrolet an' I'm afraid I tore it.

[*The women descend into store: laconic greetings, interest focused on* VAL.]

Is it dark in here or am I losin' my eyesight? I been painting all day, finished a picture in a ten-hour stretch, just stopped a few minutes fo' coffee and went back to it again while I had a clear vision. I think I got it this time. But I'm so exhausted I could drop in my tracks. There's nothing more exhausting than that kind of work on earth, it's not so much that it tires your body out, but it leaves you drained inside. Y'know what I mean? Inside? Like you was burned out by something? Well! Still! —You feel you've accomplished something when you're through with it, sometimes you feel—*elevated!* How are you, Dolly?

DOLLY: All right, Mrs. Talbott.

VEE: That's good. How are *you,* Beulah?

BEULAH: Oh, I'm all right, I reckon.

VEE: Still can't make out much. Who is that there? [*Indicates* CAROL'S *figure by the window. A significant silence greets this question.* VEE, *suddenly:*]

Oh! I thought her folks had got her out of the county . . .

[CAROL *utters a very light, slightly rueful laugh, her eyes drifting back to* VAL *as she moves back into confectionery.*]

Jabe and Lady back yet?

DOLLY: Pee Wee an' Dawg have gone to the depot to meet 'em.

VEE: Aw. Well, I'm just in time. I brought my new picture with me, the paint isn't dry on it yet. I thought that Lady might want to hang it up in Jabe's room while he's convalescin' from the operation, cause after a close shave with death, people like to be reminded of spiritual things. Huh? Yes! This is the Holy Ghost ascending. . . .

DOLLY [*looking at canvas*]: You didn't put a head on it.

VEE: The head was a blaze of light, that's all I saw in my vision.

DOLLY: Who's the young man with yuh?

VEE: Aw, excuse me, I'm too worn out to have manners. This is Mr. Valentine Xavier, Mrs. Hamma and Mrs.—I'm sorry, Beulah. I never *can* get y' last *name!*

BEULAH: I fo'give you. My name is Beulah Binnings.

VAL: What shall I do with this here?

VEE: Oh, that bowl of sherbet. I thought that Jabe might need something light an' digestible so I brought a bowl of sherbet.

DOLLY: What flavor is it?

VEE: Pineapple.

DOLLY: Oh, goody, I love pineapple. Better put it in the icebox before it starts to melt.

BEULAH [*looking under napkin that covers bowl*]: I'm afraid you're lockin' th' stable after the horse is gone.

DOLLY: Aw, is it melted already?

BEULAH: Reduced to juice.

VEE: Aw, shoot. Well, put it on ice anyhow, it might thicken up.

[*Women are still watching* VAL.]

Where's the icebox?

BEULAH: In the confectionery.

VEE: I thought that Lady had closed the confectionery.

BEULAH: Yes, but the Frigidaire's still there.

[VAL *goes out right through confectionery.*]

VEE: Mr. Xavier is a stranger in our midst. His car broke down in that storm last night and I let him sleep in the lockup. He's lookin' for work and I thought I'd introduce him to Lady an' Jabe because if Jabe can't work they're going to need somebody to help out in th' store.

BEULAH: That's a good idea.

DOLLY: Uh-huh.

BEULAH: Well, come on in, you all, it don't look like they're comin' straight home from the depot anyhow.

DOLLY: Maybe that wasn't the Cannonball Express.

BEULAH: Or maybe they stopped off fo' Pee Wee to buy some liquor.

DOLLY: Yeah . . . at Ruby Lightfoot's.

[*They move past* CAROL *and out of sight.* CAROL *has risen. Now she crosses into the main store area, watching* VAL *with the candid curiosity of one child observing another. He pays no attention but concentrates on his belt buckle, which he is repairing with a pocketknife.*]

CAROL: What're you fixing?

VAL: Belt buckle.

CAROL: Boys like you are always fixing something. Could you fix my slipper?

VAL: What's wrong with your slipper?

243

CAROL: Why are you pretending not to remember me?

VAL: It's hard to remember someone you never met.

CAROL: Then why'd you look so startled when you saw me?

VAL: Did I?

CAROL: I thought for a moment you'd run back out the door.

VAL: The sight of a woman can make me walk in a hurry but I don't think it's ever made me run.—You're standing in my light.

CAROL [*moving aside slightly*]: Oh, excuse me. Better?

VAL: Thanks. . . .

CAROL: Are you afraid I'll snitch?

VAL: Do what?

CAROL: Snitch? I wouldn't; I'm not a snitch. But I can prove that I know you if I have to. It was New Year's Eve in New Orleans.

VAL: I need a small pair of pliers. . . .

CAROL: You had on that jacket and a snake ring with a ruby eye.

VAL: I never had a snake ring with a ruby eye.

CAROL: A snake ring with an emerald eye?

VAL: I never had a snake ring with any kind of an eye. . . . [*Begins to whistle softly, his face averted.*]

CAROL [*smiling gently*]: Then maybe it was a dragon ring with an emerald eye or a diamond or a ruby eye. You told us that it was a gift from a lady osteopath that you'd met somewhere in your travels and that any time you were broke you'd wire this lady osteopath collect, and no matter how far you were or how long it was since you'd seen her, she'd send you a money order for twenty-five dollars with the same sweet message each time. "I love you. When will you come back?" And to prove the story, not that it was difficult to believe it, you took the latest of these sweet messages from your wallet for us to see. . . . [*She throws back her head with soft laughter. He looks away still further and busies himself with the belt buckle.*]—We followed you through five places before we made contact with you and I was the one that made contact. I went up to the bar where you were standing and touched your jacket and said, "What stuff is this made of?" and when you said it was snakeskin, I said, "I wish you'd told me before I touched it." And you said something not nice. You said, "Maybe that will learn you to hold back your hands." I was drunk by that time, which was after midnight. Do you remember what I said to you? I said, "What on earth can you do on this earth but catch at whatever comes near you, with both your hands, until your fingers are broken?" I'd never said that before, or even consciously thought it, but afterwards it seemed like the truest thing that my lips had ever spoken, what on earth can you do but catch at whatever comes near you with both your hands until your fingers are broken. . . . You gave me a quick, sober look. I think you nodded slightly, and then you picked up your guitar and began to sing. After singing you passed the kitty. Whenever paper money was dropped in the kitty you blew a whistle. My cousin Bertie and I dropped in five dollars, you blew the whistle five times and then sat down at our table for a drink, Schenley's with Seven Up. You showed us all those signatures on your guitar. . . . Any correction so far?

VAL: Why are you so anxious to prove I know you?

CAROL: Because I want to know you better and better! I'd like to go out jooking with you tonight.

VAL: What's jooking?

CAROL: Oh, don't you know what that is? That's where you get in a car and drink a little and drive a little and stop and dance a little to a juke box and then you drink a little more and drive a little more and stop and dance a little more to a juke box and then you stop dancing and you just drink and drive and then you stop driving and just drink, and then, finally, you stop drinking. . . .

VAL:—What do you do, then?

CAROL: That depends on the weather and who you're jooking with. If it's a clear night you spread a blanket among the memorial stones on Cypress Hill, which is the local bone orchard, but if it's not a fair night, and this one certainly isn't, why, usually then you go to the Idlewild cabins between here and Sunset on the Dixie Highway. . . .

VAL:—That's about what I figured. But I don't go that route. Heavy drinking and smoking the weed and shacking with strangers is okay for kids in their twenties but this is my thirtieth birthday and I'm all through with that route. [*Looks up with dark eyes.*] I'm not young any more.

CAROL: You're young at thirty—I hope so! I'm twenty-nine!

VAL: Naw, you're not young at thirty if you've been on a goddam party since you were fifteen!

[*Picks up his guitar and sings and plays "Heavenly Grass." CAROL has taken a pint of bourbon from her trench coat pocket and she passes it to him.*]

CAROL: Thanks. That's lovely. Many happy returns of your birthday, Snakeskin.

[*She is very close to him.* VEE *enters and says sharply:*]

VEE: Mr. Xavier don't drink.

CAROL: Oh, ex-cuse *me!*

VEE: And if you behaved yourself better your father would not be paralyzed in bed!

[*Sound of car out front. Women come running with various cries.* LADY *enters, nodding to the women, and holding the door open for her husband and the men following him. She greets the women in almost toneless murmurs, as if too tired to speak. She could be any age between thirty-five and forty-five, in appearance, but her figure is youthful. Her face taut. She is a woman who met with emotional disaster in her girlhood; verges on hysteria under strain. Her voice is often shrill and her body tense. But when in repose, a girlish softness emerges again and she looks ten years younger.*]

LADY: Come in, Jabe. We've got a reception committee here to meet us. They've set up a buffet supper.

[JABE *enters. A gaunt, wolfish man, gray and yellow. The women chatter idiotically.*]

BEULAH: Well, look who's here!

DOLLY: Well, *Jabe!*

BEULAH: I don't think he's been sick. I think he's been to Miami. Look at that wonderful color in his face!

DOLLY: I never seen him look better in my life!

BEULAH: Who does he think he's foolin'? Ha ha ha!— not *me!*

JABE: Whew, Jesus—I'm mighty—tired. . . .

[*An uncomfortable silence, everyone staring greedily at the dying man with his tense, wolfish smile and nervous cough.*]

PEE WEE: Well, Jabe, we been feedin' lots of nickels to those one-arm bandits in there.

DOG: An' that pinball machine is hotter'n a pistol.

PEE WEE: Ha ha.

[EVA TEMPLE *appears on stairs and screams for her sister.*]

EVA: Sistuh! Sistuh! Sistuh! Cousin Jabe's here!

[*A loud clatter upstairs and shrieks.*]

JABE: Jesus. . . .

[EVA *rushing at him—stops short and bursts into tears.*]

LADY: Oh, cut that out, Eva Temple!—What were you doin' upstairs?

EVA: I can't help it, it's so good to see him, it's so wonderful to see our cousin again, oh, Jabe, *blessed!*

SISTER: Where's Jabe, where's precious Jabe? Where's our precious cousin?

EVA: Right here, Sister!

SISTER: Well, bless your old sweet life, and lookit the color he's got in his face, will you?

BEULAH: I just told him he looks like he's been to Miami and got a Florida suntan, haha ha!

[*The preceding speeches are very rapid, all overlapping.*]

JABE: I ain't been out in no sun an' if you all will excuse me I'm gonna do my celebratin' upstairs in bed because I'm kind of—worn out. [*Goes creakily to foot of steps while* EVA *and* SISTER *sob into their handkerchiefs behind him.*]—I see they's been some changes made here. Uh-huh. Uh-huh. How come the shoe department's back here now? [*Instant hostility as if habitual between them.*]

LADY: We always had a problem with light in this store.

JABE: So you put the shoe department further away from the window? That's sensible. A very intelligent solution to the problem, Lady.

LADY: Jabe, you know I told you we got a fluorescent tube coming to put back here.

JABE: Uh-huh. Uh-huh. Well. Tomorrow I'll get me some niggers to help me move the shoe department back front.

LADY: You do whatever you want to, it's your store.

JABE: Uh-huh. Uh-huh. I'm glad you reminded me of it.

[LADY *turns sharply away. He starts up stairs.* PEE WEE *and* DOG *follow him up. The women huddle and whisper in the store.* LADY *sinks wearily into chair at table.*]

BEULAH: That man will never come down those stairs again!

DOLLY: Never in this world, honey.

BEULAH: He has th' death sweat on him! Did you notice that death sweat on him?

DOLLY: An' yellow as butter, just as yellow as—

[SISTER *sobs.*]

EVA: Sister, Sister!

BEULAH [*crossing to* LADY]: Lady, I don't suppose you feel much like talking about it right now but Dog and me are so worried.

DOLLY: Pee Wee and me are worried sick about it.

LADY:—About what?

BEULAH: Jabe's operation in Memphis. Was it successful?

DOLLY: Wasn't it successful?

[LADY *stares at them blindly. The women, except* CAROL, *close avidly about her, tense with morbid interest.*]

SISTER: Was it too late for surgical interference?

EVA: Wasn't it successful?

[*A loud, measured knock begins on the floor above.*]

BEULAH: Somebody told us it had gone past the knife.

DOLLY: We do hope it ain't hopeless.

EVA: We hope and pray it ain't hopeless.

[*All their faces wear faint, unconscious smiles.* LADY *looks from face to face; then utters a slight, startled laugh and springs up from the table and crosses to the stairs.*]

LADY [*as if in flight*]: Excuse me, I have to go up, Jabe's knocking for me. [LADY *goes upstairs. The women gaze after her.*]

CAROL [*suddenly and clearly, in the silence*]: Speaking of knocks, I have a knock in my engine. It goes knock, knock, and I say who's there. I don't know whether I'm in communication with some dead ancestor or the motor's about to drop out and leave me stranded in the dead of night on the Dixie Highway. Do you have any knowledge of mechanics? I'm sure you do. Would you be sweet and take a short drive with me? So you could hear that knock?

VAL: I don't have time.

CAROL: What have you got to do?

VAL: I'm waiting to see about a job in this store.

CAROL: I'm offering you a job.

VAL: I want a job that pays.

CAROL: I expect to pay you.

[*Women whisper loudly in the background.*]

VAL: Maybe sometime tomorrow.

CAROL: I can't stay here overnight; I'm not allowed to stay overnight in this county.

[*Whispers rise. The word "corrupt" is distinguished.*]

[*Without turning, smiling very brightly:*] What are they saying about me? Can you hear what those women are saying about me?

VAL:—Play it cool. . . .

CAROL: I don't like playing it cool! What are they saying about me? That I'm corrupt?

VAL: If you don't want to be talked about, why do you make up like that, why do you—

CAROL: *To show off!*

VAL: What?

CAROL: *I'm an exhibitionist!* I want to be noticed, seen, heard, felt! I want them to know I'm alive! Don't you want them to know you're alive?

VAL: I want to live and I don't care if they know I'm alive or not.

CAROL: Then why do you play a guitar?

VAL: Why do you make a goddam show of yourself?

CAROL: That's right, for the same reason.

VAL: We don't go the same route. . . . [*He keeps moving away from her; she continually follows him. Her speech is compulsive.*]

CAROL: I used to be what they call a Christ-bitten reformer. You know what that is?—A kind of benign exhibitionist. . . . I delivered stump speeches, wrote letters of protest about the gradual massacre of the colored majority in the county. I thought it was wrong for pellagra and slow starvation to cut them down when the cotton crop failed from army worm or boll weevil or too much rain in summer. I wanted to, tried to, put up free clinics, I squandered the money my mother left me on it. And when that Willie McGee thing came along—

251

he was sent to the chair for having improper relations with a white whore—[*Her voice is like a passionate incantation.*] I made a fuss about it. I put on a potato sack and set out for the capital on foot. This was in winter. I walked barefoot in this burlap sack to deliver a personal protest to the governor of the state. Oh, I suppose it was partly exhibitionism on my part, but it wasn't completely exhibitionism; there was something else in it, too. You know how far I got? Six miles out of town—hooted, jeered at, even spit on!—every step of the way—and then arrested! Guess what for? Lewd vagrancy! Uh-huh, that was the charge, "lewd vagrancy," because they said that potato sack I had on was not a respectable garment. . . . Well, all that was a pretty long time ago, and now I'm not a reformer any more. I'm just a "lewd vagrant." And I'm showing the "S.O.B.S." how lewd a "lewd vagrant" can be if she puts her whole heart in it like I do mine! All right. I've told you my story, the story of an exhibitionist. Now I want you to do something for me. Take me out to Cypress Hill in my car. And we'll hear the dead people talk. They do talk there. They chatter together like birds on Cypress Hill, but all they say is one word and that one word is "live," they say "Live, live, live, live, live!" It's all they've learned, it's the only advice they can give.—Just live. . . . [*She opens the door.*] Simple!—a very simple instruction. . . .

[*Goes out. Women's voices rise from the steady, indistinct murmur, like hissing geese.*]

WOMEN'S VOICES:—No, not liquor! Dope!

—Something not normal all right!

—Her father and brother were warned by the Vigilantes to keep her out of this county.

—She's absolutely degraded!

—Yes, corrupt!

—Corrupt! (Etc., etc.)

[*As if repelled by their hissing voices,* VAL *suddenly picks up his guitar and goes out of the store as—*VEE TALBOTT *appears on the landing and calls down to him.*]

VEE: Mr. Xavier! Where is Mr. Xavier?

BEULAH: Gone, honey.

DOLLY: You might as well face it, Vee. This is one candidate for salvation that you have lost to the opposition.

BEULAH: He's gone off to Cypress Hill with the Cutrere girl.

VEE [*descending*]:—If some of you older women in Two River County would set a better example there'd be more decent young people!

BEULAH: What was that remark?

VEE: I mean that people who give drinkin' parties an' get so drunk they don't know which is their husband and which is somebody else's and people who serve on the altar guild and still play cards on Sundays—

BEULAH: Just stop right there! Now I've discovered the source of that dirty gossip!

VEE: I'm only repeating what I've been told by others. I never been to these parties!

BEULAH: No, and you never will! You're a public kill-joy, a professional hypocrite!

VEE: I try to build up characters! You and your drinkin' parties are only concerned with tearin' characters down! I'm goin' upstairs, I'm goin' back upstairs! [*Rushes upstairs.*]

BEULAH: Well, I'm glad I said what I said to that woman. I've got no earthly patience with that sort of hypocriticism.

253

Dolly, let's put this perishable stuff in the Frigidaire and leave
here. I've never been so thoroughly disgusted!

DOLLY: Oh, my Lawd. [*Pauses at stairs and shouts:*] PEE
WEE! [*Goes off with the dishes.*]

SISTER: Both of those wimmen are as common as dirt.

EVA: Dolly's folks in Blue Mountain are nothin' at all but
the poorest kind of white trash. Why, Lollie Tucker told me
the old man sits on the porch with his shoes off drinkin' beer
out of a bucket!—Let's take these flowers with us to put on
the altar.

SISTER: Yes, we can give Jabe credit in the parish notes.

EVA: I'm going to take these olive-nut sandwiches, too.
They'll come in handy for the Bishop Adjutant's tea.

[DOLLY *and* BEULAH *cross through.*]

DOLLY: We still have time to make the second show.

BEULAH [*shouting*]: Dog!

DOLLY: Pee Wee! [*They rush out of store.*]

EVA: Sits on the porch with his shoes off?

SISTER: Drinkin' beer out of a bucket! [*They go out with
umbrellas, etc. Men descend stairs.*]

SHERIFF TALBOTT: Well, it looks to me like Jabe will more
than likely go under before the cotton comes up.

PEE WEE: He never looked good.

DOG: Naw, but now he looks worse.

[*They cross to door.*]

SHERIFF: Vee!

VEE [*from landing*]: Hush that bawling. I had to speak to
Lady about that boy and I couldn't speak to her in front of

254

Jabe because he thinks he's gonna be able to go back to work himself.

SHERIFF: Well, move along, quit foolin'.

VEE: I think I ought to wait till that boy gits back.

SHERIFF: I'm sick of you making a goddam fool of yourself over every stray bastard that wanders into this county.

[*Car horn honks loudly.* VEE *follows her husband out. Sound of cars driving off. Dogs bay in distance as lights dim to indicate short passage of time.*]

*A couple of hours later that night. Through the great window
the landscape is faintly luminous under a scudding moonlit
sky. Outside a girl's laughter,* CAROL'S, *rings out high and clear
and is followed by the sound of a motor, rapidly going off.*

VAL *enters the store before the car sound quite fades out
and while a dog is still barking at it somewhere along the
highway. He says "Christ" under his breath, goes to the buffet
table and scrubs lipstick stain off his mouth and face with a
paper napkin, picks up his guitar, which he had left on a
counter.*

Footsteps descending: LADY *appears on the landing in a
flannel robe, shivering in the cold air; she snaps her fingers
impatiently for the old dog, Bella, who comes limping down
beside her. She doesn't see* VAL, *seated on the shadowy counter,
and she goes directly to the phone near the stairs. Her manner
is desperate, her voice harsh and shrill.*

LADY: Ge' me the drugstore, will you? I know the drugstore's closed, this is Mrs. Torrance, my store's closed, too, but
I got a sick man here, just back from the hospital, yeah, yeah,
an emergency, wake up Mr. Dubinsky, keep ringing till he
answers, it's an emergency! [*Pause: she mutters under her
breath:*] —*Porca la miseria!*—I wish I was dead, dead,
dead. . . .

VAL [*quietly*]: No, you don't, lady.

[*She gasps, turning and seeing him, without leaving the
phone, she rings the cashbox open and snatches out something.*]

LADY: What're you doin' here? You know this store is
closed!

VAL: I seen a light was still on and the door was open so
I come back to—

LADY: You see what I got in my hand? [*Raises revolver above level of counter.*]

VAL: You going to shoot me?

LADY: You better believe it if you don't get out of here, mister!

VAL: That's all right, Lady, I just come back to pick up my guitar.

LADY: To pick up your guitar?

[*He lifts it gravely.*]

—Huh. . . .

VAL: Miss Talbott brought me here. I was here when you got back from Memphis, don't you remember?

LADY:—Aw. Aw, yeah. . . . You been here all this time?

VAL: No. I went out and come back.

LADY [*into the phone*]: I told you to keep ringing till he answers! Go on, keep ringing, keep ringing! [*Then to* VAL:] You went out and come back?

VAL: Yeah.

LADY: What for?

VAL: You know that girl that was here?

LADY: Carol Cutrere?

VAL: She said she had car trouble and could I fix it.

LADY:—Did you fix it?

VAL: She didn't have no car trouble, that wasn't her trouble, oh, she had trouble, all right, but *that* wasn't it. . . .

LADY: What was her trouble?

VAL: She made a mistake about me.

LADY: What mistake?

VAL: She thought I had a sign "Male at Stud" hung on me.

LADY: She thought you—? [*Into phone suddenly:*] Oh, Mr. Dubinsky, I'm sorry to wake you up but I just brought my husband back from the Memphis hospital and I left my box of Luminal tablets in the—I got to have some! I ain't slep' for three nights, I'm going to pieces, you hear me, I'm going to pieces, I ain't slept in three nights, I got to have some tonight. Now you look here, if you want to keep my trade, you send me over some tablets. Then bring them yourself, God damn it, excuse my French! Because I'm going to pieces right this minute! [*Hangs up violently.*]—*Mannage la miseria!*—Christ. . . . I'm shivering!—It's cold as a goddam ice plant in this store, I don't know why, it never seems to hold heat, the ceiling's too high or something, it don't hold heat at all.—Now what do you want? I got to go upstairs.

VAL: Here. Put this on you.

[*He removes his jacket and hands it to her. She doesn't take it at once, stares at him questioningly and then slowly takes the jacket in her hands and examines it, running her fingers curiously over the snakeskin.*]

LADY: What is this stuff this thing's made of? It looks like it was snakeskin.

VAL: Yeah, well, that's what it is.

LADY: What're you doing with a snakeskin jacket?

VAL: It's a sort of a trademark; people call me Snakeskin.

LADY: Who calls you Snakeskin?

VAL: Oh, in the bars, the sort of places I work in—but I've quit that. I'm through with that stuff now. . . .

LADY: You're a—entertainer?

VAL: I sing and play the guitar.

LADY:—Aw? [*She puts the jacket on as if to explore it.*] It feels warm all right.

VAL: It's warm from my body, I guess. . . .

LADY: You must be a warm-blooded boy. . . .

VAL: That's right. . . .

LADY: Well, what in God's name are you lookin' for around here?

VAL:—Work.

LADY: Boys like you don't work.

VAL: What d'you mean by boys like me?

LADY: Ones that play th' guitar and go around talkin' about how warm they are. . . .

VAL: That happens t' be the truth. My temperature's always a couple degrees above normal the same as a dog's, it's normal for me the same as it is for a dog, that's the truth. . . .

LADY:—Huh!

VAL: You don't believe me?

LADY: I have no reason to doubt you, but what about it?

VAL:—Why—nothing. . . .

[LADY *laughs softly and suddenly;* VAL *smiles slowly and warmly.*]

LADY: You're a peculiar somebody all right, you sure are! How did you get around here?

VAL: I was driving through here last night and an axle broke on my car, that stopped me here, and I went to the county jail for a place to sleep out of the rain. Mizz Talbott

259

took me in and give me a cot in the lockup and said if I hung around till you got back that you might give me a job in the store to help out since your husband was tooken sick.

LADY:—Uh-huh. Well—she was wrong about that. . . . If I took on help here it would have to be local help, I couldn't hire no stranger with a—snakeskin jacket and a guitar . . . and that runs a temperature as high as a dog's! [*Throws back her head in another soft, sudden laugh and starts to take off the jacket.*]

VAL: Keep it on.

LADY: No, I got to go up now and you had better be going . . .

VAL: I got nowhere to go.

LADY: Well, everyone's got a problem and that's yours.

VAL:—What nationality are you?

LADY: Why do you ask me that?

VAL: You seem to be like a foreigner.

LADY: I'm the daughter of a Wop bootlegger burned to death in his orchard!—Take your jacket. . . .

VAL: What was that you said about your father?

LADY: Why?

VAL:—A "Wop bootlegger"?

LADY:—They burned him to death in his orchard! What about it? The story's well known around here.

[JABE *knocks on ceiling.*]

I got to go up, I'm being called for.

[*She turns out light over counter and at the same moment he begins to sing softly with his guitar: "Heavenly Grass." He suddenly stops short and says abruptly:*]

VAL: I do electric repairs.

[LADY *stares at him softly.*]

I can do all kinds of odd jobs. Lady, I'm thirty today and I'm through with the life that I've been leading. [*Pause. Dog bays in distance.*] I lived in corruption but I'm not corrupted. Here is why. [*Picks up his guitar.*] My life's companion! It washes me clean like water when anything unclean has touched me. . . . [*Plays softly, with a slow smile.*]

LADY: What's all that writing on it?

VAL: Autographs of musicians I run into here and there.

LADY: Can I see it?

VAL: Turn on that light above you.

[*She switches on green-shaded bulb over counter.* VAL *holds the instrument tenderly between them as if it were a child; his voice is soft, intimate, tender.*]

See this name? Leadbelly?

LADY: Leadbelly?

VAL: Greatest man ever lived on the twelve-string guitar! Played it so good he broke the stone heart of a Texas governor with it and won himself a pardon out of jail. . . . And see this name Oliver? King Oliver? That name is immortal, Lady. Greatest man since Gabriel on a horn. . . .

LADY: What's this name?

VAL: Oh. That name? That name is also immortal. The name Bessie Smith is written in the stars!—Jim Crow killed her, John Barleycorn and Jim Crow killed Bessie Smith but that's another story. . . . See this name here? That's another immortal!

LADY: Fats Waller? Is his name written in the stars, too?

261

VAL: Yes, his name is written in the stars, too. . . .

[*Her voice is also intimate and soft: a spell of softness between them, their bodies almost touching, only divided by the guitar.*]

LADY: You had any sales experience?

VAL: All my life I been selling something to someone.

LADY: So's everybody. You got any character reference on you?

VAL: I have this—letter.

[*Removes a worn, folded letter from a wallet, dropping a lot of snapshots and cards of various kinds on the floor. He passes the letter to her gravely and crouches to collect the dropped articles while she peruses the character reference.*]

LADY [*reading slowly aloud*]: "This boy worked for me three months in my auto repair shop and is a real hard worker and is good and honest but is a peculiar talker and that is the reason I got to let him go but would like to—[*Holds letter closer to light.*]—would like to—keep him. Yours truly."

[VAL *stares at her gravely, blinking a little.*]

Huh!—Some reference!

VAL:—Is that what it says?

LADY: Didn't you know what it said?

VAL: No.—The man sealed the envelope on it.

LADY: Well, that's not the sort of character reference that will do you much good, boy.

VAL: Naw. I guess it ain't.

LADY:—However. . . .

VAL:—What?

LADY: What people say about you don't mean much. Can you read shoe sizes?

VAL: I guess so.

LADY: What does 75 David mean?

[VAL *stares at her, shakes head slowly.*]

75 means seven and one half long and David mean "D" wide. You know how to make change?

VAL: Yeah, I could make change in a store.

LADY: Change for better or worse? Ha ha!—Well— [*Pause.*] Well—you see that other room there, through that arch there? That's the confectionery; it's closed now but it's going to be reopened in a short while and I'm going to compete for the night life in this county, the after-the-movies trade. I'm going to serve setups in there and I'm going to redecorate. I got it all planned. [*She is talking eagerly now, as if to herself.*] Artificial branches of fruit trees in flower on the walls and ceilings!—It's going to be like an orchard in the spring!—My father, he had an orchard on Moon Lake. He made a wine garden of it. We had fifteen little white arbors with tables in them and they were covered with—grapevines and—we sold Dago red wine an' bootleg whiskey and beer. —They burned it up! My father was burned up in it. . . .

[JABE *knocks above more loudly and a hoarse voice shouts* "Lady!" *Figure appears at the door and calls:* "Mrs. Torrance?"]

Oh, that's the sandman with my sleeping tablets. [*Crosses to door.*] Thanks, Mr. Dubinsky, sorry I had to disturb you, sorry I—

[*Man mutters something and goes. She closes the door.*]

Well, go to hell, then, old bastard. . . . [*Returns with package.*]—You ever have trouble sleeping?

VAL: I can sleep or not sleep as long or short as I want to.

LADY: Is that right?

VAL: I can sleep on a concrete floor or go without sleeping, without even feeling sleepy, for forty-eight hours. And I can hold my breath three minutes without blacking out; I made ten dollars betting I could do it and I did it! And I can go a whole day without passing water.

LADY [*startled*]: Is *that* a *fact?*

VAL [*very simply as if he'd made an ordinary remark*]: That's a fact. I served time on a chain gang for vagrancy once and they tied me to a post all day and I stood there all day without passing water to show the sons of bitches that I could do it.

LADY:—I see what that auto repair man was talking about when he said this boy is a peculiar talker! Well—what else can you do? Tell me some more about your self-control!

VAL [*grinning*]: Well, they say that a woman can burn a man down. But I can burn down a woman.

LADY: Which woman?

VAL: Any two-footed woman.

LADY [*throws back her head in sudden friendly laughter as he grins at her with the simple candor of a child*]:—Well, there's lots of two-footed women round here that might be willin' to test the truth of that statement.

VAL: I'm saying I could. I'm not saying I would.

LADY: Don't worry, boy. I'm one two-footed woman that you don't have to convince of your perfect controls.

VAL: No, I'm done with all that.

LADY: What's the matter? Have they tired you out?

VAL: I'm not tired. I'm disgusted.

264

LADY: Aw, you're disgusted, huh?

VAL: I'm telling you, Lady, there's people bought and sold in this world like carcasses of hogs in butcher shops!

LADY: You ain't tellin' me nothin' I don't know.

VAL: You might think there's many and many kinds of people in this world but, Lady, there's just two kinds of people, the ones that are bought and the buyers! No!—there's one other kind . . .

LADY: What kind's that?

VAL: The kind that's never been branded.

LADY: You will be, man.

VAL: They got to catch me first.

LADY: Well, then, you better not settle down in this county.

VAL: You know they's a kind of bird that don't have legs so it can't light on nothing but has to stay all its life on its wings in the sky? That's true. I seen one once, it had died and fallen to earth and it was light-blue colored and its body was tiny as your little finger, that's the truth, it had a body as tiny as your little finger and so light on the palm of your hand it didn't weigh more than a feather, but its wings spread out this wide but they was transparent, the color of the sky and you could see through them. That's what they call protection coloring. Camouflage, they call it. You can't tell those birds from the sky and that's why the hawks don't catch them, don't see them up there in the high blue sky near the sun!

LADY: How about in gray weather?

VAL: They fly so high in gray weather the goddam hawks would get dizzy. But those little birds, they don't have no legs at all and they live their whole lives on the wing, and they sleep on the wind, that's how they sleep at night, they just

265

spread their wings and go to sleep on the wind like other birds fold their wings and go to sleep on a tree. . . . [*Music fades in.*]—They sleep on the wind and . . . [*His eyes grow soft and vague and he lifts his guitar and accompanies the very faint music.*]—never light on this earth but one time when they die!

LADY:—I'd like to be one of those birds.

VAL: So'd I like to be one of those birds; they's lots of people would like to be one of those birds and never be—corrupted!

LADY: If one of those birds ever dies and falls on the ground and you happen to find it, I wish you would show it to me because I think maybe you just imagine there is a bird of that kind in existence. Because I don't think nothing living has ever been that free, not even nearly. Show me one of them birds and I'll say, Yes, God's made one perfect creature!—I sure would give this mercantile store and every bit of stock in it to be that tiny bird the color of the sky . . . for one night to sleep on the wind and—float!—around under th'—stars . . .

[JABE *knocks on floor.* LADY'S *eyes return to* VAL.]

—Because I sleep with a son of a bitch who bought me at a fire sale, and not in fifteen years have I had a single good dream, not one—oh!—*Shit* . . . I don't know why I'm—telling a stranger—this. . . . [*She rings the cashbox open.*] Take this dollar and go eat at the Al-Nite on the highway and come back here in the morning and I'll put you to work. I'll break you in clerking here and when the new confectionery opens, well, maybe I can use you in there.—That door locks when you close it!—But let's get one thing straight.

VAL: What thing?

LADY: I'm not interested in your perfect functions, in fact you don't interest me no more than the air that you stand in.

266

If that's understood we'll have a good working relation, but otherwise trouble!—Of course I know you're crazy, but they's lots of crazier people than you are still running loose and some of them in high positions, too. Just remember. No monkey business with me. Now go. Go eat, you're hungry.

VAL: Mind if I leave this here? My life's companion? [*He means his guitar.*]

LADY: Leave it here if you want to.

VAL: Thanks, Lady.

LADY: Don't mention it.

[*He crosses toward the door as a dog barks with passionate clarity in the distance. He turns to smile back at her and says:*]

VAL: I don't know nothing about you except you're nice but you are just about the nicest person that I have ever run into! And I'm going to be steady and honest and hard-working to please you and any time you have any more trouble sleeping, I know how to fix that for you. A lady osteo-path taught me how to make little adjustments in the neck and spine that give you sound, natural sleep. Well, g'night, now.

[*He goes out. Count five. Then she throws back her head and laughs as lightly and gaily as a young girl. Then she turns and wonderingly picks up and runs her hands tenderly over his guitar as the curtain falls.*]

ACT TWO

*The store, afternoon, a few weeks later. The table and chair
are back in the confectionery.* LADY *is hanging up the phone.*
VAL *is standing just outside the door. He turns and enters.
Outside on the highway a mule team is laboring to pull a big
truck back on the icy pavement. A Negro's voice shouts:
"Hyyyyyyyyy-up."*

VAL [*moving to right window*]: One a them big Diamond
T trucks an' trailors gone off the highway last night and a
six-mule team is tryin' t' pull it back on. . . . [*He looks out
window.*]

LADY [*coming from behind to right of counter*]: Mister,
we just now gotten a big fat complaint about you from a
woman that says if she wasn't a widow her husband would
come in here and beat the tar out of you.

VAL [*taking a step toward her*]: Yeah?—Is this a small
pink-headed woman?

LADY: *Pin*-headed woman did you say?

VAL: Naw, I said, "Pink!"—A little pink-haired woman,
in a checkered coat with pearl buttons this big on it.

LADY: I talked to her on the phone. She didn't go into such
details about her appearance but she did say you got familiar.
I said, "How? by his talk or behavior?" And she said, "Both!"
—Now I was afraid of this when I warned you last week,
"No monkey business here, boy!"

VAL: This little pink-headed woman bought a valentine
from me and all I said is my *name* is Valentine to her. Few
minutes later a small colored boy come in and delivered the
valentine to me with something wrote on it an' I believe I
still got it. . . . [*Finds and shows it to* LADY *who goes to him.*

LADY *reads it, and tears it fiercely to pieces. He lights a cigarette.*]

LADY: Signed it with a lipstick kiss? You didn't show up for this date?

VAL: No, ma'am. That's why she complained. [*Throws match on floor.*]

LADY: Pick that match up off the floor.

VAL: Are you bucking for sergeant, or something?

[*He throws match out the door with elaborate care. Her eyes follow his back.* VAL *returns lazily toward her.*]

LADY: Did you walk around in front of her that way?

VAL [*at counter*]: What way?

LADY: Slew-foot, slew-foot!

[*He regards her closely with good-humored perplexity.*]

Did you stand in front of her like that? That close? In that, that—*position?*

VAL: What position?

LADY: Ev'rything you do is suggestive!

VAL: Suggestive of what?

LADY: Of what you said you was through with—somethin' —*Oh, shoot, you know what I mean.*—Why'd 'ya think I give you a plain, dark business suit to work in?

VAL [*sadly*]: Un-hun. . . . [*Sighs and removes his blue jacket.*]

LADY: Now what're you takin' that off for?

VAL: I'm giving the suit back to you. I'll change my pants in the closet. [*Gives her the jacket and crosses into alcove.*]

269

LADY: Hey! I'm sorry! You hear me? I didn't sleep well last night. Hey! I said I'm sorry! You hear me? [*She enters alcove and returns immediately with* VAL'S *guitar and crosses to downstage right. He follows.*]

VAL: Le' me have my guitar, Lady. You find too many faults with me and I tried to do good.

LADY: I told you I'm sorry. You want me to get down and lick the dust off your shoes?

VAL: Just give me back my guitar.

LADY: I ain't dissatisfied with you. I'm pleased with you, sincerely!

VAL: You sure don't show it.

LADY: My nerves are all shot to pieces. [*Extends hand to him.*] Shake.

VAL: You mean I ain't fired, so I don't have to quit?

[*They shake hands like two men. She hands him guitar— then silence falls between them.*]

LADY: You see, we don't know each other, we're, we're— just gettin'—acquainted.

VAL: That's right, like a couple of animals sniffin' around each other. . . .

[*The image embarrasses her. He crosses to counter, leans over and puts guitar behind it.*]

LADY: Well, not exactly like that, but—!

VAL: We don't know each other. How do people get to know each other? I used to think they did it by touch.

LADY: By what?

VAL: By touch, by touchin' each other.

LADY [*moving up and sitting on shoe-fitting chair which has been moved to right window*]: Oh, you mean by close —contact!

VAL: But later it seemed like that made them more strangers than ever, uhh, huh, more strangers than ever. . . .

LADY: Then how d'you think they get to know each other?

VAL [*sitting on counter*]: Well, in answer to your last question, I would say this: Nobody ever gets to know *no body!* We're all of us sentenced to solitary confinement inside our own skins, for life! You understand me, Lady?—I'm tellin' you it's the truth, we got to face it, we're under a life-long sentence to solitary confinement inside our own lonely skins for as long as we live on this earth!

LADY [*rising and crossing to him*]: Oh, no, I'm not a big optimist but I cannot agree with something as sad as that statement!

[*They are sweetly grave as two children; the store is some-what dusky. She sits in chair R. of counter.*]

VAL: *Listen!*—When I was a kid on Witches Bayou? After my folks all scattered away like loose chicken's feathers blown around by the wind?—I stayed there alone on the bayou, hunted and trapped out of season and hid from the law!— *Listen!*—All that time, all that lonely time, I felt I was— waiting for something!

LADY: What for?

VAL: What does anyone wait for? For something to happen, for anything to happen, to make things make more sense. . . . It's hard to remember what that feeling was like because I've lost it now, but I was waiting for something like if you ask a question you wait for someone to answer, but you ask the wrong question or you ask the wrong person and the answer don't come.

271

Does everything stop because you don't get the answer? No, it goes right on as if the answer was given, day comes after day and night comes after night, and you're still waiting for someone to answer the question and going right on as if the question was answered. And then—well—then. . . .

LADY: Then what?

VAL: You get the make-believe answer.

LADY: What answer is that?

VAL: Don't pretend you don't know because you do!

LADY:—Love?

VAL [*placing hand on her shoulder*]: That's the make-believe answer. It's fooled many a fool besides you an' me, that's the God's truth, Lady, and you had better believe it.

[LADY *looks reflectively at* VAL *and he goes on speaking and sits on stool below counter.*]

—I met a girl on the bayou when I was fourteen. I'd had a feeling that day that if I just kept poling the boat down the bayou a little bit further I would come bang into whatever it was I'd been so long expecting!

LADY: Was she the answer, this girl that you met on the bayou?

VAL: She made me think that she was.

LADY: How did she do that?

VAL: By coming out on the dogtrot of a cabin as naked as I was in that flat-bottom boat! She stood there a while with the daylight burning around her as bright as heaven as far as I could see. You seen the inside of a shell, how white that is, pearly white? Her naked skin was like that.—Oh, God, I remember a bird flown out of the moss and its wings made a shadow on her, and then it sung a single, high clear note, and as if she was waiting for that as a kind of a signal to catch me, she turned and smiled, and walked on back in the cabin. . . .

LADY: You followed?

VAL: Yes, I followed, I followed, like a bird's tail follows a bird, I followed!

I thought that she give me the answer to the question, I'd been waiting for, but afterwards I wasn't sure that was it, but from that time the question wasn't much plainer than the answer and—

LADY:—What?

VAL: At fifteen I left Witches Bayou. When the dog died I sold my boat and the gun. . . . I went to New Orleans in this snakeskin jacket. . . . It didn't take long for me to learn the score.

LADY: What did you learn?

VAL: I learned that I had something to sell besides snakeskins and other wild things' skins I caught on the bayou. I was corrupted! That's the answer. . . .

LADY: Naw, that ain't the answer!

VAL: Okay, *you* tell me the answer!

LADY: I don't know the answer, I just know corruption ain't the answer. I know that much. If I thought that was the answer I'd take Jabe's pistol or his morphine tablets and—

[*A woman bursts into store.*]

WOMAN: I got to use your pay-phone!

LADY: Go ahead. Help yourself.

[*Woman crosses to phone, deposits coin.* LADY *crosses to confectionery. To* VAL:]

Get me a coke from the cooler.

273

[VAL *crosses and goes out right. During the intense activity among the choral women,* LADY *and* VAL *seem bemused, as if they were thinking back over their talk before. For the past minute or two a car horn has been heard blowing repeatedly in the near distance.*]

WOMAN [*at phone*]: Cutrere place, get me the Cutrere place, will yuh? David Cutrere or his wife, whichever comes to the phone!

[BEULAH *rushes in from the street to right-center.*]

BEULAH: Lady, Lady, where's Lady! Carol Cutrere is—!

WOMAN: Quiet, please! I am callin' her brother about her!

[LADY *sits at table in confectionery.*]

[*At phone:*] Who's this I'm talking to? Good! I'm calling about your sister, Carol Cutrere. She is blowing her car horn at the Red Crown station, she is blowing and blowing her car horn at the Red Crown station because my husband give the station attendants instructions not to service her car, and she is blowing and blowing and blowing on her horn, drawing a big crowd there and, Mr. Cutrere, I thought that you and your father had agreed to keep that girl out of Two River County for good, that's what we all understood around here.

[*Car horn.*]

BEULAH [*Listening with excited approval*]: Good! Good! Tell him that if—

[DOLLY *enters.*]

DOLLY: She's gotten out of the car and—

BEULAH: *Shhh!*

WOMAN: Well, I just wanted to let you know she's back here in town makin' another disturbance and my husband's on the phone now at the Red Crown station—

[DOLLY *goes outside and looks off.*]
ιrying to get the Sheriff, so if she gits picked up again by th'
law, you can't say I didn't warn you, Mr. Cutrere.

[*Car horn.*]

DOLLY [*coming back in*]: Oh, good! Good!

BEULAH: Where is she, where's she gone now?

WOMAN: You better be quick about it. Yes, I do. I sym-
pathize with you and your father and with Mrs. Cutrere, but
Carol cannot demand service at our station, we just refuse to
wait on her, she's not—Hello? Hello? [*She jiggles phone
violently.*]

BEULAH: What's he doin'? Comin' to pick her up?

DOLLY: Call the Sheriff's office!

[BEULAH *goes outside again.* VAL *comes back with a bottle
of Coca-Cola—hands it to* LADY *and leans on juke box.*]

[*Going out to* BEULAH] What's goin' on now?

BEULAH [*outside*]: Look, look, they're pushing her out of
the station driveway.

[*They forget* LADY *in this new excitement. Ad libs con-
tinual. The short woman from the station charges back out
of the store.*]

DOLLY: Where is Carol?

BEULAH: Going into the White Star Pharmacy!

[DOLLY *rushes back in to the phone.*]

BEULAH [*crossing to* LADY]: Lady, I want you to give me
your word that if that Cutrere girl comes in here, you won't
wait on her! You hear me?

LADY: No.

BEULAH:—What? Will you refuse to wait on her?

275

LADY: I can't refuse to wait on anyone in this store.

BEULAH: Well, I'd like to know why you can't.

DOLLY: Shhh! I'm on the phone!

BEULAH: Who you phonin' Dolly?

DOLLY: That White Star Pharmacy! I want to make sure that Mr. Dubinsky refuses to wait on that girl! [*Having found and deposited coin*] I want the White Far Starmacy. I mean the—[*Stamps foot.*]—White Star Pharmacy!—I'm so upset my tongue's twisted!

[LADY *hands coke to* VAL. BEULAH *is at the window.*]

I'm getting a busy signal. Has she come out yet?

BEULAH: No, she's still in the White Star!

DOLLY: Maybe they're not waiting on her.

BEULAH: Dubinsky'd wait on a purple-bottom baboon if it put a dime on th' counter an' pointed at something!

DOLLY: I know she sat at a table in the Blue Bird Café half'n hour last time she was here and the waitresses never came near her!

BEULAH: That's different. They're not foreigners there!

[DOLLY *crosses to counter.*]

You can't ostracize a person out of this county unless everybody cooperates. Lady just told me that she was going to wait on her if she comes here.

DOLLY: Lady wouldn't do that.

BEULAH: *Ask* her! She told *me* she would!

LADY [*rising and turning at once to the women and shouting at them*]: Oh, for God's sake, no! I'm not going to refuse to wait on her because you all don't like her! Besides I'm

delighted that wild girl is givin' her brother so much trouble!
[*After this outburst she goes back of the counter.*]

DOLLY [*at phone*]: Hush! Mr. Dubinsky! This is Dolly
Hamma, Mr. "Dog" Hamma's wife!

[CAROL *quietly enters the front door.*]

I want to ask you, is Carol Cutrere in your drugstore?

BEULAH [*warningly*]: Dolly!

CAROL: No. She isn't.

DOLLY:—What?

CAROL: She's here.

[BEULAH *goes   into confectionery.* CAROL *moves toward*
VAL *to downstage right.*]

DOLLY:—Aw!—Never mind, Mr. Dubinsky, I—[*Hangs
up furiously and crosses to door.*]

[*A silence in which they all stare at the girl from various
positions about the store. She has been on the road all night
in an open car: her hair is blown wild, her face flushed and
eyes bright with fever. Her manner in the scene is that of
a wild animal at bay, desperate but fearless.*]

LADY [*finally and quietly*]: Hello, Carol.

CAROL: Hello, Lady.

LADY [*defiantly cordial*]: I thought that you were in New
Orleans, Carol.

CAROL: Yes, I was. Last night.

LADY: Well, you got back fast.

CAROL: I drove all night.

LADY: In that storm?

CAROL: The wind took the top off my car but I didn't stop.

277

[*She watches* VAL *steadily; he steadily ignores her; turns away and puts bottles of Coca-Cola on a table.*]

LADY [*with growing impatience*]: Is something wrong at home, is someone sick?

CAROL [*absently*]: No. No, not that I know of, I wouldn't know if there was, they—may I sit down?

LADY: Why, sure.

CAROL [*crossing to chair at counter and sitting*]:—They pay me to stay away so I wouldn't know. . . .

[*Silence.* VAL *walks deliberately past her and goes into alcove.*]

—I think I have a fever, I feel like I'm catching pneumonia, everything's so far away. . . .

[*Silence again except for the faint, hissing whispers of* BEULAH *and* DOLLY *at the back of the store.*]

LADY [*with a touch of exasperation*]: Is there something you want?

CAROL: Everything seems miles away. . . .

LADY: Carol, I said is there anything you want here?

CAROL: Excuse me!—yes. . . .

LADY: Yes, what?

CAROL: Don't bother now. I'll wait.

[VAL *comes out of alcove with the blue jacket on.*]

LADY: Wait for what, what are you waiting for! You don't have to wait for nothing, just say what you want and if I got it in stock I'll give it to you!

[*Phone rings once.*]

CAROL [*vaguely*]:—Thank you—no. . . .

LADY [*to* VAL]: Get that phone, Val.

[DOLLY *crosses and hisses something inaudible to* BEULAH.]

BEULAH [*rising*]: I just want to wait here to see if she does or she don't.

DOLLY: She just said she would!

BEULAH: Just the same, I'm gonna wait!!

VAL [*at phone*]: Yes, sir, she is.—I'll tell her. [*Hangs up and speaks to* LADY:] Her brother's heard she's here and he's coming to pick her up.

LADY: *David Cutrere is not coming in this store!*

DOLLY: Aw-aw!

BEULAH: David Cutrere used to be her lover.

DOLLY: I remember you told me.

LADY [*wheels about suddenly toward the women*]: Beulah! Dolly! Why're you back there hissing together like geese? [*Coming from behind counter to right-center.*] Why don't you go to th'—Blue Bird and—have some hot coffee—talk there!

BEULAH: It looks like we're getting what they call the bum's rush.

DOLLY: I never stay where I'm not wanted and when I'm not wanted somewhere I never come back!

[*They cross out and slam door.*]

LADY [*after a pause*]: What did you come here for?

CAROL: To deliver a message.

LADY: To me?

CAROL: No.

LADY: Then who?

279

[CAROL *stares at* LADY *gravely a moment, then turns slowly to look at* VAL.]

—Him?—Him?

[CAROL *nods slowly and slightly.*]

OK, then, give him the message, deliver the message to him.

CAROL: It's a private message. Could I speak to him alone, please?

[LADY *gets a shawl from a hook.*]

LADY: Oh, for God's sake! Your brother's plantation is ten minutes from here in that sky-blue Cadillac his rich wife give him. Now look, he's on his way here but I won't let him come in, I don't even want his hand to touch the door-handle. I know your message, this boy knows your message, there's nothing private about it. But I tell you, that this boy's not for sale in my store!—Now—I'm going out to watch for the sky-blue Cadillac on the highway. When I see it, I'm going to throw this door open and holler and when I holler, I want you out of this door like a shot from a pistol!—that fast! Understand?

[NOTE: *Above scene is overextended. This can be remedied by a very lively performance. It might also help to indicate a division between the Lady-Val scene and the group scene that follows.*]

[LADY *slams door behind her. The loud noise of the door-slam increases the silence that follows.* VAL'S *oblivious attitude is not exactly hostile, but deliberate. There's a kind of purity in it; also a kind of refusal to concern himself with a problem that isn't his own. He holds his guitar with a specially tender concentration, and strikes a soft chord on it. The girl stares at* VAL; *he whistles a note and tightens a guitar string to the pitch of the whistle, not looking at*

*the girl. Since this scene is followed by the emotional scene
between* LADY *and* DAVID, *it should be keyed somewhat
lower than written; it's important that* VAL *should not seem
brutal in his attitude toward* CAROL; *there should be an air
between them of two lonely children.*]

VAL [*in a soft, preoccupied tone*]: You told the lady I work
for that you had a message for me. Is that right, miss? Have
you got a message for me?

CAROL [*she rises, moves a few steps toward him, hesitantly.*
VAL *whistles, plucks guitar string, changes pitch*]: You've
spilt some ashes on your new blue suit.

VAL: Is that the message?

CAROL [*moves away a step*]: No. No, that was just an
excuse to touch you. The message is—

VAL: What?

[*Music fades in—guitar.*]

CAROL:—I'd love to hold something the way you hold your
guitar, that's how I'd love to hold something, with such—
tender protection! I'd love to hold *you* that way, with that
same—*tender protection!* [*Her hand has fallen onto his knee,
which he has drawn up to rest a foot on the counter stool.*]—
Because you hang the moon for me!

VAL [*he speaks to her, not roughly but in a tone that holds
a long history that began with a romantic acceptance of such
declarations as she has just made to him, and that turned
gradually to his present distrust. He puts guitar down and
goes to her*]: Who're you tryin' t' fool beside you'self? You
couldn't stand the weight of a man's body on you. [*He
casually picks up her wrist and pushes the sleeve back from
it.*] What's this here? A human wrist with a bone? It feels
like a twig I could snap with two fingers. . . . [*Gently, negli-*

281

gently, pushes collar of her trench coat back from her bare throat and shoulders. Runs a finger along her neck tracing a vein.] Little girl, you're transparent, I can see the veins in you. A man's weight on you would break you like a bundle of sticks. . . .

[*Music fades out.*]

CAROL [*gazes at him, startled by his perception*]: Isn't it funny! You've hit on the truth about me. The act of love-making is almost unbearably painful, and yet, of course, I do bear it, because to be not alone, even for a few moments, is worth the pain and the danger. It's dangerous for me because I'm not built for childbearing.

VAL: Well, then, fly away, little bird, fly away before you— get broke. [*He turns back to his guitar.*]

CAROL: Why do you dislike me?

VAL [*turning back*]: I never dislike nobody till they inter- fere with me.

CAROL: How have I interfered with you? Did I snitch when I saw my cousin's watch on you?

VAL [*Beginning to remove his watch*]:—You won't take my word for a true thing I told you. I'm thirty years old and I'm done with the crowd you run with and the places you run to. The Club Rendezvous, the Starlite Lounge, the Music Bar, and all the night places. Here—[*Offers watch.*]— take this Rolex Chronometer that tells the time of the day and the day of the week and the month and all the crazy moon's phases. I never stole nothing before. When I stole that I known it was time for me to get off the party, so take it back, now, to Bertie. . . . [*He takes her hand and tries to force the watch into her fist. There is a little struggle, he can't open her fist. She is crying, but staring fiercely into his eyes.*

He draws a hissing breath and hurls watch violently across the floor.]

—That's my message to you and the pack you run with!

CAROL [*flinging coat away*]: *I RUN WITH NOBODY!*

—I hoped I could run with you. . . . [*Music stops short.*] You're in danger here, Snakeskin. You've taken off the jacket that said: "I'm wild, I'm alone!" and put on the nice blue uniform of a convict! . . . Last night I woke up thinking about you again. I drove all night to bring you this warning of danger. . . . [*Her trembling hand covers her lips.*]—The message I came here to give you was a warning of danger! I hoped you'd hear me and let me take you away before it's —too late.

[*Door bursts open.* LADY *rushes inside, crying out:*]

LADY: *Your brother's coming, go out! He can't come in!*

[CAROL *picks up coat and goes into confectionery, sobbing.* VAL *crosses toward door.*]

Lock that door! Don't let him come in my store!

[CAROL *sinks sobbing at table.* LADY *runs up to the landing of the stairs as* DAVID CUTRERE *enters the store. He is a tall man in hunter's clothes. He is hardly less handsome now than he was in his youth but something has gone: his power is that of a captive who rules over other captives. His face, his eyes, have something of the same desperate, unnatural hardness that* LADY *meets the world with.*]

DAVID: Carol?

VAL: She's in there. [*He nods toward the dim confectionery into which the girl has retreated.*]

DAVID [*crossing*]: Carol!

[*She rises and advances a few steps into the lighted area of the stage.*]

283

You broke the agreement.

[CAROL *nods slightly, staring at* VAL.]

[*Harshly:*] All right. I'll drive you back. Where's your coat?

[CAROL *murmurs something inaudible, staring at* VAL.]

Where is her coat, where is my sister's coat?

[VAL *crosses below and picks up the coat that* CAROL *has dropped on the floor and hands it to* DAVID. *He throws it roughly about* CAROL'S *shoulders and propels her forcefully toward store entrance.* VAL *moves away to downstage right.*]

LADY [*suddenly and sharply*]: *Wait, please!*

[DAVID *looks up at the landing; stands frozen as* LADY *rushes down the stairs.*]

DAVID [*softly, hoarsely*]: How—*are* you, Lady?

LADY [*turning to* VAL]: Val, go out.

DAVID [*to* CAROL]: Carol, will you wait for me in my car?

[*He opens the door for his sister; she glances back at* VAL *with desolation in her eyes.* VAL *crosses quickly through the confectionery. Sound of door closing in there.* CAROL *nods slightly as if in sad response to some painful question and goes out of the store. Pause.*]

LADY: I told you once to never come in this store.

DAVID: I came for my sister. . . . [*He turns as if to go.*]

LADY: No, wait!

DAVID: I don't dare leave my sister alone on the road.

LADY: I have something to tell you I never told you before. [*She crosses to him.* DAVID *turns back to her, then moves away to downstage right-center.*]

—I—carried your child in my body the summer you quit me.

[*Silence.*]

DAVID:—I—didn't know.

LADY: No, no, I didn't write you no letter about it; I was proud then; I had pride. But I had your child in my body the summer you quit me, that summer they burned my father in his wine garden, and you, you washed your hands clean of any connection with a Dago bootlegger's daughter and—[*Her breathless voice momentarily falters and she makes a fierce gesture as she struggles to speak.*]—took that—society girl that—restored your homeplace and give you such—[*Catches breath.*]—well-born children. . . .

DAVID:—I—didn't know.

LADY: Well, now you do know, you know now. I carried your child in my body the summer you quit me but I had it cut out of my body, and they cut my heart out with it!

DAVID:—I—didn't know.

LADY: I wanted death after that, but death don't come when you *want* it, it comes when you don't want it! I wanted death, then, but I took the next best thing. *You* sold *yourself*. *I* sold *my* self. *You* was bought. *I* was bought. You made whores of us both!

DAVID:—I—didn't know. . . .

[*Mandolin, barely audible,* "Dicitencello Vuoi."]

LADY: But that's all a long time ago. Some reason I drove by there a few nights ago; the shore of the lake where my father had his wine garden? You remember? You remember the wine garden of my father?

[DAVID *stares at her. She turns away.*]

No, you don't? You don't remember it even?

285

DAVID:—Lady, I don't—remember—anything else. . . .

LADY: The mandolin of my father, the songs that I sang with my father in my father's wine garden?

DAVID: Yes, I don't remember anything else. . . .

LADY: *Core Ingrata! Come Le Rose!* And we disappeared and he would call, *"Lady? Lady?"* [*Turns to him.*] *How could I answer him with two tongues in my mouth!* [*A sharp hissing intake of breath, eyes opened wide, hand clapped over her mouth as if what she said was unendurable to her. He turns instantly, sharply away.*]

[*Music stops short.* JABE *begins to knock for her on the floor above. She crosses to stairs, stops, turns.*]

I hold hard feelings!—Don't ever come here again. If your wild sister comes here, send somebody else for her, not you, not you. Because I hope never to feel this knife again in me. [*Her hand is on her chest; she breathes with difficulty.*]

[*He turns away from her; starts toward the door. She takes a step toward him.*]

And don't pity me neither. I haven't gone down so terribly far in the world. I got a going concern in this mercantile store, in there's the confectionery which'll reopen this spring, it's being done over to make it the place that all the young people will come to, it's going to be like—

[*He touches the door, pauses with his back to her.*]

—the wine garden of my father, those wine-drinking nights when you had something better than anything you've had since!

DAVID: Lady—*That's*—

LADY:—*What?*

DAVID:—*True!* [*Opens door.*]

LADY: Go now. I just wanted to tell you my life ain't over.

[*He goes out as* JABE *continues knocking. She stands, stunned, motionless till* VAL *quietly re-enters the store. She becomes aware of his return rather slowly; then she murmurs:*]

I made a fool of myself. . . .

VAL: What?

[*She crosses to stairs.*]

LADY: *I made a fool of myself!*

[*She goes up the stairs with effort as the lights change slowly to mark a division of scenes.*]

SCENE TWO

Sunset of that day. VAL *is alone in the store, as if preparing to go. The sunset is fiery. A large woman opens the door and stands there looking dazed. It is* VEE TALBOTT.

VAL [*turning*]: Hello, Mrs. Talbott.

VEE: Something's gone wrong with my eyes. I can't see nothing.

VAL [*going to her*]: Here, let me help you. You probably drove up here with that setting sun in your face. [*Leading her to shoe-fitting chair at right window.*] There now. Set down right here.

VEE: Thank you—so—much. . . .

VAL: I haven't seen you since that night you brought me here to ask for this job.

VEE: Has the minister called on you yet? Reverend Tooker? I made him promise he would. I told him you were new around here and weren't affiliated to any church yet. I want you to go to ours.

VAL:—That's—mighty kind of you.

VEE: The Church of the Resurrection, it's Episcopal.

VAL: Uh, huh.

VEE: Unwrap that picture, please.

VAL: Sure. [*He tears paper off canvas.*]

VEE: It's the Church of the Resurrection. I give it a sort of imaginative treatment. You know, Jabe and Lady have never darkened a church door. I thought it ought to be hung where Jabe could look at it, it might help to bring that poor dying man to Jesus. . . .

288

[VAL *places it against chair right of counter and crouches before the canvas, studying it long and seriously.* VEE *coughs nervously, gets up, bends to look at the canvas, sits uncertainly back down.* VAL *smiles at her warmly, then back to the canvas.*]

VAL [*at last*]: What's this here in the picture?

VEE: The steeple.

VAL: Aw.—Is the church steeple red?

VEE: Why—no, but—

VAL: Why'd you paint it red, then?

VEE: Oh, well, you see, I—[*Laughs nervously, childlike in her growing excitement.*]—I just, just *felt* it that way! I paint a thing how I feel it instead of always the way it actually is. Appearances are misleading, nothing is what it looks like to the eyes. You got to have—*vision*—to see!

VAL:—Yes. Vision. Vision!—to see. . . . [*Rises, nodding gravely, emphatically.*]

VEE: I paint from vision. They call me a visionary.

VAL: Oh.

VEE [*with shy pride*]: That's what the New Orleans and Memphis newspaper people admire so much in my work. They call it a primitive style, the work of a visionary. One of my pictures is hung on the exhibition in Audubon Park museum and they have asked for others. I can't turn them out fast enough!—I have to wait for—visions, no, I—I can't paint without—visions . . . I couldn't *live* without visions!

VAL: Have you always had visions?

VEE: No, just since I was born, I—[*Stops short, startled by the absurdity of her answer. Both laugh suddenly, then she rushes on, her great bosom heaving with curious excitement,*

289

twisting in her chair, gesturing with clenched hands.] I was born, I was born with a caul! A sort of thing like a veil, a thin, thin sort of a web was over my eyes. They call that a caul. It's a sign that you're going to have visions, and I did, I had them! [*Pauses for breath; light fades.*]—When I was little my baby sister died. Just one day old, she died. They had to baptize her at midnight to save her soul.

VAL: Uh-huh. [*He sits opposite her, smiling, attentive.*]

VEE: The minister came at midnight, and after the baptism service, he handed the bowl of holy water to me and told me, "Be sure to empty this out on the ground!"—I didn't. I was scared to go out at midnight, with, with—death! in the— house and—I sneaked into the kitchen; I emptied the holy water into the kitchen sink—thunder struck!—the kitchen sink turned black, the kitchen sink turned absolutely black!

[SHERIFF TALBOTT *enters the front door.*]

TALBOTT: Mama! What're you doin'?

VEE: Talkin'.

TALBOTT: I'm gonna see Jabe a minute, you go out and wait in th' car. [*He goes up. She rises slowly, picks up canvas and moves to counter.*]

VEE:—Oh, I—tell you!—since I got into this painting, my whole outlook is different. I can't explain how it is, the difference to me.

VAL: You don't have to explain. I know what you mean. Before you started to paint, it didn't make sense.

VEE:—What—what didn't?

VAL: Existence!

VEE [*slowly and softly*]: No—no, it didn't . . . existence didn't make sense. . . . [*She places canvas on guitar on counter and sits in chair.*]

VAL [*rising and crossing to her*]: You lived in Two River County, the wife of the county sheriff. You saw awful things take place.

VEE: Awful! Things!

VAL: Beatings!

VEE: Yes!

VAL: Lynchings!

VEE: Yes!

VAL: Runaway convicts torn to pieces by hounds!

[*This is the first time she could express this horror.*]

VEE: *Chain-gang dogs!*

VAL: Yeah?

VEE: Tear fugitives!

VAL: Yeah?

VEE:—to *pieces.* . . .

[*She had half risen: now sinks back faintly.* VAL *looks beyond her in the dim store, his light eyes have a dark gaze. It may be that his speech is too articulate: counteract this effect by groping, hesitations.*]

VAL [*moving away a step*]: But violence ain't quick always. Sometimes it's slow. Some tornadoes are slow. Corruption—rots men's hearts and—rot is slow. . . .

VEE:—How do you—?

VAL: Know? I been a witness, I know!

VEE: *I* been a witness! *I* know!

VAL: We seen these things from seats down front at the show. [*He crouches before her and touches her hands in her lap. Her breath shudders.*] And so you begun to paint your

291

visions. Without no plan, no training, you started to paint as if God touched your fingers. [*He lifts her hands slowly, gently from her soft lap.*] You made some beauty out of this dark country with these two, soft, woman hands. . . .

[TALBOTT *appears on the stair landing, looks down, silent.*] Yeah, you made some beauty! [*Strangely, gently, he lifts her hands to his mouth. She gasps.* TALBOTT *calls out:*]

TALBOTT: *Hey!*

[VEE *springs up, gasping.*]

[*Descending*] *Cut this crap!*

[VAL *moves away to right-center.*]

[*To* VEE:] Go out. Wait in the car. [*He stares at* VAL *till* VEE *lumbers out as if dazed. After a while:*]

Jabe Torrance told me to take a good look at you. [*Crosses to* VAL.] Well, now, I've taken that look. [*Nods shortly. Goes out of store. The store is now very dim. As door closes on* TALBOTT, VAL *picks up painting; he goes behind counter and places it on a shelf, then picks up his guitar and sits on counter. Lights go down to mark a division as he sings and plays "Heavenly Grass."*]

As VAL *finishes the song,* LADY *descends the stair. He rises and turns on a green-shaded light bulb.*

VAL [*to* LADY]: You been up there a long time.

LADY:—I gave him morphine. He must be out of his mind. He says such awful things to me. He says I want him to die.

VAL: You sure you don't?

LADY: I don't want no one to die. Death's terrible, Val. [*Pause. She wanders to right front window. He takes his guitar and crosses to the door.*] You gotta go now?

VAL: I'm late.

LADY: Late for what? You got a date with somebody?

VAL:—No. . . .

LADY: Then stay a while. Play something. I'm all unstrung. . . .

[*He crosses back and leans against counter; the guitar is barely audible, under the speeches.*]

I made a terrible fool of myself down here today with—

VAL:—That girl's brother?

LADY: Yes, I—threw away——pride. . . .

VAL: His sister said she'd come here to give me a warning. I wonder what of?

LADY [*sitting in shoe-fitting chair*]:—I said things to him I should of been too proud to say. . . .

[*Both are pursuing their own reflections; guitar continues softly.*]

VAL: Once or twice lately I've woke up with a fast heart, shouting something, and had to pick up my guitar to calm myself down. . . . Somehow or other I can't get used to this place, I don't feel safe in this place, but I—want to stay. . . .

[*Stops short; sound of wild baying.*]

LADY: The chain-gang dogs are chasing some runaway convict. . . .

VAL: *Run boy! Run fast, brother! If they catch you, you never will run again! That's*—[*He has thrust his guitar under his arm on this line and crossed to the door.*]—for sure. . . . [*The baying of the dogs changes, becomes almost a single savage note.*]—Uh-huh—the dogs've got him. . . . [*Pause.*] They're tearing him to pieces! [*Pause. Baying continues. A shot is fired. The baying dies out. He stops with his hand on the door; glances back at her; nods; draws the door open. The wind sings loud in the dusk.*]

LADY: *Wait!*

VAL:—Huh?

LADY:—Where do you stay?

VAL:—When?

LADY: Nights.

VAL: I stay at the Wildwood cabins on the highway.

LADY: You like it there?

VAL: Uh-huh.

LADY:—Why?

VAL: I got a comfortable bed, a two-burner stove, a shower and icebox there.

LADY: You want to save money?

VAL: I never could in my life.

LADY: You could if you stayed on the place.

VAL: What place?

LADY: This place.

VAL: Whereabouts on this place?

LADY [*pointing to alcove*]: Back of that curtain.

VAL:—Where they try on clothes?

LADY: There's a cot there. A nurse slept on it when Jabe had his first operation, and there's a washroom down here and I'll get a plumber to put in a hot an' cold shower! I'll—fix it up nice for you. . . . [*She rises, crosses to foot of stairs. Pause. He lets the door shut, staring at her.*]

VAL [*moving downstage center*]:—I—don't like to be—obligated.

LADY: There wouldn't be no obligation, you'd do me a favor. I'd feel safer at night with somebody on the place. I would; it would cost you nothing! And you could save up that money you spend on the cabin. How much? Ten a week? Why, two or three months from now you'd—save enough money to—[*Makes a wide gesture with a short laugh as if startled.*] Go on! Take a look at it! See if it don't suit you! —All right. . . .

[*But he doesn't move; he appears reflective.*]

LADY [*shivering, hugging herself*]: Where does heat go in this building?

VAL [*reflectively*]:—Heat rises. . . .

LADY: You with your dog's temperature, don't feel cold, do you? I do! I turn blue with it!

VAL:—Yeah. . . .

[*The wait is unendurable to* LADY.]

LADY: *Well, aren't you going to look at it, the room back there, and see if it suits you or not?!*

295

VAL:—I'll go and take a look at it. . . .

[*He crosses to the alcove and disappears behind the curtain.
A light goes on behind it, making its bizarre pattern translucent: a gold tree with scarlet fruit and white birds in it,
formally designed. Truck roars; lights sweep the frosted
window.* LADY *gasps aloud; takes out a pint bottle and a
glass from under the counter, setting them down with a
crash that makes her utter a startled exclamation: then a
startled laugh. She pours a drink and sits in chair right
of counter. The lights turn off behind alcove curtain and*
VAL *comes back out. She sits stiffly without looking at him
as he crosses back lazily, goes behind counter, puts guitar
down. His manner is gently sad as if he had met with a
familiar, expected disappointment. He sits down quietly on
edge of counter and takes the pint bottle and pours himself
a shot of the liquor with a reflective sigh. Boards creak
loudly, contracting with the cold.* LADY'S *voice is harsh and
sudden, demanding:*]

LADY: *Well, is it okay or—what!*

VAL: I never been in a position where I could turn down
something I got for nothing in my life. I like that picture in
there. That's a famous picture, that "September Morn" picture
you got on the wall in there. Ha ha! I might have trouble
sleeping in a room with that picture. I might keep turning
the light on to take another look at it! The way she's cold
in that water and sort of crouched over in it, holding her body
like that, that—might—ha ha!—sort of keep me awake. . . .

LADY: Aw, you with your dog's temperature and your
control of all functions, it would take more than a picture to
keep you awake!

VAL: I was just kidding.

LADY: I was just kidding too.

VAL: But you know how a single man is. He don't come home every night with just his shadow.

[*Pause. She takes a drink.*]

LADY: You bring girls home nights to the Wildwood cabins, do you?

VAL: I ain't so far. But I would like to feel free to. That old life is what I'm used to. I always worked nights in cities and if you work nights in cities you live in a different city from those that work days.

LADY: Yes. I know, I—imagine. . . .

VAL: The ones that work days in cities and the ones that work nights in cities, they live in different cities. The cities have the same name but they are different cities. As different as night and day. There's something wild in the country that only the night people know. . . .

LADY: Yeah, I know!

VAL: I'm thirty years old!—but sudden changes don't work, it takes—

LADY:—Time—yes. . . .

[*Slight pause which she finds disconcerting. He slides off counter and moves around below it.*]

VAL: You been good to me, Lady.—Why d'you want me to stay here?

LADY [*defensively*]: I told you why.

VAL: For company nights?

LADY: Yeah, to, to!—*guard the store,* nights!

VAL: To be a night watchman?

LADY: Yeah, to be a night *watchman.*

VAL: You feel nervous alone here?

LADY: Naturally now!—Jabe sleeps with a pistol next to him but if somebody broke in the store, he couldn't git up and all I could do is holler!—Who'd *hear* me? They got a telephone girl on the night shift with—sleepin' sickness, I think! Anyhow, why're you so suspicious? You look at me like you thought I was *plottin'*.—Kind people *exist:* Even me! [*She sits up rigid in chair, lips and eyes tight closed, drawing in a loud breath which comes from a tension both personal and vicarious.*]

VAL: I understand, Lady, but. . . . Why're you sitting up so stiff in that chair?

LADY: Ha! [*Sharp laugh; she leans back in chair.*]

VAL: You're still unrelaxed.

LADY: I know.

VAL: Relax. [*Moving around close to her.*] I'm going to show you some tricks I learned from a lady osteopath that took me in, too.

LADY: What tricks?

VAL: How to manipulate joints and bones in a way that makes you feel like a loose piece of string. [*Moves behind her chair. She watches him.*] Do you trust me or don't you?

LADY: Yeah, I trust you completely, but—

VAL: Well then, lean forward a little and raise your arms up and turn sideways in the chair.

[*She follows these instructions.*]

Drop your head. [*He manipulates her head and neck.*] Now the spine, Lady. [*He places his knee against the small of her backbone and she utters a sharp, startled laugh as he draws her backbone hard against his kneecap.*]

LADY: Ha, ha!—That makes a sound like, like, like!—boards contracting with cold in the building, ha, ha!

298

[*He relaxes.*]

VAL: Better?

LADY: Oh, yes!—much . . . thanks. . . .

VAL [*stroking her neck*]: Your skin is like silk. You're light skinned to be Italian.

LADY: Most people in this country think Italian people are dark. Some are but not all are! Some of them are fair . . very fair. . . . My father's people were dark but my mother's people were fair. Ha ha!

[*The laughter is senseless. He smiles understandingly at her as she chatters to cover confusion. He turns away, then goes above and sits on counter close to her.*]

My mother's mother's sister—come here from Monte Cassino, to die, with relations!—but I think people always die alone . . . with or without relations. I was a little girl then and I remember it took her such a long, long time to die we almost forgot her.—And she was so quiet . . . in a corner. . . . And I remember asking her one time, Zia Teresa, how does it feel to die?—Only a little girl would ask such a question, ha ha! Oh, and I remember her answer. She said— "It's a lonely feeling."

I think she wished she had stayed in Italy and died in a place that she knew. . . . [*Looks at him directly for the first time since mentioning the alcove.*] Well, there is a washroom, and I'll get the plumber to put in a hot and cold shower! Well—[*Rises, retreats awkwardly from the chair. His interest seems to have wandered from her.*] I'll go up and get some clean linen and make up that bed in there.

[*She turns and walks rapidly, almost running, to stairs. He appears lost in some private reflection but as soon as she has disappeared above the landing, he says something under*

*his breath and crosses directly to the cashbox. He coughs
loudly to cover the sound of ringing it open; scoops out
a fistful of bills and coughs again to cover the sound of
slamming drawer shut. Picks up his guitar and goes out
the front door of store.* LADY *returns downstairs, laden with
linen. The outer darkness moans through the door left open.
She crosses to the door and a little outside it, peering both
ways down the dark road. Then she comes in furiously,
with an Italian curse, shutting the door with her foot or
shoulder, and throws the linen down on counter. She
crosses abruptly to cashbox, rings it open and discovers
theft. Slams drawer violently shut.*]

Thief! Thief!

[*Turns to phone, lifts receiver. Holds it a moment, then
slams it back into place. Wanders desolately back to the
door, opens it and stands staring out into the starless night
as the scene dims out. Music: blues—guitar.*]

SCENE FOUR

Late that night. VAL *enters the store, a little unsteadily, with his guitar; goes to the cashbox and rings it open. He counts some bills off a big wad and returns them to the cashbox and the larger wad to the pocket of his snakeskin jacket. Sudden footsteps above; light spills onto stair landing. He quickly moves away from the cashbox as* LADY *appears on the landing in a white sateen robe; she carries a flashlight.*

LADY: Who's that?

[*Music fades out.*]

VAL:—Me.

[*She turns the flashlight on his figure.*]

LADY: Oh, my God, how you scared me!

VAL: You didn't expect me?

LADY: How'd I know it was you I heard come in?

VAL: I thought you give me a room here.

LADY: You left without letting me know if you took it or not. [*She is descending the stairs into store, flashlight still on him.*]

VAL: Catch me turning down something I get for nothing.

LADY: Well, you might have said something so I'd expect you or not.

VAL: I thought you took it for granted.

LADY: I don't take nothing for granted.

[*He starts back to the alcove.*]

Wait!—I'm coming downstairs. . . . [*She descends with the flashlight beam on his face.*]

VAL: You're blinding me with that flashlight.

301

[*He laughs. She keeps the flashlight on him. He starts back again toward the alcove.*]

LADY: The bed's not made because I didn't expect you.

VAL: That's all right.

LADY: I brought the linen downstairs and you'd cut out.

VAL:—Yeah, well—

[*She picks up linen on counter.*]

Give me that stuff. I can make up my own rack. Tomorrow you'll have to get yourself a new clerk. [*Takes it from her and goes again toward alcove.*] I had a lucky night. [*Exhibits a wad of bills.*]

LADY: *Hey!*

[*He stops near the curtain. She goes and turns on green-shaded bulb over cashbox.*]

—*Did you just open this cashbox?*

VAL:—Why you ask that?

LADY: I thought I heard it ring open a minute ago, that's why I come down here.

VAL:—In your—white satin—kimona?

LADY: *Did you just open the cashbox?!*

VAL:—I wonder who did if I didn't. . . .

LADY: Nobody did if you didn't, but somebody did! [*Opens cashbox and hurriedly counts money. She is trembling violently.*]

VAL: How come you didn't lock the cash up in the safe this evening, Lady?

LADY: Sometimes I forget to.

VAL: That's careless.

LADY:—Why'd you open the cashbox when you come in?

VAL: I opened it twice this evening, once before I went out and again when I come back. I borrowed some money and put it back in the box an' got all this left over! [*Shows her the wad of bills.*] I beat a blackjack dealer five times straight. With this much loot I can retire for the season. . . . [*He returns money to pocket.*]

LADY: *Chicken feed!*—I'm sorry for you.

VAL: You're sorry for me?

LADY: I'm sorry for you because nobody can help you. I was touched by your—strangeness, your strange talk.—That thing about birds with no feet so they have to sleep on the wind?—I said to myself, "This boy is a bird with no feet so he has to sleep on the wind," and that softened my fool Dago heart and I wanted to help you. . . . Fool, me!—I got what I should of expected. You robbed me while I was upstairs to get sheets to make up your bed!

[*He starts out toward the door.*]

I guess I'm a fool to even feel disappointed.

VAL [*stopping center and dropping linen on counter*]: You're disappointed in me. I was disappointed in you.

LADY [*coming from behind counter*]:—How did I disappoint you?

VAL: There wasn't no cot behind that curtain before. You put it back there for a purpose.

LADY: It was back there!—folded behind the mirror.

VAL: It wasn't back of no mirror when you told me three times to go and—

LADY [*cutting in*]: I left that money in the cashbox on purpose, to find out if I could trust you.

303

VAL: You got back th' . . .

LADY: No, no, no, I can't trust you, now I know I can't trust you, I got to trust anybody or I don't want him.

VAL: That's OK, I don't expect no character reference from you.

LADY: I'll give you a character reference. I'd say this boy's a peculiar talker! But I wouldn't say a real hard worker or honest. I'd say a peculiar slew-footer that sweet talks you while he's got his hand in the cashbox.

VAL: I took out less than you owed me.

LADY: Don't mix up the issue. I see through you, mister!

VAL: I see through you, Lady.

LADY: What d'you see through me?

VAL: You sure you want me to tell?

LADY: I'd love for you to.

VAL: —A not so young and not so satisfied woman, that hired a man off the highway to do double duty without paying overtime for it. . . . I mean a store clerk days and a stud nights, and—

LADY: God, no! You—! [*She raises her hand as if to strike at him.*] Oh, God no . . . you cheap little—[*Invectives fail her so she uses her fists, hammering at him with them. He seizes her wrists. She struggles a few moments more, then collapses, in chair, sobbing. He lets go of her gently.*]

VAL: It's natural. You felt—lonely. . . .

[*She sobs brokenly against the counter.*]

LADY: Why did you come back here?

VAL: To put back the money I took so you wouldn't re-member me as not honest or grateful—[*He picks up his guitar and starts to the door nodding gravely. She catches her breath; rushes to intercept him, spreading her arms like a crossbar over the door.*]

LADY: NO, NO, DON'T GO . . . I NEED YOU!!!

[*He faces her for five beats. The true passion of her outcry touches him then, and he turns about and crosses to the alcove. . . . As he draws the curtain across it he looks back at her.*]

TO LIVE. . . . TO GO ON LIVING!!!

[*Music fades in—"Lady's Love Song"—guitar. He closes the curtain and turns on the light behind it, making it translucent. Through an opening in the alcove entrance, we see him sitting down with his guitar.* LADY *picks up the linen and crosses to the alcove like a spellbound child. Just outside it she stops, frozen with uncertainty, a conflict of feelings, but then he begins to whisper the words of a song so tenderly that she is able to draw the curtain open and enter the alcove. He looks up gravely at her from his guitar. She closes the curtain behind her. Its bizarre design, a gold tree with white birds and scarlet fruit in it, is softly translucent with the bulb lighted behind it. The guitar continues softly for a few moments; stops; the stage darkens till only the curtain of the alcove is clearly visible.*]

CURTAIN

ACT THREE

An early morning. The Saturday before Easter. The sleeping alcove is lighted. VAL *is smoking, half dressed, on the edge of the cot.* LADY *comes running, panting downstairs, her hair loose, in dressing robe and slippers and calls out in a panicky, shrill whisper.*

LADY: Val! Val, he's comin' downstairs!

VAL [*hoarse with sleep*]: Who's—what?

LADY: Jabe!

VAL: Jabe?

LADY: I swear he is, he's coming downstairs!

VAL: What of it?

LADY: Jesus, will you get up and put some clothes on? The damned nurse told him that he could come down in the store to check over the stock! You want him to catch you half dressed on that bed there?

VAL: Don't he know I sleep here?

LADY: Nobody knows you sleep here but you and me.

[*Voices above.*]

Oh, God!—they've started.

NURSE: Don't hurry now. Take one step at a time.

[*Footsteps on stairs, slow, shuffling. The professional, nasal cheer of a nurse's voice.*]

LADY [*panicky*]: Get your shirt on! Come out!

NURSE: That's right. One step at a time, one step at a time, lean on my shoulder and take one step at a time.

306

[VAL *rises, still dazed from sleep.* LADY *gasps and sweeps the curtain across the alcove just a moment before the descending figures enter the sight-lines on the landing.* LADY *breathes like an exhausted runner as she backs away from the alcove and assumes a forced smile.* JABE *and the nurse,* MISS PORTER, *appear on the landing of the stairs and at the same moment scudding clouds expose the sun. A narrow window on the landing admits a brilliant shaft of light upon the pair. They have a bizarre and awful appearance, the tall man, his rusty black suit hanging on him like an empty sack, his eyes burning malignantly from his yellow face, leaning on a stumpy little woman with bright pink or orange hair, clad all in starched white, with a voice that purrs with the faintly contemptuous cheer and sweetness of those hired to care for the dying.*]

NURSE: Aw, now, just look at that, that nice bright sun comin' out.

LADY: Miss Porter? It's—it's cold down here!

JABE: What's she say?

NURSE: She says it's cold down here.

LADY: The—the—the air's not warm enough yet, the air's not heated!

NURSE: He's determined to come right down, Mrs. Torrance.

LADY: I know but—

NURSE: Wild horses couldn't hold him a minute longer.

JABE [*exhausted*]:—Let's—rest here a minute. . . .

LADY [*eagerly*]: Yes! Rest there a minute!

NURSE: Okay. We'll rest here a minute. . . .

[*They sit down side by side on a bench under the artificial palm tree in the shaft of light.* JABE *glares into the light like a fierce dying old beast. There are sounds from the alcove. To cover them up,* LADY *keeps making startled, laughing sounds in her throat, half laughing, half panting, chafing her hands together at the foot of the stairs, and coughing falsely.*]

JABE: Lady, what's wrong? Why are you so excited?

LADY: It seems like a miracle to me.

JABE: What seems like a miracle to you?

LADY: You coming downstairs.

JABE: You never thought I would come downstairs again?

LADY: Not this quick! Not as quick as this, Jabe! Did you think he would pick up as quick as this, Miss Porter?

[JABE *rises.*]

NURSE: Ready?

JABE: Ready.

NURSE: He's doing fine, knock wood.

LADY: Yes, knock wood, knock wood!

[*Drums counter loudly with her knuckles.* VAL *steps silently from behind the alcove curtain as the* NURSE *and* JABE *resume their slow, shuffling descent of the stairs.*]

[*Moving back to downstage right-center.*] You got to be careful not to overdo. You don't want another setback. Ain't that right, Miss Porter?

NURSE: Well, it's my policy to mobilize the patient.

LADY [*to* VAL *in a shrill whisper*]: Coffee's boiling, take the goddamm coffeepot off the burner! [*She gives* VAL *a panicky signal to go in the alcove.*]

JABE: Who're you talking to, Lady?

LADY: To—to—to Val, the clerk! I told him to—get you a—chair!

JABE: Who's that?

LADY: Val, Val, the clerk, you know Val!

JABE: Not yet. I'm anxious to meet him. Where is he?

LADY: Right here, right here, here's Val!

[VAL *returns from the alcove.*]

JABE: He's here bright and early.

LADY: The early bird catches the worm!

JABE: That's right. Where is the worm?

LADY [*loudly*]: Ha ha!

NURSE: Careful! One step at a time, Mr. Torrance.

LADY: Saturday before Easter's our biggest sales-day of the year, I mean second biggest, but sometimes it's even bigger than Christmas Eve! So I told Val to get here a half hour early.

[JABE *misses his step and stumbles to foot of stairs.* LADY *screams.* NURSE *rushes down to him.* VAL *advances and raises the man to his feet.*]

VAL: Here. Here.

LADY: Oh, my God.

NURSE: Oh, oh!

JABE: I'm all right.

NURSE: Are you sure?

LADY: Are you sure?

JABE: Let me go! [*He staggers to lean against counter, panting, glaring, with a malignant smile.*]

309

LADY: Oh, my God. Oh, my—God. . . .

JABE: This is the boy that works here?

LADY: Yes, this is the clerk I hired to help us out, Jabe.

JABE: How is he doing?

LADY: Fine, fine.

JABE: He's mighty good looking. Do women give him much trouble?

LADY: When school lets out the high-school girls are thick as flies in this store!

JABE: How about older women? Don't he attract older women? The older ones are the buyers, they got the money. They sweat it out of their husbands and throw it away! What's your salary, boy, how much do I pay you?

LADY: Twenty-two fifty a week.

JABE: You're getting him cheap.

VAL: I get—commissions.

JABE: Commissions?

VAL: Yes. One percent of all sales.

JABE: Oh? Oh? I didn't know about that.

LADY: I knew he would bring in trade and he brings it in.

JABE: I bet.

LADY: Val, get Jabe a chair, he ought to sit down.

JABE: No, I don't want to sit down. I want to take a look at the new confectionery.

LADY: Oh, yes, yes! Take a look at it! Val, Val, turn on the lights in the confectionery! I want Jabe to see the way I done it over! I'm—real—*proud!*

[VAL *crosses and switches on light in confectionery. The bulbs in the arches and the juke box light up.*]

Go in and look at it, Jabe. I am real proud of it!

[*He stares at* LADY *a moment; then shuffles slowly into the spectral radiance of the confectionery.* LADY *moves downstage center. At the same time a calliope becomes faintly audible and slowly but steadily builds.* MISS PORTER *goes with the patient, holding his elbow.*]

VAL [*returning to* LADY]: He looks like death.

LADY [*moving away from him*]: *Hush!*

[VAL *goes up above counter and stands in the shadows.*]

NURSE: Well, isn't this artistic.

JABE: Yeh. Artistic as hell.

NURSE: I never seen anything like it before.

JABE: Nobody else did either.

NURSE [*coming back to upstage right-center*]: Who done these decorations?

LADY [*defiantly*]: I did them, all by myself!

NURSE: What do you know. It sure is something artistic.

[*Calliope is now up loud.*]

JABE [*coming back to downstage right*]: Is there a circus or carnival in the county?

LADY: What?

JABE: That sounds like a circus calliope on the highway.

LADY: That's no circus calliope. It's advertising the gala opening of the Torrance Confectionery tonight!

JABE: Doing what did you say?

LADY: It's announcing the opening of our confectionery, it's going all over Glorious Hill this morning and all over Sunset and Lyon this afternoon. Hurry on here so you can

311

see it go by the store. [*She rushes excitedly to open the front door as the ragtime music of the calliope approaches.*]

JABE: I married a live one, Miss Porter. How much does that damn thing cost me?

LADY: You'll be surprised how little. [*She is talking with an hysterical vivacity now.*] I hired it for a song!

JABE: How much of a song did you hire it for?

LADY [*closing door*]: Next to nothing, seven-fifty an hour! And it covers three towns in Two River County!

[*Calliope fades out.*]

JABE [*with a muted ferocity*]: Miss Porter, I married a live one! Didn't I marry a live one? [*Switches off lights in confectionery*] Her daddy "The Wop" was just as much of a live one till he burned up.

[LADY *gasps as if struck.*]

[*With a slow, ugly grin:*] He had a wine garden on the north shore of Moon Lake. The new confectionery sort of reminds me of it. But he made a mistake, he made a bad mistake, one time, selling liquor to niggers. We burned him out. We burned him out, house and orchard and vines and "The Wop" was burned up trying to fight the fire. [*He turns.*] I think I better go up.

LADY:—Did you say "WE"?

JABE:—I have a kind of a cramp. . . .

NURSE [*taking his arm*]: Well, let's go up.

JABE:—Yes, I better go up. . . .

[*They cross to stairs. Calliope fades in.*]

LADY [*almost shouting as she moves downstage center*]: Jabe, did you say "WE" did it, did you say "WE" did it?

312

JABE [*at foot of stairs, stops, turns*]: Yes, I said *"We"* did it. You heard me, Lady.

NURSE: One step at a time, one step at a time, take it easy.

[*They ascend gradually to the landing and above. The calliope passes directly before the store and a clown is seen, or heard, shouting through megaphone.*]

CLOWN: Don't forget tonight, folks, the gala opening of the Torrance Confectionery, free drinks and free favors, don't forget it, the gala opening of the confectionery.

[*Fade.* JABE *and the* NURSE *disappear above the landing. Calliope gradually fades. A hoarse cry above. The* NURSE *runs back downstairs, exclaiming:*]

NURSE: He's bleeding, he's having a hemm'rhage! [*Runs to phone.*] Dr. Buchanan's office! [*Turns again to* LADY.] Your husband is having a hemm'rhage!

[*Calliope is loud still.* LADY *appears not to hear. She speaks to* VAL:]

LADY: Did you hear what he said? He said "We" did it, "WE" burned—house—vines—orchard—"The Wop" burned fighting the fire. . . .

[*The scene dims out; calliope fades out.*]

Sunset of the same day. At rise VAL *is alone. He is standing
stock-still down center stage, almost beneath the proscenium,
in the tense, frozen attitude of a wild animal listening to
something that warns it of danger, his head turned as if he
were looking off stage left, out over the house, frowning
slightly, attentively. After a moment he mutters something
sharply, and his body relaxes; he takes out a cigarette and
crosses to the store entrance, opens the door and stands looking out. It has been raining steadily and will rain again in a
while, but right now it is clearing: the sun breaks through,
suddenly, with great brilliance; and almost at the same instant,
at some distance, a woman cries out a great hoarse cry of terror
and exaltation; the cry is repeated as she comes running nearer.*

VEE TALBOTT *appears through the window as if blind and
demented, stiff, groping gestures, shielding her eyes with one
arm as she feels along the store window for the entrance,
gasping for breath.* VAL *steps aside, taking hold of her arm
to guide her into the store. For a few moments she leans
weakly, blindly panting for breath against the oval glass of
the door, then calls out.*

VEE: I'm—*struck blind!*

VAL: You can't see?

VEE:—No! Nothing....

VAL [*assisting her to stool below counter*]: Set down here,
Mrs. Talbott.

VEE:—Where?

VAL [*pushing her gently*]: Here.

[VEE *sinks moaning onto stool.*]

What hurt your eyes, Mrs. Talbott, what happened to your
eyes?

VEE [*drawing a long, deep breath*]: The vision I waited and prayed for all my life long!

VAL: You had a vision?

VEE: I saw the eyes of my Savior!—They struck me blind. [*Leans forward, clasping her eyes in anguish.*] Ohhhh, they burned out my eyes!

VAL: Lean back.

VEE: Eyeballs burn like fire. . . .

VAL [*going off right*]: I'll get you something cold to put on your eyes.

VEE: I knew a vision was coming, oh, I had many signs!

VAL [*in confectionery*]: It must be a terrible shock to have a vision. . . . [*He speaks gravely, gently, scooping chipped ice from the soft-drink cooler and wrapping it in his handkerchief.*]

VEE [*with the naïveté of a child, as* VAL *comes back to her*]: I *thought* I would see my Savior on the day of His passion, which was yesterday, Good Friday, that's when I expected to see Him. But I was mistaken, I was—disappointed. Yesterday passed and nothing, nothing much happened but—today—

[VAL *places handkerchief over her eyes.*]

—this afternoon, somehow I pulled myself together and walked outdoors and started to go to pray in the empty church and meditate on the Rising of Christ tomorrow. Along the road as I walked, thinking about the mysteries of Easter, veils!

—[*She makes a long shuddering word out of "veils."*]—

seemed to drop off my eyes! Light, oh, light! I never have seen such brilliance! It *PRICKED* my eyeballs like *NEEDLES!*

VAL:—Light?

VEE: Yes, yes, light. YOU know, you know we live in light and shadow, that's, that's what we *live* in, a world of—*light* and—*shadow....*

VAL: Yes. In light and shadow. [*He nods with complete understanding and agreement. They are like two children who have found life's meaning, simply and quietly, along a country road.*]

VEE: A world of light and shadow is what we live in, and —it's—confusing....

[*A man is peering in at store window.*]

VAL: Yeah, they—*do* get—*mixed....*

VEE: Well, and then—[*Hesitates to recapture her vision.*] —I heard this clap of thunder! Sky!—Split open!—And there in the split-open sky, I saw, I tell you, I *saw* the TWO HUGE BLAZING EYES OF JESUS CHRIST RISEN!—Not crucified but Risen! I mean Crucified and *then* RISEN!—The blazing eyes of Christ Risen! And then a great—[*Raises both arms and makes a great sweeping motion to describe an apocalyptic disturbance of the atmosphere.*]—His hand!—*Invisible!* —I didn't *see* his hand!—But it *touched* me—*here!* [*She seizes* VAL'S *hand and presses it to her great heaving bosom.*]

TALBOTT [*appearing right in confectionery, furiously*]: VEE!

[*She starts up, throwing the compress from her eyes. Utters a sharp gasp and staggers backward with terror and blasted ecstacy and dismay and belief, all confused in her look.*]

VEE: You!

TALBOTT: VEE!

VEE: *You!*

TALBOTT [*advancing*]: VEE!

VEE [*making two syllables of the word "eyes"*]:—The Ey —es! [*She collapses, forward, falls to her knees, her arms*

316

thrown about VAL. *He seizes her to lift her. Two or three men are peering in at the store window.*]

TALBOTT [*pushing* VAL *away*]: Let go of her, don't put your hands on my wife! [*He seizes her roughly and hauls her to the door.* VAL *moves up to help* VEE.] Don't move. [*At door, to* VAL:] I'm coming back.

VAL: I'm not goin' nowhere.

TALBOTT [*to* DOG, *as he goes off left with* VEE]: Dog, go in there with that boy.

VOICE [*outside*]: Sheriff caught him messin' with his wife.

[*Repeat:* ANOTHER VOICE *at a distance.* "DOG" HAMMA *enters and stands silently beside the door while there is a continued murmur of excited voices on the street. The following scene should be underplayed, played almost casually, like the performance of some familiar ritual.*]

VAL: What do you want?

[DOG *says nothing but removes from his pocket and opens a spring-blade knife and moves to D.R.* PEE WEE *enters. Through the open door—voices.*]

VOICES [*outside*]:—Son of a low-down bitch foolin' with—

—That's right, ought to be—

—Cut the son of a—

VAL: What do you—?

[PEE WEE *closes the door and silently stands beside it, opening a spring-blade knife.* VAL *looks from one to the other.*]

—It's six o'clock. Store's closed.

[*Men chuckle like dry leaves rattling.* VAL *crosses toward the door; is confronted by* TALBOTT; *stops short.*]

TALBOTT: Boy, I said stay here.

VAL: I'm not—goin' nowhere. . . .

TALBOTT: Stand back under that light.

VAL: Which light?

TALBOTT: That light.

[*Points.* VAL *goes behind counter.*]

I want to look at you while I run through some photos of men wanted.

VAL: I'm not wanted.

TALBOTT: A good-looking boy like you is always wanted.

[*Men chuckle.* VAL *stands in hot light under green-shaded bulb.* TALBOTT *shuffles through photos he has removed from his pocket.*]

—How tall are you, boy?

VAL: Never measured.

TALBOTT: How much do you weigh?

VAL: Never weighed.

TALBOTT: Got any scars or marks of identification on your face or body?

VAL: No, sir.

TALBOTT: Open your shirt.

VAL: What for? [*He doesn't.*]

TALBOTT: Open his shirt for him, Dog.

[DOG *steps quickly forward and rips shirt open to waist.* VAL *starts forward; men point knives; he draws back.*]

That's right, stay there, boy. What did you do before?

[PEE WEE *sits on stairs.*]

VAL: Before—what?

TALBOTT: Before you come here?

VAL:—Traveled and—played. . . .

TALBOTT: Played?

DOG [*advancing to center*]: What?

PEE WEE: With wimmen?

[DOG *laughs.*]

VAL: No. Played guitar—and sang.. . . .

[VAL *touches guitar on counter.*]

TALBOTT: Let me see that guitar.

VAL: Look at it. But don't touch it. I don't let nobody but musicians touch it.

[*Men come close.*]

DOG: What're you smiling for, boy?

PEE WEE: He ain't smiling, his mouth's just twitching like a dead chicken's foot.

[*They laugh.*]

TALBOTT: What is all that writing on the guitar?

VAL:—Names. . . .

TALBOTT: What of?

VAL: Autographs of musicians dead and living.

[*Men read aloud the names printed on the guitar: Bessie Smith, Leadbelly, Woody Guthrie, Jelly Roll Morton, etc. They bend close to it, keeping the open knife blades pointed at* VAL'S *body;* DOG *touches neck of the guitar, draws it toward him.* VAL *suddenly springs, with catlike agility, onto the counter. He runs along it, kicking at their hands as they catch at his legs. The* NURSE *runs down to the landing.*]

MISS PORTER: *What's going on?*

319

TALBOTT [*at the same time*]: *Stop that!*

[JABE *calls hoarsely above.*]

MISS PORTER [*excitedly, all in one breath, as* JABE *calls*]: Where's Mrs. Torrance? I got a very sick man up there and his wife's disappeared.

[JABE *calls out again.*]

I been on a whole lot of cases but never seen one where a wife showed no concern for a—

[JABE *cries out again. Her voice fades out as she returns above.*]

TALBOTT [*overlapping* NURSE'S *speech*]: Dog! Pee Wee! You all stand back from that counter. Dog, why don't you an' Pee Wee go up an' see Jabe. Leave me straighten this boy out, go on, go on up.

PEE WEE: C'mon, Dawg. . . .

[*They go up.* VAL *remains panting on counter.*]

TALBOTT [*sits in shoe chair at right window. In his manner there is a curious, half-abashed gentleness, when alone with the boy, as if he recognized the purity in him and was, truly, for the moment, ashamed of the sadism implicit in the occurrence*]: Awright, boy. Git on down off th' counter, I ain't gonna touch y'r guitar.

[VAL *jumps off counter.*]

But I'm gonna tell you something. They's a certain county I know of which has a big sign at the county line that says, "Nigger, don't let the sun go down on you in this county." That's all it says, it don't threaten nothing, it just says, "Nigger, don't let the sun go down on you in this county!" [*Chuckles hoarsely. Rises and takes a step toward* VAL.]

Well, son! You ain't a nigger and this is not that county, but, son, I want you to just imagine that you seen a sign that said to you: "Boy, don't let the sun rise on you in this county." I said "rise," not "go down" because it's too close to sunset for you to git packed an' move on before that. But I think if you value that instrument in your hands as much as you seem to, you'll simplify my job by not allowing the sun tomorrow to rise on you in this county. 'S that understood, now, boy?

[VAL *stares at him, expressionless, panting.*]

[*Crossing to door*] I *hope* so. I don't like *violence*. [*He looks back and nods at* VAL *from the door. Then goes outside in the fiery afterglow of the sunset. Dogs bark in the distance. Music fades in: "Dog Howl Blues"—minor—guitar. Pause in which* VAL *remains motionless, cradling guitar in his arms. Then* VAL'S *faraway, troubled look is resolved in a slight, abrupt nod of his head. He sweeps back the alcove curtain and enters the alcove and closes the curtain behind him. Lights dim down to indicate a division of scenes.*]

SCENE THREE

*Half an hour later. The lighting is less realistic than in the
previous scenes of the play. The interior of the store is so dim
that only the vertical lines of the pillars and such selected items
as the palm tree on the stair landing and the ghostly paper
vineyard of the confectionery are plainly visible. The view
through the great front window has virtually become the background of the action: A singing wind sweeps clouds before the
moon so that the witchlike country brightens and dims and
brightens again. The marshal's hounds are restless: their
baying is heard now and then. A lamp outside the door sometimes catches a figure that moves past with mysterious urgency,
calling out softly and raising an arm to beckon, like a shade
in the under kingdom.*

*At rise, or when the stage is lighted again, it is empty but
footsteps are descending the stairs as* DOLLY *and* BEULAH
rush into the store and call out, in soft shouts:

DOLLY: Dawg?

BEULAH: Pee Wee?

EVA TEMPLE [*appearing on landing and calling down
softly in the superior tone of a privileged attendant in a
sick-chamber*]: Please don't shout!—Mr. Binnings and Mr.
Hamma [*Names of the two husbands*] are upstairs sitting with
Jabe. . . . [*She continues her descent. Then* EVA TEMPLE
appears, sobbing, on landing.]

—Come down carefully, Sister.

SISTER: Help me, I'm all to pieces. . . .

[EVA *ignores this request and faces the two women.*]

BEULAH: Has the bleedin' quit yit?

EVA: The hemorrhage seems to have stopped. Sister, Sister, pull yourself together, we all have to face these things sometime in life.

DOLLY: Has he sunk into a coma?

EVA: No. Cousin Jabe is conscious. Nurse Porter says his pulse is remarkably strong for a man that lost so much blood. Of course he's had a transfusion.

SISTER: Two of 'em.

EVA [*crossing to* DOLLY]: Yais, an' they put him on glucose. His strength came back like magic.

BEULAH: She up there?

EVA: *Who?*

BEULAH: Lady!

EVA: No! When last reported she had just stepped into the Glorious Hill Beauty Parlor.

BEULAH: You don't mean it.

EVA: Ask Sister!

SISTER: She's planning to go ahead with—!

EVA:—The gala opening of the confectionery. Switch on the lights in there, Sister.

[SISTER *crosses and switches on lights and moves off right. The decorated confectionery is lighted.* DOLLY *and* BEULAH *exclaim in awed voices.*]

—Of course it's not normal behavior; it's downright lunacy, but still that's no excuse for it! And when she called up at five, about one hour ago, it wasn't to ask about Jabe, oh, no, she didn't mention his name. She asked if Ruby Lightfoot had delivered a case of Seagram's. Yais, she just shouted that question and hung up the phone, before I could—[*She crosses and goes off R.*]

BEULAH [*going into confectionery*]: *Oh, I understand, now! Now I see what she's up to!* Electric moon, cutout silver-paper stars and artificial vines? Why, it's her father's wine garden on Moon Lake she's turned this room into!

DOLLY [*suddenly as she sits in shoe chair*]: *Here she comes, here she comes!*

[*The* TEMPLE SISTERS *retreat from view in confectionery as* LADY *enters the store. She wears a hooded rain-cape and carries a large paper shopping bag and paper carton box.*]

LADY: Go on, ladies, don't stop, my ears are burning!

BEULAH [*coming to upstage right-center*]:—Lady, oh, Lady, Lady. . . .

LADY: Why d'you speak my name in that pitiful voice? Hanh? [*Throws back hood of cape, her eyes blazing, and places bag and box on counter.*] *Val? Val!* Where is that boy that works here?

[DOLLY *shakes her head.*]

I guess he's havin' a T-bone steak with French fries and coleslaw fo' ninety-five cents at the Blue Bird. . . .

[*Sounds in confectionery.*]

Who's in the confectionery, is that you, Val?

[TEMPLE SISTERS *emerge and stalk past her.*]

Going, girls?

[*They go out of store.*]

Yes, gone! [*She laughs and throws off rain-cape, onto counter, revealing a low-cut gown, triple strand of pearls and a purple satin-ribboned corsage.*]

BEULAH [*sadly*]: How long have I known you, Lady?

LADY [*going behind counter, unpacks paper hats and whistles*]: A long time, Beulah. I think you remember when my people come here on a banana boat from Palermo, Sicily, by way of Caracas, Venezuela, yes, with a grind-organ and a monkey my papa had bought in Venezuela. I was not much bigger than the monkey, ha ha! You remember the monkey? The man that sold Papa the monkey said it was a very young monkey, but he was a liar, it was a very old monkey, it was on its last legs, ha ha ha! But it was a well-dressed monkey. [*coming to right of counter*] It had a green velvet suit and a little red cap that it tipped and a tambourine that it passed around for money, ha ha ha. . . . The grind-organ played and the monkey danced in the sun, ha ha!—"*O Sole Mio, Da Da Da daaa . . . !*" [*She sits in chair at counter.*]—One day, the monkey danced too much in the sun and it was a very old monkey and it dropped dead. . . . My Papa, he turned to the people, he made them a bow and he said, "The show is over, the monkey is dead." Ha ha!

[*Slight pause. Then* DOLLY *pipes up venomously:*]

DOLLY: Ain't it wonderful Lady can be so brave?

BEULAH: Yaiss, wonderful! Hanh. . . .

LADY: For me the show is not over, the monkey is not dead yet! [*Then suddenly:*] *Val, is that you, Val?*

[*Someone has entered the confectionery door, out of sight, and the draught of air has set the wind-chimes tinkling wildly.* LADY *rushes forward but stops short as* CAROL *appears. She wears a trench coat and a white sailor's cap with a turned-down brim, inscribed with the name of a vessel and a date, past or future, memory or anticipation.*]

DOLLY: Well, here's your first customer, Lady.

LADY [*going behind counter*]:—Carol, that room ain't open.

CAROL: There's a big sign outside that says "Open Tonite!"

325

LADY: It ain't open to you.

CAROL: I have to stay here a while. They stopped my car, you see, I don't have a license; my license has been revoked and I have to find someone to drive me across the river.

LADY: You can call a taxi.

CAROL: I heard that the boy that works for you is leaving tonight and I—

LADY: *Who said he's leaving?*

CAROL [*crossing to counter*]: Sheriff Talbott. The county marshal suggested I get him to drive me over the river since he'd be crossing it too.

LADY: You got some mighty wrong information!

CAROL: Where is he? I don't see him?

LADY: Why d'you keep coming back here bothering that boy? He's not interested in you! Why would he be leaving here tonight?

[*Door opens off as she comes from behind counter.*]

Val, is that you, Val?

[CONJURE MAN *enters through confectionery, mumbling rapidly, holding out something.* BEULAH *and* DOLLY *take flight out the door with cries of revulsion.*]

No conjure stuff, go away!

[*He starts to withdraw.*]

CAROL [*crossing to upstage right-center*]: Uncle! The Choctaw cry! I'll give you a dollar for it.

[LADY *turns away with a gasp, with a gesture of refusal. The* NEGRO *nods, then throws back his turkey neck and utters a series of sharp barking sounds that rise to a sustained cry of great intensity and wildness. The cry produces*] *a violent reaction in the building.* BEULAH *and* DOLLY *run out of the store.* LADY *does not move but she catches her breath.* DOG *and* PEE WEE *run down the stairs with ad libs and hustle the* NEGRO *out of the store, ignoring* LADY, *as their wives call:* "PEE WEE!" *and* "DAWG!" *outside on the walk.* VAL *sweeps back the alcove curtain and appears as if the cry were his cue. Above, in the sick room, hoarse, outraged shouts that subside with exhaustion.* CAROL *crosses downstage and speaks to the audience and to herself:*]

CAROL: Something is still wild in the country! This country used to be wild, the men and women were wild and there was a wild sort of sweetness in their hearts, for each other, but now it's sick with neon, it's broken out sick, with neon, like most other places. . . . I'll wait outside in my car. It's the fastest thing on wheels in Two River County!

[*She goes out of the store right.* LADY *stares at* VAL *with great asking eyes, a hand to her throat.*]

LADY [*with false boldness*]: Well, ain't you going with her?

VAL: I'm going with no one I didn't come here with. And I come here with no one.

LADY: Then get into your white jacket. I need your services in that room there tonight.

[VAL *regards her steadily for several beats.*]

[*Clapping her hands together twice*] Move, move, stop goofing! The Delta Brilliant lets out in half'n hour and they'll be driving up here. You got to shave ice for the setups!

VAL [*as if he thought she'd gone crazy*]: "Shave ice for the setups"? [*He moves up to counter.*]

LADY: Yes, an' call Ruby Lightfoot, tell her I need me a dozen more half-pints of Seagram's. They all call for Seven-

327

and-Sevens. You know how t' sell bottle goods under a counter? It's OK. We're gonna git paid for protection. [*Gasps, touching her diaphragm*] But one thing you gotta watch out for is sellin' to minors. Don't serve liquor to minors. Ask for his driver's license if they's any doubt. Anybody born earlier than—let's see, twenty-one from—oh, I'll figure it later. Hey! Move! Move! Stop goofing!

VAL [*placing guitar on counter*]:—You're the one that's goofing, not me, Lady.

LADY: Move, I said, *move!*

VAL: What kick are you on, are you on a benny kick, Lady? 'Ve you washed down a couple of bennies with a pot of black coffee t' make you come on strong for th' three o'clock show? [*His mockery is gentle, almost tender, but he has already made a departure; he is back in the all-night bars with the B-girls and raffish entertainers. He stands at counter as she rushes about. As she crosses between the two rooms, he reaches out to catch hold of her bare arm and he pulls her to him and grips her arms.*]

LADY: Hey!

VAL: Will you quit thrashin' around like a hooked catfish?

LADY: Go git in y'r white jacket an'—

VAL: Sit down. I want to talk to you.

LADY: I don't have time.

VAL: I got to reason with you.

LADY: It's not possible to.

VAL: You can't open a night-place here this night.

LADY: You bet your sweet life I'm *going* to!

VAL: Not *me*, not *my* sweet life!

LADY: I'm betting *my* life on it! Sweet or *not* sweet, I'm—

VAL: Yours is yours, mine is mine. . . . [*He releases her with a sad shrug.*]

LADY: You don't get the point, huh? There's a man up there that set fire to my father's wine garden and I lost my life in it, yeah, I lost my life in it, *three* lives was lost in it, two *born* lives and one—*not*. . . . I was made to commit a *murder* by him up there! [*Has frozen momentarily*]—I want that man to see the wine garden come open again when he's dying! I want him to hear it coming open again here tonight! While he's dying. It's necessary, no power on earth can stop it. Hell, I don't even want it, it's just necessary, it's just something's got to be done to square things away, to, to, to—be *not defeated! You get me? Just to be not defeated!* Ah, oh, I won't be defeated, not again, in my life! [*Embraces him*] Thank you for staying here with me!—God bless you for it. . . . Now please go and get in your white jacket . . .

[VAL *looks at her as if he were trying to decide between a natural sensibility of heart and what his life's taught him since he left Witches' Bayou. Then he sighs again, with the same slight, sad shrug, and crosses into alcove to put on a jacket and remove from under his cot a canvas-wrapped package of his belongings.* LADY *takes paper hats and carnival stuff from counter, crosses into confectionery and puts them on the tables, then starts back but stops short as she sees* VAL *come out of alcove with his snakeskin jacket and luggage.*]

LADY: That's not your white jacket, that's that snakeskin jacket you had on when you come here.

VAL: I come and I go in this jacket.

LADY: *Go,* did you say?

VAL: Yes, ma'am, I did, I said go. All that stays to be settled is a little matter of wages.

329

[*The dreaded thing's happened to her. This is what they call "the moment of truth" in the bull ring, when the matador goes in over the horns of the bull to plant the mortal sword-thrust.*]

LADY:—So you're—cutting out, are you?

VAL: My gear's all packed. I'm catchin' the southbound bus.

LADY: Uh-huh, in a pig's eye. You're not conning me, mister. She's waiting for you outside in her high-powered car and you're—

[*Sudden footsteps on stairs. They break apart,* VAL *puts suitcase down, drawing back into shadow, as* NURSE PORTER *appears on the stair landing.*]

NURSE PORTER: Mrs. Torrance, are you down there?

LADY [*crossing to foot of stairs*]: Yeah. I'm here. I'm back.

NURSE PORTER: Can I talk to you up here about Mr. Torrance?

LADY [*shouting to* NURSE]: I'll be up in a minute.

[*Door closes above.* LADY *turns to* VAL:] OK, now, mister. You're scared about something, ain't you?

VAL: I been threatened with violence if I stay here.

LADY: I got paid for protection in this county, plenty paid for it, and it covers you too.

VAL: No, ma'am. My time is up here.

LADY: Y' say that like you'd served a sentence in jail.

VAL: I got in deeper than I meant to, Lady.

LADY: Yeah, and how about me?

VAL [*going to her*]: I would of cut out before you got back to the store, but I wanted to tell you something I never told

330

no one before. [*Places hand on her shoulder.*] I feel a true love for you, Lady! [*He kisses her.*] I'll wait for you out of this county, just name the time and the . . .

LADY [*moving back*]: Oh, don't talk about love, not to me. It's easy to say "Love, Love!" with fast and free transportation waiting right out the door for you!

VAL: D'you remember some things I told you about me the night we met here?

LADY [*crossing to right-center*]: Yeah, many things. Yeah, temperature of a dog. And some bird, oh, yeah, without legs so it had to sleep on the wind!

VAL [*through her speech*]: Naw, not that; not that.

LADY: And how you could burn down a woman? I said "Bull!" I take that back. You can! You can burn down a woman and stamp on her ashes to make sure the fire is put out!

VAL: I mean what I said about gettin' away from . . .

LADY: How long've you held this first steady job in your life?

VAL: Too long, too long!

LADY: Four months and five days, mister. All right! How much pay have you took?

VAL: I told you to keep out all but—

LADY: Y'r living expenses. I can give you the figures to a dime. Eighty-five bucks, no, ninety? Chicken feed, mister! Y'know how much you got coming? IF you get it? I don't need paper to figure, I got it all in my head. You got five hundred and eighty-six bucks coming to you, not, not chicken feed, that. But, mister. [*Gasps for breath*]—If you try to walk out on me, now, tonight, without notice!—You're going to get just nothing! A great big zero. . . .

331

Somebody hollers at door off right: "Hey! You open?"
She rushes toward it shouting, "CLOSED! CLOSED! GO
*AWAY!"—*VAL *crosses to the cashbox. She turns back*
toward him, gasps:]

Now you watch your next move and I'll watch mine. You
open that cashbox and I swear I'll throw open that door and
holler, clerk's robbing the store!

VAL:—Lady?

LADY [*fiercely*]: Hanh?

VAL:—Nothing, you've—

LADY:—Hanh?

VAL: Blown your stack. I will go without pay.

LADY [*coming to center*]: Then you ain't understood me!
With or without pay, you're staying!

VAL: I've got my gear. [*Picks up suitcase. She rushes to
seize his guitar.*]

LADY: Then I'll go up and git mine! And take this with
me, just t'make sure you wait till I'm—[*She moves back to
R.C. He puts suitcase down.*]

VAL [*advancing toward her*]: Lady, what're you—?

LADY [*entreating with guitar raised*]: Don't—!

VAL:—Doing with—

LADY:—*Don't!*

VAL:—my guitar!

LADY: *Holding it for security while I—*

VAL: Lady, you been a lunatic since this morning!

LADY: Longer, longer than morning! I'm going to keep
hold of your "life companion" while I pack! I am! I am goin'
to pack an' go, if you go, where you go!

[*He makes a move toward her. She crosses below and around to counter.*]

You didn't think so, you actually didn't think so? What was I going to do, in your opinion? What, in your opinion, would I be doing? Stay on here in a store full of bottles and boxes while you go far, while you go fast and far, without me having your—forwarding address!—even?

VAL: I'll—give you a forwarding address. . . .

LADY: Thanks, oh, thanks! Would I take your forwarding address back of that curtain? "Oh, dear forwarding address, hold me, kiss me, be faithful!" [*Utters grotesque, stifled cry; presses fist to mouth.*]

[*He advances cautiously, hand stretched toward the guitar. She retreats above to upstage right-center, biting lip, eyes flaring. JABE knocks above.*]

Stay back! You want me to smash it!

VAL [*downstage center*]: He's—knocking for you. . . .

LADY: I know! Death's knocking for me! Don't you think I hear him, knock, knock, knock? It sounds like what it is! Bones knocking bones. . . . Ask me how it felt to be coupled with death up there, and I can tell you. My skin crawled when he touched me. But I endured it. I guess my heart knew that somebody must be coming to take me out of this hell! You did. You came. Now look at me! I'm alive once more! [*Convulsive sobbing controlled: continues more calmly and harshly:*]

—*I won't wither in dark!* Got that through your skull? Now. Listen! Everything in this rotten store is yours, not just your pay, but everything Death's scraped together down here! —but Death has got to die before we can go. . . . You got that memorized, now?—Then get into your white jacket!—

333

*Tonight is the gala opening—[Rushes through confectionery.]
—of the confectionery—*

[VAL *runs and seizes her arm holding guitar. She breaks
violently free.*]

*Smash me against a rock and I'll smash your guitar! I will,
if you—*

[*Rapid footsteps on stairs.*]

Oh, Miss Porter!

[*She motions* VAL *back. He retreats into alcove.* LADY *puts
guitar down beside juke box.* MISS PORTER *is descending
the stairs.*]

NURSE PORTER [*descending watchfully*]: You been out a
long time.

LADY [*moving upstage right-center*]: Yeah, well, I had lots
of—[*Her voice expires breathlessly. She stares fiercely, blindly, into the other's hard face.*]

NURSE PORTER:—Of what?

LADY: Things to—things to—take care of. . . . [*Draws a
deep, shuddering breath, clenched fist to her bosom.*]

NURSE PORTER: Didn't I hear you shouting to someone
just now?

LADY:—Uh-huh. Some drunk tourist made a fuss because I
wouldn't sell him no—liquor. . . .

NURSE [*crossing to the door*]: Oh. Mr. Torrance is sleeping
under medication.

LADY: That's good. [*She sits in shoe-fitting chair.*]

NURSE: I gave him a hypo at five.

LADY:—Don't all that morphine weaken the heart, Miss
Porter?

NURSE: Gradually, yes.

LADY: How long does it usually take for them to let go?

NURSE: It varies according to the age of the patient and the condition his heart's in. Why?

LADY: Miss Porter, don't people sort of help them let go?

NURSE: How do you mean, Mrs. Torrance?

LADY: Shorten their suffering for them?

NURSE: Oh, I see what you mean. [*Snaps her purse shut.*] —I see what you mean, Mrs. Torrance. But killing is killing, regardless of circumstances.

LADY: Nobody said killing.

NURSE: You said "shorten their suffering."

LADY: Yes, like merciful people shorten an animal's suffering when he's. . . .

NURSE: A human being is not the same as an animal, Mrs. Torrance. And I don't hold with what they call—

LADY [*overlapping*]: *Don't give me a sermon*, Miss Porter I just wanted to know if—

NURSE [*overlapping*]: I'm not giving a sermon. I just answered your question. If you want to get somebody to shorten your husband's life—

LADY [*jumping up; overlapping*]: Why, how dare you say that I—

NURSE: I'll be back at ten-thirty.

LADY: Don't!

NURSE: What?

LADY [*crossing behind counter*]: Don't come back at ten-thirty, don't come back.

335

NURSE: I'm always discharged by the doctors on my cases.

LADY: This time you're being discharged by the patient's wife.

NURSE: That's something we'll have to discuss with Dr. Buchanan.

LADY: I'll call him myself about it. I don't like you. I don't think you belong in the nursing profession, you have cold eyes; I think you like to watch pain!

NURSE: I know why you don't like my eyes. [*Snaps purse shut.*] You don't like my eyes because you know they see clear.

LADY: Why are you staring at *me?*

NURSE: I'm not staring at you, I'm staring at the curtain. There's something burning in there, smoke's coming out! [*Starts toward alcove.*] Oh.

LADY: Oh, no, you don't. [*Seizes her arm.*]

NURSE [*pushes her roughly aside and crosses to the curtain.* VAL *rises from cot, opens the curtain and faces her coolly*]: Oh, excuse me! [*She turns to* LADY.]—The moment I looked at you when I was called on this case last Friday morning I knew that you were pregnant.

[LADY *gasps.*]

I also knew the moment I looked at your husband it wasn't by him. [*She stalks to the door.* LADY *suddenly cries out:*]

LADY: Thank you for telling me what I hoped for is true.

MISS PORTER: You don't seem to have any shame.

LADY [*exalted*]: No. I don't have shame. I have—great— *joy!*

MISS PORTER [*venomously*]: Then why don't you get the calliope and the clown to make the announcement?

LADY: You do it for me, save me the money! Make the announcement, all over!

[NURSE *goes out.* VAL *crosses swiftly to the door and locks it. Then he advances toward her, saying:*]

VAL: Is it true what she said?

[LADY *moves as if stunned to the counter; the stunned look gradually turns to a look of wonder. On the counter is a heap of silver and gold paper hats and trumpets for the gala opening of the confectionery.*]

VAL [*in a hoarse whisper*]: Is it true or not true, what that woman told you?

LADY: You sound like a scared little boy.

VAL: She's gone out to tell.

[*Pause.*]

LADY: You gotta go now—it's dangerous for you to stay here. . . . Take your pay out of the cashbox, you can go. Go, go, take the keys to my car, cross the river into some other county. You've done what you came here to do. . . .

VAL:—It's true then, it's—?

LADY [*sitting in chair of counter*]: True as God's word! I have life in my body, this dead tree, my body, has burst in flower! You've given me life, you can go!

[*He crouches down gravely opposite her, gently takes hold of her knotted fingers and draws them to his lips, breathing on them as if to warm them. She sits bolt upright, tense, blind as a clairvoyant.*]

VAL:—Why didn't you tell me before?

LADY:—When a woman's been childless as long as I've been childless, it's hard to believe that you're still able to bear! —We used to have a little fig tree between the house and the orchard. It never bore any fruit, they said it was barren. Time went by it, spring after useless spring, and it almost started to—die. . . . Then one day I discovered a small green fig on the tree they said wouldn't bear! [*She is clasping a gilt paper horn.*] I ran through the orchard. I ran through the wine garden shouting, "Oh, Father, it's going to bear, the fig tree is going to bear!"—It seemed such a wonderful thing, after those ten barren springs, for the little fig tree to bear, it called for a celebration—I ran to a closet, I opened a box that we kept Christmas ornaments in!—I took them out, glass bells, glass birds, tinsel, icicles, stars. . . . And I hung the little tree with them, I decorated the fig tree with glass bells and glass birds, and silver icicles and stars, because it won the battle and it would bear! [*Rises, ecstatic*] Unpack the box! Unpack the box with the Christmas ornaments in it, put them on me, glass bells and glass birds and stars and tinsel and snow! [*In a sort of delirium she thrusts the conical gilt paper hat on her head and runs to the foot of the stairs with the paper horn. She blows the horn over and over, grotesquely mounting the stairs, as* VAL *tries to stop her. She breaks away from him and runs up to the landing, blowing the paper horn and crying out:*] I've won, I've won, Mr. Death, I'm going to bear! [*Then suddenly she falters, catches her breath in a shocked gasp and awkwardly retreats to the stairs. Then turns screaming and runs back down them, her cries dying out as she arrives at the floor level. She retreats haltingly as a blind person, a hand stretched out to* VAL, *as slow, clumping footsteps and hoarse breathing are heard on the stairs. She moans:*]—Oh, God, oh —God. . . .

[JABE *appears on the landing, by the artificial palm tree in its dully lustrous green jardiniere, a stained purple robe hangs loosely about his wasted yellowed frame. He is Death's self, and malignancy, as he peers, crouching, down into the store's dimness to discover his quarry.*]

JABE: Buzzards! Buzzards! [*Clutching the trunk of the false palm tree, he raises the other hand holding a revolver and fires down into the store.* LADY *screams and rushes to cover* VAL'S *motionless figure with hers.* JABE *scrambles down a few steps and fires again and the bullet strikes her, expelling her breath in a great "Hah!" He fires again; the great "Hah!" is repeated. She turns to face him, still covering* VAL *with her body, her face with all the passions and secrets of life and death in it now, her fierce eyes blazing, knowing, defying and accepting. But the revolver is empty; it clicks impotently and* JABE *hurls it toward them; he descends and passes them, shouting out hoarsely:*] I'll have you burned! I burned her father and I'll have you burned! [*He opens the door and rushes out onto the road, shouting hoarsely:*] The clerk is robbing the store, he shot my wife, the clerk is robbing the store, he killed my wife!

VAL:—Did it—?

LADY:—Yes!—it did. . . .

[*A curious, almost formal, dignity appears in them both. She turns to him with the sort of smile that people offer in apology for an awkward speech, and he looks back at her gravely, raising one hand as if to stay her. But she shakes her head slightly and points to the ghostly radiance of her make-believe orchard and she begins to move a little unsteadily toward it. Music.* LADY *enters the confectionery and looks about it as people look for the last time at a loved place they are deserting.*]

The show is over. The monkey is dead . . .

[*Music rises to cover whatever sound Death makes in the confectionery. It halts abruptly. Figures appear through the great front window of the store, pocket-lamps stare through the glass and someone begins to force the front door open.* VAL *cries out:*]

339

VAL: Which way!

[*He turns and runs through the dim radiance of the confectionery, out of our sight. Something slams. Something cracks open. Men are in the store and the dark is full of hoarse, shouting voices.*]

VOICES OF MEN [*shouting*]:—Keep to the walls! He's armed!

—Upstairs, Dog!

—Jack, the confectionery!

[*Wild cry back of store.*]

Got him. GOT HIM!

—They got him!

—Rope, git rope!

—Git rope from th' hardware section!

—I got something better than rope!

—What've you got?

—What's that, what's he got?

—A BLOWTORCH!

—Christ. . . .

[*A momentary hush.*]

—Come on, what in hell are we waiting for?

—Hold on a minute, I wanta see if it works!

—Wait, Wait!

—LOOK here!

[*A jet of blue flame stabs the dark. It flickers on* CAROL'S *figure in the confectionery. The men cry out together in hoarse passion crouching toward the fierce blue jet of fire, their faces lit by it like the faces of demons.*]

—Christ!

—It works!

[*They rush out. Confused shouting behind. Motors start. Fade quickly. There is almost silence, a dog bays in the distance. Then—the* CONJURE MAN *appears with a bundle of garments which he examines, dropping them all except the snakeskin jacket, which he holds up with a toothless mumble of excitement.*]

CAROL [*quietly, gently*]: What have you got there, Uncle? Come here and let me see.

[*He crosses to her.*]

Oh yes, his snakeskin jacket. I'll give you a gold ring for it.

[*She slowly twists ring off her finger. Somewhere there is a cry of anguish. She listens attentively till it fades out, then nods with understanding.*]

—Wild things leave skins behind them, they leave clean skins and teeth and white bones behind them, and these are tokens passed from one to another, so that the fugitive kind can always follow their kind. . . .

[*The cry is repeated more terribly than before. It expires again. She draws the jacket about her as if she were cold, nods to the old* NEGRO, *handing him the ring. Then she crosses toward the door, pausing halfway as* SHERIFF TALBOTT *enters with his pocket-lamp.*]

SHERIFF: Don't no one move, don't move!

[*She crosses directly past him as if she no longer saw him, and out the door. He shouts furiously:*]

341

Stay here!

[*Her laughter rings outside. He follows the girl, shouting:*]

Stop! Stop!

[*Silence. The* NEGRO *looks up with a secret smile as the curtain falls slowly.*]

SUDDENLY LAST SUMMER

TO ANNE MEACHAM

Copyright © 1958 by Tennessee Williams

Suddenly Last Summer, with *Something Unspoken,* were presented together under the collective title of *Garden District* at the York Theatre on First Avenue in New York on January 7, 1958, by John C. Wilson and Warner Le Roy. It was directed by Herbert Machiz; the stage set was designed by Robert Soule and the costumes by Stanley Simmons. Lighting was by Lee Watson and the incidental music was by Ned Rorem. *Something Unspoken* was added to the 1953 edition of *27 Wagons Full of Cotton and Other Plays.*

CAST OF CHARACTERS

MRS. VENABLE	HORTENSE ALDEN
DR. CUKROWICZ	ROBERT LANSING
MISS FOXHILL	DONNA CAMERON
MRS. HOLLY	ELEANOR PHELPS
GEORGE HOLLY	ALAN MIXON
CATHARINE HOLLY	ANNE MEACHAM
SISTER FELICITY	NANON-KIAM

Hortense Alden as Mrs. Venable, Robert Lansing as
Dr. Cukrowicz and Anne Meacham as Catherine Holly
in SUDDENLY LAST SUMMER. *Photo by Friedman-Abeles*

SCENE ONE

The set may be as unrealistic as the decor of a dramatic ballet. It represents part of a mansion of Victorian Gothic style in the Garden District of New Orleans on a late afternoon, between late summer and early fall. The interior is blended with a fantastic garden which is more like a tropical jungle, or forest, in the prehistoric age of giant fern-forests when living creatures had flippers turning to limbs and scales to skin. The colors of this jungle-garden are violent, especially since it is steaming with heat after rain. There are massive tree-flowers that suggest organs of a body, torn out, still glistening with undried blood; there are harsh cries and sibilant hissings and thrashing sounds in the garden as if it were inhabited by beasts, serpents and birds, all of savage nature. . . .

The jungle tumult continues a few moments after the curtain rises; then subsides into relative quiet, which is occasionally broken by a new outburst.

A lady enters with the assistance of a silver-knobbed cane. She has light orange or pink hair and wears a lavender lace dress, and over her withered bosom is pinned a starfish of diamonds.

She is followed by a young blond Doctor, all in white, glacially brilliant, very, very good looking, and the old lady's manner and eloquence indicate her undeliberate response to his icy charm.

MRS. VENABLE:

Yes, this was Sebastian's garden. The Latin names of the plants were printed on tags attached to them but the print's fading out. Those ones there—[*She draws a deep breath.*]— are the oldest plants on earth, survivors from the age of the giant fern-forests. Of course in this semitropical climate— [*She takes another deep breath.*]—some of the rarest plants, such as the Venus's-flytrap—you know what this is, Doctor? The Venus's-flytrap?

DOCTOR:

An insectivorous plant?

MRS. VENABLE:

Yes, it feeds on insects. It has to be kept under glass from early fall to late spring and when it went under glass, my son, Sebastian, had to provide it with fruit flies flown in at great expense from a Florida laboratory that used fruit flies for experiments in genetics. Well, I can't do that, Doctor. [*She takes a deep breath.*] I can't, I just can't do it! It's not the expense but the—

DOCTOR:

Effort.

MRS. VENABLE:

Yes. So goodbye, Venus's-flytrap—like so much else. . . . Whew! . . . [*She draws breath.*]—I don't know why, but—! I already feel I can lean on your shoulder, Doctor—Cu?—Cu?

350

DOCTOR:

Cu-kro-wicz. It's a Polish word that means sugar, so let's make it simple and call me Doctor Sugar.

[*He returns her smile.*]

MRS. VENABLE:

Well, now, Doctor Sugar, you've seen Sebastian's garden.

[*They are advancing slowly to the patio area.*]

DOCTOR:

It's like a well-groomed jungle. . . .

MRS. VENABLE:

That's how he meant it to be, nothing was accidental, everything was planned and designed in Sebastian's life and his— [*She dabs her forehead with her handkerchief which she had taken from her reticule.*]—work!

DOCTOR:

What was your son's work, Mrs. Venable?—besides this garden?

MRS. VENABLE:

As many times as I've had to answer that question! D'you know it still shocks me a little?—to realize that Sebastian Venable the poet is still unknown outside of a small coterie of friends, including his mother.

DOCTOR:

Oh.

MRS. VENABLE:

You see, strictly speaking, his *life* was his occupation.

DOCTOR:

I see.

MRS. VENABLE:

No, you *don't* see, yet, but before I'm through, you will.—

Sebastian was a poet! That's what I meant when I said his life was his work because the work of a poet is the life of a poet and—vice versa, the life of a poet is the work of a poet, I mean you can't separate them, I mean—well, for instance, a salesman's work is one thing and his life is another—or can be. The same thing's true of—doctor, lawyer, merchant, *thief*! —But a poet's life is his work and his work is his life in a special sense because—oh, I've already talked myself breathless and dizzy.

[*The Doctor offers his arm.*]

Thank you.

DOCTOR:
Mrs. Venable, did your doctor okay this thing?

MRS. VENABLE [*breathless*]:
What thing?

DOCTOR:
Your meeting this girl that you think is responsible for your son's death?

MRS. VENABLE:
I've waited months to face her because I couldn't get to St. Mary's to face her—I've had her brought here to my house. I won't collapse! She'll collapse! I mean her lies will collapse —not my truth—not the truth. . . . *Forward march, Doctor Sugar!*

[*He conducts her slowly to the patio.*]

Ah, we've *made* it, *ha ha*! I didn't know that I was so weak on my pins! Sit down, Doctor. I'm not afraid of using every last ounce and inch of my little, leftover strength in doing just what I'm doing. I'm devoting all that's left of my life, Doctor, to the defense of a dead poet's reputation. Sebastian had no public name as a poet, he didn't want one, he refused to have one. He *dreaded, abhorred*!—false values that come from being publicly known, from fame, from personal—exploitation. . . . Oh, he'd say to me: "Violet? Mother?—You're going to outlive me!!"

DOCTOR:
What made him think that?

MRS. VENABLE:
Poets are always clairvoyant!—And he had rheumatic fever when he was fifteen and it affected a heart-valve and he wouldn't stay off horses and out of water and so forth. . . . "Violet? Mother? You're going to live longer than me, and then, when I'm gone, it will be yours, in your hands, to do whatever you please with!"—Meaning, of course, his future recognition!—That he *did* want, he wanted it after his death when it couldn't disturb him; then he did want to offer his work to the world. All right. Have I made my point, Doctor? Well, here is my son's work, Doctor, here's his life going *on*!

[*She lifts a thin gilt-edged volume from the patio table as if elevating the Host before the altar. Its gold leaf and lettering catch the afternoon sun. It says* Poem of Summer. *Her face suddenly has a different look, the look of a visionary, an exalted* religieuse. *At the same instant a bird sings clearly and purely in the garden and the old lady seems to be almost young for a moment.*]

DOCTOR [*reading the title*]:
Poem of Summer?

MRS. VENABLE:
Poem of Summer, and the date of the summer, there are twenty-five of them, he wrote one poem a year which he printed himself on an eighteenth-century hand press at his—atelier in the—French—Quarter—so no one but he could see it. . . .

[*She seems dizzy for a moment.*]

DOCTOR:
He wrote one poem a year?

MRS. VENABLE:
One for each summer that we traveled together. The other nine months of the year were really only a preparation.

DOCTOR:
Nine months?

MRS. VENABLE:
The length of a pregnancy, yes. . . .

DOCTOR:
The poem was hard to deliver?

MRS. VENABLE:
Yes, even with me! *Without* me, *impossible*, Doctor!—he wrote no poem last summer.

DOCTOR:
He died last summer?

MRS. VENABLE:
Without me he died last summer, that was his last summer's poem.

[*She staggers; he assists her toward a chair. She catches her breath with difficulty.*]

One long-ago summer—now, why am I thinking of this?—my son, Sebastian, said, "Mother?—Listen to this!"—He read me Herman Melville's description of the Encantadas, the Galapagos Islands. Quote—take five and twenty heaps of cinders dumped here and there in an outside city lot. Imagine some of them magnified into mountains, and the vacant lot, the sea. And you'll have a fit idea of the general aspect of the Encantadas, the Enchanted Isles—extinct volcanos, looking

much as the world at large might look—after a last con-
flagration—end quote. He read me that description and said
that we had to go there. And so we did go there that summer
on a chartered boat, a four-masted schooner, as close as possible to the sort of a boat that Melville must have sailed
on. . . . We saw the Encantadas, but on the Encantadas we
saw something Melville *hadn't* written about. We saw the
great sea turtles crawl up out of the sea for their annual
egg-laying. . . . Once a year the female of the sea turtle crawls
up out of the equatorial sea onto the blazing sand-beach of a
volcanic island to dig a pit in the sand and deposit her eggs
there. It's a long and dreadful thing, the depositing of the eggs
in the sand pits, and when it's finished the exhausted female
turtle crawls back to the sea half dead. She never sees her
offspring, but we did. Sebastian knew exactly when the sea
turtle eggs would be hatched out and we returned in time for
it. . . .

DOCTOR:
You went back to the—?

MRS. VENABLE:
Terrible Encantadas, those heaps of extinct volcanos, in time
to witness the hatching of the sea turtles and their desperate
flight to the sea!

[*There is a sound of harsh bird-cries in the air. She looks
up.*]

—The narrow beach, the color of caviar, was all in motion!
But the sky was in motion, too. . . .

DOCTOR:
The sky was in motion, too?

MRS. VENABLE:
—Full of flesh-eating birds and the noise of the birds, the
horrible savage cries of the—

DOCTOR:
Carnivorous birds?

MRS. VENABLE:
Over the narrow black beach of the Encantadas as the just-hatched sea turtles scrambled out of the sand pits and started their race to the sea. . . .

DOCTOR:
Race to the sea?

MRS. VENABLE:
To escape the flesh-eating birds that made the sky almost as black as the beach!

[*She gazes up again: we hear the wild, ravenous, harsh cries of the birds. The sound comes in rhythmic waves like a savage chant.*]

And the sand all alive, all alive, as the hatched sea-turtles made their dash for the sea, while the birds hovered and swooped to attack and hovered and—swooped to attack! They were diving down on the hatched sea turtles, turning them over to expose their soft undersides, tearing the undersides open and rending and eating their flesh. Sebastian guessed that possibly only a hundredth of one per cent of their number would escape to the sea. . . .

DOCTOR:
What was it about this spectacle on the beach that fascinated your son?

MRS. VENABLE:
My son was looking for—

[*Stops short: continues evasively—*]

Let's just say he was interested in sea turtles.

DOCTOR:
You started to say that your son was looking for something.

MRS. VENABLE:

[*defiantly*]

All right, I started to say that my son was looking for God and I stopped myself because I was afraid that if I said he was looking for God, you'd say to yourself, "Oh, a pretentious young crack pot!"—which Sebastian was not. All poets look for God, all good poets do, and they have to look harder for Him than priests do since they don't have the help of such famous guidebooks and well-organized expeditions as priests have with their scriptures and churches. All right! Well, now I've said it, my son was looking for God. I mean for a clear image of Him. He spent that whole blazing equatorial day in the crow's nest of the schooner watching that thing on the beach of the Endantadas till it was too dark to see it, and when he came back down the rigging, he said, Well, now I've seen Him!—and he meant God . . .

DOCTOR:

I see.

MRS. VENABLE:

For several days after that he had a fever, he was delirious with it. I took command of the ship and we sailed north by east into cooler waters . . .

[*Miss Foxhill comes out silently on rubber-soled white oxfords, and waits to be noticed. She carries a water glass.*]

Next? India, China!—In the Himalayas—

[*Notices Miss Foxhill.*]

What? Oh, elixir of—ha!—Isn't it kind of the drugstore to keep me alive!

[*Tosses down medicine with a wry face and dismisses Miss Foxhill with a slight gesture.*]

Where was I?

DOCTOR:

In the Himalayas.

MRS. VENABLE:

Oh yes, that long-ago summer. . . . In the Himalayas he almost entered a Buddhist monastery, had gone so far as to shave his head and eat just rice out of a wood bowl on a grass mat. He'd promised those sly Buddhist monks that he would give up the world and himself and all his worldly possessions to their mendicant order.—Well, I cabled his father, "For God's sake notify bank to freeze Sebastian's accounts!"—I got back this cable from my late husband's lawyer: "Mr. Venable critically ill Stop Wants you Stop Needs you Stop Immediate return advised most strongly. Stop. Cable time of arrival. . . ."

DOCTOR:

Did you go back to your husband?

MRS. VENABLE:

I made the hardest decision of my life. I stayed with my son. I got him through that crisis too. In less than a month he got up off the filthy grass mat and threw the rice bowl away— and booked us into Shepheard's Hotel in Cairo and the Ritz in Paris—. And from then on, oh, we—still lived in a—world of light and shadow. . . .

[*She turns vaguely with empty glass. He rises and takes it from her.*]

But the shadow was almost as luminous as the light.

DOCTOR:

Don't you want to sit down now?

MRS. VENABLE:

Yes, indeed I do, before I fall down.

[*He assists her into wheelchair.*]

—Are your hindlegs still on you?

DOCTOR [*still concerned over her agitation*]:
—My what? Oh—hind legs!—Yes . . .

MRS. VENABLE:
Well, then you're not a donkey, you're certainly not a donkey because I've been talking the hindlegs off a donkey—several donkeys. . . . But I had to make it clear to you that the world lost a great deal too when I lost my son last summer. . . . You would have liked my son, he would have been charmed by you. My son, Sebastian, was not a family snob or a money snob but he was a snob, all right. He was a snob about personal charm in people, he insisted upon good looks in people around him, and, oh, he had a perfect little court of young and beautiful people around him always, wherever he was, here in New *Orleans* or New York or on the Riviera or in Paris and Venice, he always had a little entourage of the beautiful and the talented and the young!

DOCTOR:
Your son was young, Mrs. Venable?

MRS. VENABLE:
Both of us were young, and stayed young, Doctor.

DOCTOR:
Could I see a photograph of your son, Mrs. Venable?

MRS. VENABLE:
Yes, indeed you could, Doctor. I'm glad that you asked to see one. I'm going to show you not one photograph but two. Here. Here is my son, Sebastian, in a Renaissance pageboy's costume at a masked ball in Cannes. Here is my son, Sebastian, in the same costume at a masked ball in Venice. These two pictures were taken twenty years apart. Now which is the older one, Doctor?

DOCTOR:
This photograph looks older.

MRS. VENABLE:

The photograph looks older but not the subject. It takes character to refuse to grow old, Doctor—successfully to refuse to. It calls for discipline, abstention. One cocktail before dinner, not two, four, six—a single lean chop and lime juice on a salad in restaurants famed for rich dishes.

[*Foxhill comes from the house.*]

FOXHILL:

Mrs. Venable, Miss Holly's mother and brother are—

[*Simultaneously Mrs. Holly and George appear in the window.*]

GEORGE:

Hi, Aunt Vi!

MRS. HOLLY:

Violet, dear, we're here.

FOXHILL:

They're here.

MRS. VENABLE:

Wait upstairs in my upstairs living room for me.

[*To Miss Foxhill:*]

Get them upstairs. I don't want them at that window during this talk.

[*To the Doctor:*]

Let's get away from the window.

[*He wheels her to stage center.*]

DOCTOR:

Mrs. Venable? Did your son have a—well—what kind of a *personal*, well, *private* life did—

MRS. VENABLE:
That's a question I wanted you to ask me.

DOCTOR:
Why?

MRS. VENABLE:
I haven't heard the girl's story except indirectly in a watered-down version, being too ill to go to hear it directly, but I've gathered enough to know that it's a hideous attack on my son's moral character which, being dead, he can't defend himself from. I have to be the defender. Now. Sit down. Listen to me . . .

[*The Doctor sits.*]

. . . before you hear whatever you're going to hear from the girl when she gets here. My son, Sebastian, was chaste. Not c-h-a-s-e-d! Oh, he was chased in that way of spelling it, too, we had to be very fleet-footed I can tell you, with his looks and his charm, to keep ahead of pursuers, every kind of pursuer!—I mean he was c-h-a-s-t-e!—Chaste. . . .

DOCTOR:
I understood what you meant, Mrs. Venable.

MRS. VENABLE:
And you *believe* me, don't you?

DOCTOR:
Yes, but—

MRS. VENABLE:
But *what*?

DOCTOR:
Chastity at—what age was your son last summer?

MRS. VENABLE:
Forty, maybe. We really didn't count birthdays. . . .

DOCTOR:
He lived a celibate life?

MRS. VENABLE:
As strictly as if he'd *vowed* to! This sounds like vanity, Doctor, but really I was actually the only one in his life that satisfied the demands he made of people. Time after time my son would let people go, dismiss them!—because their, their, their!—*attitude* toward him was—

DOCTOR:
Not as pure as—

MRS. VENABLE:
My son, Sebastian, demanded! We were a famous couple. People didn't speak of Sebastian and his mother or Mrs. Venable and her son, they said "Sebastian and Violet, Violet and Sebastian are staying at the Lido, they're at the Ritz in Madrid. Sebastian and Violet, Violet and Sebastian have taken a house at Biarritz for the season," and every appearance, every time we appeared, attention was centered on *us*! —*everyone else*! *Eclipsed*! Vanity? Ohhhh, no, Doctor, you can't call it that—

DOCTOR:
I didn't call it that.

MRS. VENABLE:
—It wasn't *folie de grandeur*, it was grandeur.

DOCTOR:
I see.

MRS. VENABLE:
An attitude toward life that's hardly been known in the world since the great Renaissance princes were crowded out of their palaces and gardens by successful shopkeepers!

DOCTOR:
I see.

MRS. VENABLE:
Most people's lives—what are they but trails of debris, each day more debris, more debris, long, long trails of debris with nothing to clean it all up but, finally, death. . . .

[*We hear lyric music.*]

My son, Sebastian, and I constructed our days, each day, we would—carve out each day of our lives like a piece of sculpture.—Yes, we left behind us a trail of days like a gallery of sculpture! But, last summer—

[*Pause: the music continues.*]

I can't forgive him for it, not even now that he's paid for it with his life!—he let in this—*vandal*! This—

DOCTOR:
The girl that—?

MRS. VENABLE:
That you're going to meet here this afternoon! Yes. He admitted this vandal and with her tongue for a hatchet she's gone about smashing our legend, the memory of—

DOCTOR:
Mrs. Venable, what do you think is her reason?

MRS. VENABLE:
Lunatics don't have reason!

DOCTOR:
I mean what do you think is her—motive?

MRS. VENABLE:
What a question!—We put the bread in her mouth and the clothes on her back. People that like you for that or even forgive you for it are, are—*hen's teeth,* Doctor. The role of

363

the benefactor is worse than thankless, it's the role of a victim, Doctor, a sacrificial victim, yes, they want your blood, Doctor, they want your blood on the altar steps of their *outraged, outrageous* egos!

DOCTOR:
Oh. You mean she resented the—

MRS. VENABLE:
Loathed!—They can't shut her up at St. Mary's.

DOCTOR:
I thought she'd been there for months.

MRS. VENABLE:
I mean keep her *still* there. She *babbles*! They couldn't shut her up in Cabeza de Lobo or at the clinic in Paris—she babbled, babbled!—smashing my son's reputation.—On the *Berengaria* bringing her back to the States she broke out of the stateroom and babbled, babbled; even at the airport when she was flown down here, she babbled a bit of her story before they could whisk her into an ambulance to St. Mary's. This is a reticule, Doctor. [*She raises a cloth bag.*] A catchall, carry-all bag for an elderly lady which I turned into last summer. . . . Will you open it for me, my hands are stiff, and fish out some cigarettes and a cigarette holder.

[*He does.*]

DOCTOR:
I don't have matches.

MRS. VENABLE:
I think there's a table-lighter on the table.

DOCTOR:
Yes, there is,

[*He lights it, it flames up high.*]
My Lord, what a torch!

MRS. VENABLE [*with a sudden, sweet smile*]:
"So shines a good deed in a naughty world," Doctor—
Sugar. . . .

[*Pause. A bird sings sweetly in the garden.*]

DOCTOR:
Mrs. Venable?

MRS. VENABLE:
Yes?

DOCTOR:
In your letter last week you made some reference to a, to a—
fund of some kind, an endowment fund of—

MRS. VENABLE:
I wrote you that my lawyers and bankers and certified public
accountants were setting up the Sebastian Venable Memorial
Foundation to subsidize the work of young people like you
that are pushing out the frontiers of art and science but have
a financial problem. You have a financial problem, don't you,
Doctor?

DOCTOR:
Yes, we do have that problem. My work is such a *new* and
radical thing that people in charge of state funds are naturally
a little scared of it and keep us on a small budget, so small
that—. We need a separate ward for my patients, I need
trained assistants, I'd like to marry a girl I can't afford to
marry!—But there's also the problem of getting right patients,
not just—criminal psychopaths that the state turns over to us
for my operation!—because it's—well—risky. . . . I don't want
to turn you against my work at Lion's View but I have to be
honest with you. There is a good deal of risk in my operation.
Whenever you enter the brain with a foreign object . . .

MRS. VENABLE:
Yes.

DOCTOR:
—Even a needle-thin knife . . .

MRS. VENABLE:
Yes.

DOCTOR:
—In a skilled surgeon's fingers . . .

MRS. VENABLE:
Yes.

DOCTOR:
—There is a good deal of risk involved in—the operation. . . .

MRS. VENABLE:
You said that it pacifies them, it quiets them down, it suddenly makes them peaceful.

DOCTOR:
Yes. It does that, that much we already know, but—

MRS. VENABLE:
What?

DOCTOR:
Well, it will be ten years before we can tell if the immediate benefits of the operation will be lasting or—passing or even if there'd still be—and this is what haunts me about it!—any possibility, afterwards, of—reconstructing a—totally sound person, it may be that the person will always be limited afterwards, relieved of acute disturbances but—*limited,* Mrs. Venable. . . .

MRS. VENABLE:
Oh, but what a blessing to them, Doctor, to be just peaceful, to be just suddenly—peaceful. . . .

[*A bird sings sweetly in the garden.*]

After all that horror, after those nightmares: just to be able to lift up their eyes and see—[*She looks up and raises a hand to indicate the sky.*]—a sky not as black with savage, devouring birds as the sky that we saw in the Encantadas, Doctor.

DOCTOR:

—Mrs. Venable? I can't guarantee that a lobotomy would stop her—*babbling*!!

MRS. VENABLE:

That may be, maybe not, but after the operation, who would *believe* her, Doctor?

[*Pause: faint jungle music.*]

DOCTOR [*quietly*]:

My God. [*Pause.*]—Mrs. Venable, suppose after meeting the girl and observing the girl and hearing this story she babbles— I still shouldn't feel that her condition's—intractable enough! to justify the risks of—suppose I shouldn't feel that non-surgical treatment such as insulin shock and electric shock and—

MRS. VENABLE:

SHE'S HAD ALL THAT AT SAINT MARY'S!! Nothing else is left for her.

DOCTOR:

But if I disagreed with you? [*Pause.*]

MRS. VENABLE:

That's just part of a question: finish the question, Doctor.

DOCTOR:

Would you still be interested in my work at Lion's View? I mean would the Sebastian Venable Memorial Foundation still be interested in it?

MRS. VENABLE:

Aren't we always more interested in a thing that concerns us personally, Doctor?

DOCTOR:
Mrs. Venable!!

[*Catharine Holly appears between the lace window curtains.*]

You're such an innocent person that it doesn't occur to you, it obviously hasn't even occurred to you that anybody less innocent than you are could possibly interpret this offer of a subsidy as—well, as sort of a *bribe?*

MRS. VENABLE [*laughs, throwing her head back*]:
Name it that—I don't care—. There's just two things to remember. She's a destroyer. My son was a *creator!*—Now if my honesty's shocked you—pick up your little black bag without the subsidy in it, and run away from this garden!—Nobody's heard our conversation but you and I, Doctor Sugar. . . .

[*Miss Foxhill comes out of the house and calls.*]

MISS FOXHILL:
Mrs. Venable?

MRS. VENABLE:
What is it, what do you want, Miss Foxhill?

MISS FOXHILL:
Mrs. Venable? Miss Holly is here, with—

[*Mrs. Venable sees Catharine at the window.*]

MRS. VENABLE:
Oh, my God. There she is, in the window!—I told you I didn't want her to enter my house again, I told you to meet them at the door and lead them around the side of the house to the garden and you didn't listen. I'm not ready to face her. I have to have my five o'clock cocktail first, to fortify me. Take my chair inside. Doctor? Are you still here? I thought you'd run out of the garden. I'm going back through the

garden to the other entrance. Doctor? Sugar? You may stay in the garden if you wish to or run out of the garden if you wish to or go in this way if you wish to or do anything that you wish to but I'm going to have my five o'clock daiquiri, *frozen!*—before I face her. . . .

[*All during this she has been sailing very slowly off through the garden like a stately vessel at sea with a fair wind in her sails, a pirate's frigate or a treasure-laden galleon. The young Doctor stares at Catharine framed by the lace window curtains. Sister Felicity appears beside her and draws her away from the window. Music: an ominous fanfare. Sister Felicity holds the door open for Catharine as the Doctor starts quickly forward. He starts to pick up his bag but doesn't. Catharine rushes out, they almost collide with each other.*]

CATHARINE:
Excuse me.

DOCTOR:
I'm sorry. . . .

[*She looks after him as he goes into the house.*]

SISTER FELICITY:
Sit down and be still till your family come outside.

DIM OUT

SCENE TWO

Catharine removes a cigarette from a lacquered box on the table and lights it. The following quick, cadenced lines are accompanied by quick, dancelike movement, almost formal, as the Sister in her sweeping white habit, which should be starched to make a crackling sound, pursues the girl about the white wicker patio table and among the wicker chairs: this can be accompanied by quick music.

SISTER:
What did you take out of that box on the table?

CATHARINE:
Just a cigarette, Sister.

SISTER:
Put it back in the box.

CATHARINE:
Too late, it's already lighted.

370

SISTER:
Give it here.

CATHARINE:
Oh, please, let me smoke, Sister!

SISTER:
Give it here.

CATHARINE:
Please, Sister Felicity.

SISTER:
Catharine, give it here. You know that you're not allowed to smoke at Saint Mary's.

CATHARINE:
We're not at Saint Mary's, this is an afternoon out.

SISTER:
You're still in my charge. I can't permit you to smoke because the last time you smoked you dropped a lighted cigarette on your dress and started a fire.

CATHARINE:
Oh, I did not start a fire. I just burned a hole in my skirt because I was half unconscious under medication. [*She is now back of a white wicker chair.*]

SISTER [*overlapping her*]:
Catharine, give it here.

CATHARINE:
Don't be such a bully!

SISTER:
Disobedience has to be paid for later.

CATHARINE:
All right, I'll pay for it later.

SISTER [*overlapping*]:
Give me that cigarette or I'll make a report that'll put you

371

right back on the violent ward, if you don't. [*She claps her hands twice and holds one hand out across the table.*]

CATHARINE [*overlapping*]:
I'm not being violent, Sister.

SISTER [*overlapping*]:
Give me that cigarette, I'm holding my hand out for it!

CATHARINE:
All right, take it, here, take it!

[*She thrusts the lighted end of the cigarette into the palm of the Sister's hand. The Sister cries out and sucks her burned hand.*]

SISTER:
You burned me with it!

CATHARINE:
I'm sorry, I didn't mean to.

SISTER [*shocked, hurt*]:
You deliberately burned me!

CATHARINE [*overlapping*]:
You said give it to you and so I gave it to you.

SISTER [*overlapping*]:
You stuck the lighted end of that cigarette in my hand!

CATHARINE [*overlapping*]:
I'm *sick*, I'm *sick*!—of being *bossed* and *bullied*!

SISTER [*commandingly*]:
Sit down!

[*Catharine sits down stiffly in a white wicker chair on fore-stage, facing the audience. The Sister resumes sucking the burned palm of her hand. Ten beats. Then from inside the house the whirr of a mechanical mixer.*]

CATHARINE:
There goes the Waring Mixer, Aunt Violet's about to have her
five o'clock frozen daiquiri, you could set a watch by it! [*She
almost laughs. Then she draws a deep, shuddering breath and
leans back in her chair, but her hands remain clenched on the
white wicker arms.*]—We're in Sebastian's garden. *My God,
I can still cry!*

SISTER:
Did you have any medication before you went out?

CATHARINE:
No. I didn't have any. Will you give me some, Sister?

SISTER [*almost gently*]:
I can't. I wasn't told to. However, I think the doctor will give
you something.

CATHARINE:
The young blond man I bumped into?

SISTER:
Yes. The young doctor's a specialist from another hospital.

CATHARINE:
What hospital?

SISTER:
A word to the wise is sufficient. . . .

[*The Doctor has appeared in the window.*]

CATHARINE [*rising abruptly*]:
I knew I was being watched, he's in the window, staring out
at me!

SISTER:
Sit down and be still. Your family's coming outside.

CATHARINE [*overlapping*]:
LION'S VIEW, IS IT! DOCTOR?

[*She has advanced toward the bay window. The Doctor draws back, letting the misty white gauze curtains down to obscure him.*]

SISTER [*rising with a restraining gesture which is almost pitying*]:

Sit down, dear.

CATHARINE:

IS IT LION'S VIEW? DOCTOR?!

SISTER:

Be still. . . .

CATHARINE:

WHEN CAN I STOP RUNNING DOWN THAT STEEP WHITE STREET IN CABEZA DE LOBO?

SISTER:

Catharine, dear, sit down.

CATHARINE:

I loved him, Sister! Why wouldn't he let me save him? I tried to hold onto his hand but he struck me away and ran, ran, ran in the wrong direction, Sister!

SISTER:

Catharine, dear—be still.

[*The Sister sneezes.*]

CATHARINE:

Bless you, Sister. [*She says this absently, still watching the window.*]

SISTER:

Thank you.

CATHARINE:

The Doctor's still at the window but he's too blond to hide

374

behind window curtains, he catches the light, he shines through them. [*She turns from the window.*]—We were *going* to blonds, blonds were next on the menu.

SISTER:
Be still now. Quiet, dear.

CATHARINE:
Cousin Sebastian said he was famished for blonds, he was fed up with the dark ones and was famished for blonds. All the travel brochures he picked up were advertisements of the blond northern countries. I think he'd already booked us to—Copenhagen or—Stockholm.—Fed up with dark ones, famished for light ones: that's how he talked about people, as if they were—items on a menu.—"That one's delicious-looking, that one is appetizing," or "that one is *not* appetizing"—I think because he was really nearly half-starved from living on pills and salads. . . .

SISTER:
Stop it!—Catharine, be still.

CATHARINE:
He liked me and so I loved him. . . . [*She cries a little again.*] If he'd kept hold of my hand I could have saved him!—Sebastian suddenly said to me last summer: "Let's fly north, little bird—I want to walk under those radiant, cold northern lights—I've never *seen* the aurora borealis!"—Somebody said once or wrote, once: "We're all of us children in a vast kindergarten trying to spell God's name with the wrong alphabet blocks!"

MRS. HOLLY [*offstage*]:
Sister?

[*The Sister rises.*]

CATHARINE [*rising*]:
I think it's *me* they're calling, they call *me* "Sister," Sister!

SCENE THREE

The Sister resumes her seat impassively as the girl's mother and younger brother appear from the garden. The mother, Mrs. Holly, is a fatuous Southern lady who requires no other description. The brother, George, is typically good looking, he has the best "looks" of the family, tall and elegant of figure. They enter.

MRS. HOLLY:
Catharine, dear! Catharine—

[They embrace tentatively.]

Well, well! Doesn't she look fine, George?

GEORGE:
Uh huh.

CATHARINE:
They send you to the beauty parlor whenever you're going to have a family visit. Other times you look awful, you can't

have a compact or lipstick or anything made out of metal because they're afraid you'll swallow it.

MRS. HOLLY [*giving a tinkly little laugh*]:
I think she looks just splendid, don't you, George?

GEORGE:
Can't we talk to her without the nun for a minute?

MRS. HOLLY:
Yes, I'm sure it's all right to. Sister?

CATHARINE:
Excuse me, Sister Felicity, this is my mother, Mrs. Holly, and my brother, George.

SISTER:
How do you do.

GEORGE:
How d'ya do.

CATHARINE:
This is Sister Felicity. . . .

MRS. HOLLY:
We're so happy that Catharine's at Saint Mary's! So very grateful for all you're doing for her.

SISTER [*sadly, mechanically*]:
We do the best we can for her, Mrs. Holly.

MRS. HOLLY:
I'm sure you do. Yes, well—I wonder if you would mind if we had a little private chat with our Cathie?

SISTER:
I'm not supposed to let her out of my sight.

MRS. HOLLY:
It's just for a minute. You can sit in the hall or the garden

and we'll call you right back here the minute the private part of the little talk is over.

[*Sister Felicity withdraws with an uncertain nod and a swish of starched fabric.*]

GEORGE [*to Catharine*]:
Jesus! What are you up to? Huh? Sister? Are you trying to RUIN us?!

MRS. HOLLY:
GAWGE! WILL YOU BE QUIET. You're upsetting your sister!

[*He jumps up and stalks off a little, rapping his knee with his zipper-covered tennis racket.*]

CATHARINE:
How elegant George looks.

MRS. HOLLY:
George inherited Cousin Sebastian's wardrobe but everything else is in probate! Did you know that? That everything else is in probate and Violet can keep it in probate just as long as she wants to?

CATHARINE:
Where is Aunt Violet?

MRS. HOLLY:
George, come back here!

[*He does, sulkily.*]

Violet's on her way down.

GEORGE:
Yeah. Aunt Violet has an elevator now.

MRS. HOLLY:
Yais, she has, she's had an elevator installed where the back

stairs were, and, Sister, it's the cutest little thing you ever did see! It's paneled in Chinese lacquer, black an' gold Chinese lacquer, with lovely bird-pictures on it. But there's only room for two people at a time in it. George and I came down on foot.—I think she's havin' her frozen daiquiri now, she still has a frozen daiquiri promptly at five o'clock ev'ry afternoon in the world . . . in warm weather. . . . Sister, the horrible death of Sebastian just about *killed* her!—She's now slightly better . . . but it's a question of time.—Dear, you know, I'm sure that you understand, why we haven't been out to see you at Saint Mary's. They said you were too disturbed, and a family visit might disturb you more. But I want you to know that nobody, absolutely nobody in the city, knows a thing about what you've been through. Have they, George? Not a thing. Not a soul even knows that you've come back from Europe. When people enquire, when they question us about you, we just say that you've stayed abroad to study something or other. [*She catches her breath.*] Now. Sister?—I want you to please be *very* careful what you say to your Aunt Violet about what happened to Sebastian in Cabeza de Lobo.

CATHARINE:
What do you want me to say about what—?

MRS. HOLLY:
Just don't repeat that same fantastic story! For my sake and George's sake, the sake of your brother and mother, don't repeat that horrible story again! Not to Violet! Will you?

CATHARINE:
Then I am going to have to tell Aunt Violet what happened to her son in Cabeza de Lobo?

MRS. HOLLY:
Honey, that's why you're here. She has *INSISTED* on hearing it straight from YOU!

379

GEORGE:

You were the only witness to it, Cathie.

CATHARINE:

No, there were others. That *ran.*

MRS. HOLLY:

Oh, Sister, you've just had a little sort of a—*nightmare* about it! Now, listen to me, will you, Sister? Sebastian has left, has BEQUEATHED!—to you an' Gawge in his *will*—

GEORGE [*religiously*]:

To each of us, fifty grand, each!—AFTER! TAXES!—GET IT?

CATHARINE:

Oh, yes, but if they give me an injection—I won't have any choice but to tell exactly what happened in Cabeza de Lobo last summer. Don't you see? I won't have any choice but to tell the truth. It makes you tell the truth because it shuts something off that might make you able not to and *everything* comes out, decent or *not* decent, you have no control, but always, always the truth!

MRS. HOLLY:

Catharine, darling. I don't know the full story, but surely you're not too sick in your *head* to know in your *heart* that the story you've been telling is just—too—

GEORGE [*cutting in*]:

Cathie, Cathie, you got to forget that story! Can'tcha? For *your* fifty grand?

MRS. HOLLY:

Because if Aunt Vi contests the will, and we know she'll contest it, she'll keep it in the courts forever!—We'll be—

GEORGE:

It's in PROBATE NOW! And'll never get out of probate

380

until you drop that story—we can't afford to hire lawyers good enough to contest it! So if you don't stop telling that crazy story, we won't have a pot to—cook *greens* in!

[*He turns away with a fierce grimace and a sharp, abrupt wave of his hand, as if slapping down something. Catharine stares at his tall back for a moment and laughs wildly.*]

MRS. HOLLY:
Catharine, don't laugh like that, it scares me, Catharine.

[*Jungle birds scream in the garden.*]

GEORGE [*turning his back on his sister*]:
Cathie, the money is all tied up.

[*He stoops over sofa, hands on flannel knees, speaking directly into Catharine's face as if she were hard of hearing. She raises a hand to touch his cheek affectionately; he seizes the hand and removes it but holds it tight.*]

If Aunt Vi decided to contest Sebastian's will that leaves us all of this cash?!—Am I coming through to you?

CATHARINE:
Yes, little brother, you are.

GEORGE:
You see, Mama, she's crazy like a coyote!

[*He gives her a quick cold kiss.*]

We won't get a single damn penny, honest t' God we won't! So you've just GOT to stop tellin' that story about what you say happened to Cousin Sebastian in Cabeza de Lobo, even if it's what it *couldn't* be, TRUE!—You got to drop it, Sister, you can't tell such a story to civilized people in a civilized up-to-date country!

MRS. HOLLY:
Cathie, why, why, why!—did you invent such a tale?

381

CATHARINE:

But, Mother, I DIDN'T invent it. I know it's a hideous story but it's a true story of our time and the world we live in and what did truly happen to Cousin Sebastian in Cabeza de Lobo. . . .

GEORGE:

Oh, then you are going to tell it. Mama, she *IS* going to tell it! Right to Aunt Vi, and lose us a hundred thousand! —Cathie? You are a BITCH!

MRS. HOLLY:

GAWGE!

GEORGE:

I repeat it, a bitch! She isn't crazy, Mama, she's no more crazy than I am, she's just, just—PERVERSE! Was ALWAYS!— perverse. . . .

[*Catharine turns away and breaks into quiet sobbing.*]

MRS. HOLLY:

Gawge, Gawge, apologize to Sister, this is no way for you to talk to your sister. You come right back over here and tell your sweet little sister you're sorry you spoke like that to her!

GEORGE [*turning back to Catharine*]:

I'm sorry, Cathie, but you know we NEED that money! Mama and me, we—Cathie? I got *ambitions*! And, Cathie, I'm YOUNG!—I *want* things, I *need* them, Cathie! So will you please think about ME? Us?

MISS FOXHILL [*offstage*]:

Mrs. Holly? Mrs. Holly?

MRS. HOLLY:

Somebody's callin' fo' me. Catharine, Gawge put it very badly but you know that it's TRUE! WE DO HAVE TO GET

382

WHAT SEBASTIAN HAS LEFT US IN HIS WILL, DEAR-
EST! AND YOU WON'T LET US DOWN? PROMISE?
YOU WON'T? LET US DOWN?

GEORGE [*fiercely shouting*]: HERE COMES AUNT VI!
Mama, Cathie, Aunt Violet's—here is Aunt Vi!

SCENE FOUR

Mrs. Venable enters downstage area. Entrance music.

MRS. HOLLY:
Cathie! Here's Aunt Vi!

MRS. VENABLE:
She sees me and I see her. That's all that's necessary. Miss
Foxhill, put my chair in this corner. Crank the back up a
little.

[*Miss Foxhill does this business.*]

More. More. Not that much!—Let it back down a little. All
right. Now, then. I'll have my frozen daiquiri, now. . . . Do
any of you want coffee?

GEORGE:
I'd like a chocolate malt.

MRS. HOLLY:
Gawge!

MRS. VENABLE:
This isn't a drugstore.

MRS. HOLLY:
Oh, Gawge is just being Gawge.

MRS. VENABLE:
That's what I *thought* he was being!

[*An uncomfortable silence falls. Miss Foxhill creeps out like a burglar. She speaks in a breathless whisper, presenting a cardboard folder toward Mrs. Venable.*]

MISS FOXHILL:
Here's the portfolio marked Cabeza de Lobo. It has all your correspondence with the police there and the American consul.

MRS. VENABLE:
I asked for the *English transcript*! It's in a separate—

MISS FOXHILL:
Separate, yes, here it is!

MRS. VENABLE:
Oh . . .

MISS FOXHILL:
And here's the report of the private investigators and here's the report of—

MRS. VENABLE:
Yes, yes, yes! Where's the doctor?

MISS FOXHILL:
On the phone in the library!

MRS. VENABLE:
Why does he choose such a moment to make a phone-call?

MISS FOXHILL:
He didn't make a phone-call, he received a phone-call from—

MRS. VENABLE:

Miss Foxhill, why are you talking to me like a burglar!?

[*Miss Foxhill giggles a little desperately.*]

CATHARINE:

Aunt Violet, she's frightened.—Can I move? Can I get up and move around till it starts?

MRS. HOLLY:

Cathie, Cathie, dear, did Gawge tell you that he received bids from every good fraternity on the Tulane campus and went Phi Delt because Paul Junior did?

MRS. VENABLE:

I see that he had the natural tact and good taste to come here this afternoon outfitted from head to foot in clothes that belonged to my son!

GEORGE:

You gave 'em to me, Aunt Vi.

MRS. VENABLE:

I didn't know you'd parade them in front of me, George.

MRS. HOLLY [*quickly*]:

Gawge, tell Aunt Violet how grateful you are for—

GEORGE:

I found a little Jew tailor on Britannia Street that makes alterations so good you'd never guess that they weren't cut *out* for me to *begin* with!

MRS. HOLLY:

AND so reasonable!—Luckily, since it seems that Sebastian's wonderful, wonderful bequest to Gawge an' Cathie is going to be tied up a while!?

GEORGE:

Aunt Vi? About the will?

[*Mrs. Holly coughs.*]

I was just wondering if we can't figure out some way to, to—

MRS. HOLLY:
Gawge means to EXPEDITE it! To get through the red tape quicker?

MRS. VENABLE:
I understand his meaning. Foxhill, get the Doctor.

[*She has risen with her cane and hobbled to the door.*]

MISS FOXHILL [*exits calling*]:
Doctor!

MRS. HOLLY:
Gawge, no more about money.

GEORGE:
How do we know we'll ever see her again?

[*Catharine gasps and rises; she moves downstage, followed quickly by Sister Felicity.*]

SISTER [*mechanically*]:
What's wrong, dear?

CATHARINE:
I think I'm just dreaming this, it doesn't seem real!

[*Miss Foxhill comes back out, saying:*]

FOXHILL:
He had to answer an urgent call from Lion's View.

[*Slight, tense pause.*]

MRS. HOLLY:
Violet! *Not* Lion's View!

[*Sister Felicity had started conducting Catharine back to the patio; she stops her, now.*]

SISTER:
Wait, dear.

CATHARINE:
What for? I know what's coming.

MRS. VENABLE [*at same time*]:
Why? Are you all prepared to put out a thousand a month plus extra charges for treatments to keep the girl at St. Mary's?

MRS. HOLLY:
Cathie? Cathie, dear?

[*Catharine has returned with the Sister.*]

Tell Aunt Violet how grateful you are for her makin' it possible for you to rest an' recuperate at such a sweet, sweet place as St. Mary's!

CATHARINE:
No place for lunatics is a sweet, sweet place.

MRS. HOLLY:
But the food's good there. Isn't the food good there?

CATHARINE:
Just give me written permission not to eat fried grits. I had yard privileges till I refused to eat fried grits.

SISTER:
She lost yard privileges because she couldn't be trusted in the yard without constant supervision or even with it because she'd run to the fence and make signs to cars on the highway.

CATHARINE:
Yes, I did, I did that because I've been trying for weeks to get a message out of that "sweet, sweet place."

MRS. HOLLY:
What message, dear?

CATHARINE:
I got panicky, Mother.

MRS. HOLLY:
Sister, I don't understand.

GEORGE:
What're you scared of, Sister?

CATHARINE:
What they might do to me now, after they've done all the rest!—That man in the window's a specialist from Lion's View! We get newspapers. I know what they're . . .

[*The Doctor comes out.*]

MRS. VENABLE:
Why, Doctor, I thought you'd left us with just that little black bag to remember you by!

DOCTOR:
Oh, no. Don't you remember our talk? I had to answer a call about a patient that—

MRS. VENABLE:
This is Dr. Cukrowicz. He says it means "sugar" and we can call him "Sugar"—

[*George laughs.*]

He's a specialist from Lion's View.

CATHARINE [*cutting in*]:
WHAT DOES HE SPECIALIZE IN?

MRS. VENABLE:
Something new. When other treatments have failed.

[*Pause. The jungle clamor comes up and subsides again.*]

CATHARINE:
Do you want to bore a hole in my skull and turn a knife in my brain? Everything else was done to me!

389

[*Mrs. Holly sobs. George raps his knee with the tennis racket.*]

You'd have to have my mother's permission for that.

MRS. VENABLE:
I'm paying to keep you in a private asylum.

CATHARINE:
You're not my legal guardian.

MRS. VENABLE:
Your mother's dependent on me. All of you are!—Financially. . . .

CATHARINE:
I think the situation is—clear to me, now. . . .

MRS. VENABLE:
Good! In that case. . . .

DOCTOR:
I think a quiet atmosphere will get us the best results.

MRS. VENABLE:
I don't know what you mean by a quiet atmosphere. She shouted, I didn't.

DOCTOR:
Mrs. Venable, let's try to keep things on a quiet level, now. Your niece seems to be disturbed.

MRS. VENABLE:
She has every reason to be. She took my son from me, and then she—

CATHARINE:
Aunt Violet, you're not being fair.

MRS. VENABLE:
Oh, aren't I?

CATHARINE [*to the others*]:
She's not being fair.

[*Then back to Mrs. Venable:*]

Aunt Violet, you know why Sebastian asked me to travel with him.

MRS. VENABLE:
Yes, I *do* know why!

CATHARINE:
You weren't able to travel. You'd had a—[*She stops short.*]

MRS. VENABLE:
Go on! *What* had I had? Are you afraid to say it in front of the Doctor? She meant that I had a stroke.—I DID NOT HAVE A STROKE!—I had a slight aneurism. You know what that is, Doctor? A little vascular convulsion! Not a hemorrhage, just a little convulsion of a blood vessel. I had it when I discovered that she was trying to take my son away from me. Then I had it. It gave a little temporary—muscular —contraction.—To one side of my face. . . . [*She crosses back into main acting area.*] These people are not blood relatives of mine, they're my dead husband's relations. I always detested these people, my dead husband's sister and—her two worthless children. But I did more than my duty to keep their heads above water. To please my son, whose weakness was being excessively softhearted, I went to the expense and humiliation, yes, public humiliation, of giving this girl a debut which was a fiasco. Nobody liked her when I brought her out. Oh, she had some kind of—notoriety! She had a sharp tongue that some people mistook for wit. A habit of laughing in the faces of decent people which would infuriate them, and also reflected adversely on me and Sebastian, too. But, he, Sebastian, was amused by this girl. While I was disgusted, sickened. And halfway through the season, she was dropped off the

391

party lists, yes, dropped off the lists in spite of my position. Why? Because she'd lost her head over a young married man, made a scandalous scene at a Mardi Gras ball, in the middle of the ballroom. Then everybody dropped her like a hot—rock, but—[*She loses her breath.*] My son, Sebastian, still felt sorry for her and took her with him last summer instead of me. . . .

CATHARINE [*springing up with a cry*]:
I can't change truth, I'm not God! I'm not even sure that He could, I don't think God can change truth! How can I change the story of what happened to her son in Cabeza de Lobo?

MRS. VENABLE [*at the same time*]:
She was in love with my son!

CATHARINE [*overlapping*]:
Let me go back to Saint Mary's. Sister Felicity, let's go back to Saint—

MRS. VENABLE [*overlapping*]:
Oh, no! That's not where you'll go!

CATHARINE [*overlapping*]:
All right, *Lion's View* but don't ask me to—

MRS. VENABLE [*overlapping*]:
You *know* that you were!

CATHARINE [*overlapping*]:
That I was *what,* Aunt Violet?

MRS. VENABLE [*overlapping*]:
Don't call me "Aunt," you're the niece of my dead husband, not me!

MRS. HOLLY [*overlapping*]:
Catharine, Catharine, don't upset your—Doctor? Oh, Doctor!

[*But the Doctor is calmly observing the scene, with detach-*

ment. The jungle-garden is loud with the sounds of its feathered and scaled inhabitants.]

CATHARINE:
I don't want to, I didn't want to come here! I know what she thinks, she thinks I murdered her son, she thinks that I was responsible for his death.

MRS. VENABLE:
That's right. I told him when he told me that he was going with you in my place last summer that I'd never see him again and I never did. And only you know why!

CATHARINE:
Oh, my God, I—

[*She rushes out toward garden, followed immediately by the Sister.*]

SISTER:
Miss Catharine, Miss Catharine—

DOCTOR [*overlapping*]:
Mrs. Venable?

SISTER [*overlapping*]:
Miss Catharine?

DOCTOR [*overlapping*]:
Mrs. Venable?

MRS. VENABLE:
What?

DOCTOR:
I'd like to be left alone with Miss Catharine for a few minutes.

MRS. HOLLY:
George, talk to her, George.

[*George crouches appealingly before the old lady's chair, peering close into her face, a hand on her knee.*]

393

GEORGE:
Aunt Vi? Cathie can't go to Lion's View. Everyone in the Garden District would know you'd put your niece in a state asylum, Aunt Vi.

MRS. VENABLE:
Foxhill!

GEORGE:
What do you want, Aunt Vi?

MRS. VENABLE:
Let go of my chair. Foxhill? Get me away from these people!

GEORGE:
Aunt Vi, listen, think of the talk it—

MRS. VENABLE:
I can't get up! Push me, push me away!

GEORGE [*rising but holding chair*]:
I'll push her, Miss Foxhill.

MRS. VENABLE:
Let go of my chair or—

MISS FOXHILL:
Mr. Holly, I—

GEORGE:
I got to talk to her.

[*He pushes her chair downstage.*]

MRS. VENABLE:
Foxhill!

MISS FOXHILL:
Mr. Holly, she doesn't want you to push her.

GEORGE:
I know what I'm doing, leave me alone with Aunt Vi!

MRS. VENABLE:
Let go me or I'll *strike* you!

GEORGE:
Oh, Aunt Vi!

MRS. VENABLE:
Foxhill!

MRS. HOLLY:
George—

GEORGE:
Aunt Vi?

[*She strikes at him with her cane. He releases the chair and Miss Foxhill pushes her off. He trots after her a few steps, then he returns to Mrs. Holly, who is sobbing into a handkerchief. He sighs, and sits down beside her, taking her hand. The scene fades as light is brought up on Catharine and the Sister in the garden. The Doctor comes up to them. Mrs. Holly stretches her arms out to George, sobbing, and he crouches before her chair and rests his head in her lap. She strokes his head. During this: the Sister has stood beside Catharine, holding onto her arm.*]

CATHARINE:
You don't have to hold onto me. I can't run away.

DOCTOR:
Miss Catharine?

CATHARINE:
What?

DOCTOR:
Your aunt is a very sick woman. She had a stroke last spring?

CATHARINE:
Yes, she did, but she'll never admit it. . . .

DOCTOR:
You have to understand why.

CATHARINE:
I do, I understand why. I didn't want to come here.

DOCTOR:
Miss Catharine, do you hate her?

CATHARINE:
I don't understand what hate is. How can you hate anybody and still be sane? You see, I still think I'm sane!

DOCTOR:
You think she did have a stroke?

CATHARINE:
She had a slight stroke in April. It just affected one side, the left side, of her face . . . but it was disfiguring, and after that, Sebastian couldn't use her.

DOCTOR:
Use her? Did you say use her?

[*The sounds of the jungle-garden are not loud but ominous.*]

CATHARINE:
Yes, we all use each other and that's what we think of as love, and not being able to use each other is what's—*hate.* . . .

DOCTOR:
Do you hate her, Miss Catharine?

CATHARINE:
Didn't you ask me that, once? And didn't I say that I didn't understand hate. A ship struck an iceberg at sea—everyone sinking—

DOCTOR:
Go on, Miss Catharine!

CATHARINE:
But that's no reason for everyone drowning for hating everyone drowning! Is it, Doctor?

DOCTOR:
Tell me: what was your feeling for your cousin Sebastian?

CATHARINE:
He liked me and so I loved him.

DOCTOR:
In what way did you love him?

CATHARINE:
The only way he'd accept:—a sort of motherly way. I tried
to save him, Doctor.

DOCTOR:
From what? Save him from what?

CATHARINE:
Completing!—a sort of!—*image*!—he had of himself as a
sort of!—*sacrifice* to a!—*terrible* sort of a—

DOCTOR:
—God?

CATHARINE:
Yes, a—*cruel* one, Doctor!

DOCTOR:
How did you feel about that?

CATHARINE:
Doctor, my feelings are the sort of feelings that you have in
a dream. . . .

DOCTOR:
Your life doesn't seem real to you?

CATHARINE:

Suddenly last winter I began to write my journal in the third person.

[*He grasps her elbow and leads her out upon forestage. At the same time Miss Foxhill wheels Mrs. Venable off, Mrs. Holly weeps into a handkerchief and George rises and shrugs and turns his back to the audience.*]

DOCTOR:

Something happened last winter?

CATHARINE:

At a Mardi Gras ball some—some boy that took me to it got too drunk to stand up! [*A short, mirthless note of laughter.*] I wanted to go home. My coat was in the cloakroom, they couldn't find the check for it in his pockets. I said, "Oh, hell, let it go!"—I started out for a taxi. Somebody took my arm and said, "I'll drive you home." He took off his coat as we left the hotel and put it over my shoulders, and then I looked at him and—I don't think I'd ever even seen him before then, really!—He took me home in his car but took me another place first. We stopped near the Duelling Oaks at the end of Esplanade Street. . . . Stopped!—I said, "What for?"—He didn't answer, just struck a match in the car to light a cigarette in the car and I looked at him in the car and I knew "what for"!—I think I got out of the car before he got out of the car, and we walked through the wet grass to the great misty oaks as if somebody was calling us for help there!

[*Pause. The subdued, toneless bird-cries in the garden turn to a single bird song.*]

DOCTOR:

After that?

CATHARINE:

I lost him.—He took me home and said an awful thing to

me. "We'd better forget it," he said, "my wife's expecting a child and——."—I just entered the house and sat there thinking a little and then I suddenly called a taxi and went right back to the Roosevelt Hotel ballroom. The ball was still going on. I thought I'd gone back to pick up my borrowed coat but that wasn't what I'd gone back for. I'd gone back to make a scene on the floor of the ballroom, yes, I didn't stop at the cloakroom to pick up Aunt Violet's old mink stole, no, I rushed right into the ballroom and spotted him on the floor and ran up to him and beat him as hard as I could in the face and chest with my fists till—Cousin Sebastian took me away.— After that, the next morning, I started writing my diary in the third person, singular, such as "She's still living this morning," meaning that *I* was. . . . —"WHAT'S NEXT FOR HER? GOD KNOWS!"—I couldn't go out any more. —However one morning my Cousin Sebastian came in my bedroom and said: "Get up!"—Well . . . if you're still alive after dying, well then, you're obedient, Doctor.—I got up. He took me downtown to a place for passport photos. Said: "Mother can't go abroad with me this summer. You're going to go with me this summer instead of Mother."—If you don't believe me, read my journal of Paris!—"She woke up at daybreak this morning, had her coffee and dressed and took a brief walk—"

DOCTOR:
Who did?

CATHARINE:
She did. *I* did—from the Hotel Plaza Athénée to the Place de l'Étoile as if pursued by a pack of Siberian wolves! [*She laughs her tired, helpless laugh.*]—Went right through all stop signs—couldn't wait for green signals.—"Where did she think she was going? Back to the Duelling Oaks?"—Everything chilly and dim but his hot, ravenous mouth! on—

399

DOCTOR:
Miss Catharine, let me give you something.

[*The others go out, leaving Catharine and the Doctor onstage.*]

CATHARINE:
Do I have to have the injection again, this time? What am I going to be stuck with this time, Doctor? I don't care. I've been stuck so often that if you connected me with a garden hose I'd make a good sprinkler.

DOCTOR [*preparing needle*]:
Please take off your jacket.

[*She does. The Doctor gives her an injection.*]

CATHARINE:
I didn't feel it.

DOCTOR:
That's good. Now sit down.

[*She sits down.*]

CATHARINE:
Shall I start counting backwards from a hundred?

DOCTOR:
Do you like counting backwards?

CATHARINE:
Love it! Just love it! One hundred! Ninety-nine! Ninety-eight! Ninety-seven. Ninety-six. Ninety—five—. Oh!—I already feel it! How funny!

DOCTOR:
That's right. Close your eyes for a minute.

[*He moves his chair closer to hers. Half a minute passes.*]
Miss Catharine? I want you to give me something.

CATHARINE:
Name it and it's yours, Doctor Sugar.

DOCTOR:
Give me all your resistance.

CATHARINE:
Resistance to what?

DOCTOR:
The truth. Which you're going to tell me.

CATHARINE:
The truth's the one thing I have never resisted!

DOCTOR:
Sometimes people just think they don't resist it, but still do.

CATHARINE:
They say it's at the bottom of a bottomless well, you know.

DOCTOR:
Relax.

CATHARINE:
Truth.

DOCTOR:
Don't talk.

CATHARINE:
Where was I, now? At ninety?

DOCTOR:
You don't have to count backwards.

CATHARINE:
At ninety something?

DOCTOR:
You can open your eyes.

CATHARINE:
Oh, I do feel funny!

[*Silence, pause.*]

You know what I think you're doing? I think you're trying to hypnotize me. Aren't you? You're looking so straight at me and doing something to me with your eyes and your—eyes. . . . Is that what you're doing to me?

DOCTOR:
Is that what you *feel* I'm doing?

CATHARINE:
Yes! I feel so peculiar. And it's not just the drug.

DOCTOR:
Give me all your resistance. See. I'm holding my hand out. I want you to put yours in mine and give me all your resistance. Pass all of your resistance out of your hand to mine.

CATHARINE:
Here's my hand. But there's no resistance in it.

DOCTOR:
You are totally passive.

CATHARINE:
Yes, I am.

DOCTOR:
You will do what I ask.

CATHARINE:
Yes, I will try.

DOCTOR:
You will tell the true story.

CATHARINE:
Yes, I will.

DOCTOR:
The absolutely true story. No lies, nothing not spoken. Everything told, exactly.

402

CATHARINE:
Everything. Exactly. Because I'll have to. Can I—can I stand
up?

DOCTOR:
Yes, but be careful. You might feel a little bit dizzy.

[*She struggles to rise, then falls back.*]

CATHARINE:
I can't get up! Tell me to. Then I think I could do it.

DOCTOR:
Stand up.

[*She rises unsteadily.*]

CATHARINE:
How funny! Now I can! Oh, I do feel dizzy! Help me, I'm—

[*He rushes to support her.*]

—about to fall over. . . .

[*He holds her. She looks out vaguely toward the brilliant,
steaming garden. Looks back at him. Suddenly sways toward
him, against him.*]

DOCTOR:
You see, you lost your balance.

CATHARINE:
No, I didn't. I did what I wanted to do without you telling
me to.

[*She holds him tight against her.*]

Let me! Let! Let! Let me! Let me, let me, oh, let me. . . .

[*She crushes her mouth to his violently. He tries to dis-
engage himself. She presses her lips to his fiercely, clutching
his body against her. Her brother George enters.*]

403

Please hold me! I've been so lonely. It's lonelier than death, if I've gone mad, it's lonelier than death!

GEORGE [*shocked, disgusted*]:
Cathie!—you've got a hell of a nerve.

[*She falls back, panting, covers her face, runs a few paces and grabs the back of a chair. Mrs. Holly enters.*]

MRS. HOLLY:
What's the matter, George? Is Catharine ill?

GEORGE:
No.

DOCTOR:
Miss Catharine had an injection that made her a little unsteady.

MRS. HOLLY:
What did he say about Catharine?

[*Catharine has gone out into the dazzling jungle of the garden.*]

SISTER [*returning*]:
She's gone into the garden.

DOCTOR:
That's all right, she'll come back when I call her.

SISTER:
It may be all right for you. You're not responsible for her.

[*Mrs. Venable has re-entered.*]

MRS. VENABLE:
Call her now!

DOCTOR:
Miss Catharine! Come back.

[*To the Sister:*]

Bring her back, please, Sister!

[*Catharine enters quietly, a little unsteady.*]

Now, Miss Catharine, you're going to tell the true story.

CATHARINE:
Where do I start the story?

DOCTOR:
Wherever you think it started.

CATHARINE:
I think it started the day he was born in this house.

MRS. VENABLE:
Ha! You see!

GEORGE:
Cathie.

DOCTOR:
Let's start later than that. [*Pause.*] Shall we begin with last summer?

CATHARINE:
Oh. Last summer.

DOCTOR:
Yes. Last summer.

[*There is a long pause. The raucous sounds in the garden fade into a bird song which is clear and sweet. Mrs. Holly coughs. Mrs. Venable stirs impatiently. George crosses downstage to catch Catharine's eye as he lights a cigarette.*]

CATHARINE:
Could I—?

MRS. VENABLE:
Keep that boy away from her!

GEORGE:
She wants to smoke, Aunt Vi.

CATHARINE:
Something helps in the—hands. . . .

SISTER:
Unh unh!

DOCTOR:
It's all right, Sister. [*He lights her cigarette.*] About last summer: how did it begin?

CATHARINE:
It began with his kindness and the six days at sea that took me so far away from the—Duelling Oaks that I forgot them, nearly. He was affectionate with me, so sweet and attentive to me, that some people took us for a honeymoon couple until they noticed that we had—separate staterooms, and—then in Paris, he took me to Patou and Schiaparelli's—*this* is from Schiaparelli's! [*Like a child, she indicates her suit.*]—bought me so many new clothes that I gave away my old ones to make room for my new ones in my new luggage to—travel. . . . I turned into a peacock! Of course, so was *he* one, too. . . .

GEORGE:
Ha Ha!

MRS. VENABLE:
Shh!

CATHARINE:
But then I made the mistake of responding too much to his kindness, of taking hold of his hand before he'd take hold of mine, of holding onto his arm and leaning on his shoulder, of appreciating his kindness more than he wanted me to, and, suddenly, last summer, he began to be restless, and—oh!

DOCTOR:
Go on.

CATHARINE:
The Blue Jay notebook!

DOCTOR:
Did you say notebook?

MRS. VENABLE:
I know what she means by that, she's talking about the school composition book with a Blue Jay trademark that Sebastian used for making notes and revisions on his *Poem of Summer*. It went with him everywhere that he went, in his jacket pocket, even his dinner jacket. I have the one that he had with him last summer. *Foxhill! The Blue Jay notebook!*

[*Miss Foxhill rushes in with a gasp.*]

It came with his personal effects shipped back from Cabeza de Lobo.

DOCTOR:
I don't quite get the connection between new clothes and so forth and the Blue Jay notebook.

MRS. VENABLE:
I HAVE IT!—Doctor, tell her I've found it.

[*Miss Foxhill hears this as she comes back out of house: gasps with relief, retires.*]

DOCTOR:
With all these interruptions it's going to be awfully hard to—

MRS. VENABLE:
This is important. I don't know why she mentioned the Blue Jay notebook but I want you to see it. Here it is, here! [*She holds up a notebook and leafs swiftly through the pages.*] Title? *Poem of Summer,* and the date of the summer— 1935. After that: *what? Blank pages, blank pages,* nothing but *nothing!*—last summer. . . .

DOCTOR:
What's that got to do with—?

MRS. VENABLE:

His destruction? I'll tell you. A poet's vocation is something that rests on something as thin and fine as the web of a spider, Doctor. That's all that holds him *over*!—out of destruction. . . . Few, very few are able to do it alone! Great help is needed! I *did* give it! She *didn't*.

CATHARINE:

She's right about that. I failed him. I wasn't able to keep the web from—breaking. . . . I saw it breaking but couldn't save or—repair it!

MRS. VENABLE:

There now, the truth's coming out. We had an agreement between us, a sort of contract or covenant between us which he broke last summer when he broke away from me and took her with him, not me! When he was frightened and I knew when and what of, because his hands would shake and his eyes looked in, not out, I'd reach across a table and touch his hands and say not a word, just look, and touch his hands with my hand until his hands stopped shaking and his eyes looked out, not in, and in the morning, the poem would be continued. *Continued until it was finished!*

[*The following ten speeches are said very rapidly, over-lapping.*]

CATHARINE:

I—couldn't!

MRS. VENABLE:

Naturally not! He was *mine*! I *knew* how to help him, I *could*! You didn't, you couldn't!

DOCTOR:

These interruptions—

MRS. VENABLE:

I would say "You *will*" and he *would*, I—!

CATHARINE:
Yes, you see, I failed him! And so, last summer, we went to Cabeza de Lobo, we flew down there from where he gave up writing his poem last summer....

MRS. VENABLE:
Because he'd broken our—

CATHARINE:
Yes! Yes, something had broken, that string of pearls that old mothers hold their sons by like a—sort of a—sort of— *umbilical* cord, *long—after* ...

MRS. VENABLE:
She means that I held him back from—

DOCTOR:
Please!

MRS. VENABLE:
Destruction!

CATHARINE:
All I know is that suddenly, last summer, he wasn't young any more, and we went to Cabeza de Lobo, and he suddenly switched from the evenings to the beach. . . .

DOCTOR:
From evenings? To beach?

CATHARINE:
I mean from the evenings to the afternoons and from the fa—fash—

[*Silence*: *Mrs. Holly draws a long, long painful breath. George stirs impatiently.*]

DOCTOR:
Fashionable! Is that the word you—?

409

CATHARINE:
Yes. Suddenly, last summer Cousin Sebastian changed to the afternoons and the beach.

DOCTOR:
What beach?

CATHARINE:
In Cabeza de Lobo there is a beach that's named for Sebastian's name saint, it's known as La Playa San Sebastian, and that's where we started spending all afternoon, every day.

DOCTOR:
What kind of beach was it?

CATHARINE:
It was a big city beach near the harbor.

DOCTOR:
It was a big public beach?

CATHARINE:
Yes, public.

MRS. VENABLE:
It's little statements like that that give her away.

[*The Doctor rises and crosses to Mrs. Venable without breaking his concentration on Catharine.*]

After all I've told you about his fastidiousness, can you accept such a statement?

DOCTOR:
You mustn't interrupt her.

MRS. VENABLE [*overlapping him*]:
That Sebastian would go every day to some dirty free public beach near a harbor? A man that had to go out a mile in a boat to find water fit to swim in?

410

DOCTOR:

Mrs. Venable, no matter what she says you have to let her say it without any more interruptions or this interview will be useless.

MRS. VENABLE:

I won't speak again. I'll keep still, if it kills me.

CATHARINE:

I don't want to go on. . . .

DOCTOR:

Go on with the story. Every afternoon last summer your Cousin Sebastian and you went out to this free public beach?

CATHARINE:

No, it wasn't the free one, the free one was right next to it, there was a fence between the free beach and the one that we went to that charged a small charge of admission.

DOCTOR:

Yes, and what did you do there?

[*He still stands beside Mrs. Venable and the light gradually changes as the girl gets deeper into her story: the light concentrates on Catharine, the other figures sink into shadow.*]

Did anything happen there that disturbed you about it?

CATHARINE:

Yes!

DOCTOR:

What?

CATHARINE:

He bought me a swim-suit I didn't want to wear. I laughed. I said, "I can't wear that, it's a scandal to the jay birds!"

411

DOCTOR:
What did you mean by that? That the suit was immodest?

CATHARINE:
My God, yes! It was a one-piece suit made of white lisle, the water made it transparent! [*She laughs sadly at the memory of it.*] —I didn't want to swim in it, but he'd grab my hand and drag me into the water, all the way in, and I'd come out looking naked!

DOCTOR:
Why did he do that? Did you understand why?

CATHARINE:
—Yes! To attract!—Attention.

DOCTOR:
He wanted you to attract attention, did he, because he felt you were moody? Lonely? He wanted to shock you out of your depression last summer?

CATHARINE:
Don't you understand? I was PROCURING for him!

[*Mrs. Venable's gasp is like the sound that a great hooked fish might make.*]

She used to do it, *too.*

[*Mrs. Venable cries out.*]

Not consciously! She didn't *know* that she was procuring for him in the smart, the fashionable places they used to go to before last summer! Sebastian was shy with people. She wasn't. Neither was I. We both did the same thing for him, made contacts for him, but she did it in nice places and in decent ways and I had to do it the way that I just told you! —Sebastian was lonely, Doctor, and the empty Blue Jay notebook got bigger and bigger, so big it was big and empty as

that big empty blue sea and sky. . . . I knew what I was doing.
I came out in the French Quarter years before I came out in
the Garden District. . . .

MRS. HOLLY:
Oh, Cathie! Sister . . .

DOCTOR:
Hush!

CATHARINE:
And before long, when the weather got warmer and the beach
so crowded, he didn't need me any more for that purpose. The
ones on the free beach began to climb over the fence or swim
around it, bands of homeless young people that lived on the
free beach like scavenger dogs, hungry children. . . . So now
he let me wear a decent dark suit. I'd go to a faraway empty
end of the beach, write postcards and letters and keep up my—
third-person journal till it was—five o'clock and time to meet
him outside the bathhouses, on the street. . . . He would come
out, *followed.*

DOCTOR:
Who would follow him out?

CATHARINE:
The homeless, hungry young people that had climbed over
the fence from the free beach that they lived on. He'd pass out
tips among them as if they'd all—shined his shoes or called
taxis for him. . . . Each day the crowd was bigger, noisier,
greedier!—Sebastian began to be frightened.—At last we
stopped going out there. . . .

DOCTOR:
And then? After that? After you quit going out to the public
beach?

CATHARINE:
Then one day, a few days after we stopped going out to the

413

beach—it was one of those white blazing days in Cabeza de Lobo, not a blazing hot *blue* one but a blazing hot *white* one.

DOCTOR:

Yes?

CATHARINE:

We had a late lunch at one of those open-air restaurants on the sea there.—Sebastian was white as the weather. He had on a spotless white silk Shantung suit and a white silk tie and a white panama and white shoes, white—white lizard skin—pumps! He—[*She throws back her head in a startled laugh at the recollection.*]—kept touching his face and his throat here and there with a white silk handkerchief and popping little white pills in his mouth, and I knew he was having a bad time with his heart and was frightened about it and that was the reason we hadn't gone out to the beach. . . .

[*During the monologue the lights have changed, the surrounding area has dimmed out and a hot white spot is focused on Catharine.*]

"I think we ought to go north," he kept saying, "I think we've done Cabeza de Lobo, I think we've done it, don't you?" *I* thought we'd done it!—but I had learned it was better not to seem to have an opinion because if I did, well, Sebastian, well, you know Sebastian, he always preferred to do what no one else wanted to do, and I always tried to give the impression that I was agreeing reluctantly to his wishes . . . it was a—game. . . .

SISTER:

She's dropped her cigarette.

DOCTOR:

I've got it, Sister.

[*There are whispers, various movements in the penumbra. The Doctor fills a glass for her from the cocktail shaker.*]

CATHARINE:

Where was I? Oh, yes, that five o'clock lunch at one of those fish places along the harbor of Cabeza de Lobo, it was between the city and the sea, and there were naked children along the beach which was fenced off with barbed wire from the restaurant and we had our table less than a yard from the barbed wire fence that held the beggars at bay. . . . There were naked children along the beach, a band of frightfully thin and dark naked children that looked like a flock of plucked birds, and they would come darting up to the barbed wire fence as if blown there by the wind, the hot white wind from the sea, all crying out, *"Pan, pan, pan!"*

DOCTOR [*quietly*]:
What's *pan?*

CATHARINE:

The word for bread, and they made gobbling noises with their little black mouths, stuffing their little black fists to their mouths and making those gobbling noises, with frightful grins!—Of course we were sorry that we had come to this place but it was too late to go. . . .

DOCTOR [*quietly*]:
Why was it "too late to go"?

CATHARINE:

I told you Cousin Sebastian wasn't well. He was popping those little white pills in his mouth. I think he had popped in so many of them that they had made him feel weak. . . . His, his!—eyes looked—dazed, but he said: "Don't look at those little monsters. Beggars are a social disease in this country. If you look at them, you get sick of the country, it spoils the whole country for you. . . ."

DOCTOR:
Go on.

415

CATHARINE:
I'm going on. I have to wait now and then till it gets clearer. Under the drug it has to be a vision, or nothing comes. . . .

DOCTOR:
All right?

CATHARINE:
Always when I was with him I did what he told me. I didn't look at the band of naked children, not even when the waiters drove them away from the barbed wire fence with sticks!— Rushing out through a wicket gate like an assault party in war!—and beating them screaming away from the barbed wire fence with the sticks. . . . Then! [*Pause.*]

DOCTOR:
Go on, Miss Catherine, what comes next in the vision?

CATHARINE:
The, the the!—band of children began to—serenade us. . . .

DOCTOR:
Do what?

CATHARINE:
Play for us! On instruments! Make music!—if you could call it music. . . .

DOCTOR:
Oh?

CATHARINE:
Their, their—instruments were—instruments of percussion!— Do you know what I mean?

DOCTOR [*making a note*]:
Yes. Instruments of percussion such as—*drums?*

CATHARINE:
I stole glances at them when Cousin Sebastian wasn't looking,

and as well as I could make out in the white blaze of the
sand-beach, the instruments were tin cans strung together.

DOCTOR [*slowly, writing*]:
Tin—cans—strung—together.

CATHARINE:
And, and, and, and—and!—bits of metal, other bits of metal
that had been flattened out, made into—

DOCTOR:
What?

CATHARINE:
Cymbals! You know? *Cymbals?*

DOCTOR:
Yes. Brass plates hit together.

CATHARINE:
That's right, Doctor.—Tin cans flattened out and clashed
together!—Cymbals. . . .

DOCTOR:
Yes. I understand. What's after that, in the vision?

CATHARINE [*rapidly, panting a little*]:
And others had paper bags, bags made out of—coarse paper!
—with something on a string inside the bags which they
pulled up and down, back and forth, to make a sort of a—

DOCTOR:
Sort of a—?

CATHARINE:
Noise like—

DOCTOR:
Noise like?

CATHARINE [*rising stiffly from chair*]:
Ooompa! Oompa! Oooooompa!

417

DOCTOR:
Ahhh . . . a sound like a *tuba?*

CATHARINE:
That's right!—they made a sound like a tuba. . . .

DOCTOR:
Oompa, oompa, oompa, like a tuba.

[*He is making a note of the description.*]

CATHARINE:
Oompa, oompa, oompa, like a—

[*Short pause.*]

DOCTOR:
—Tuba. . . .

CATHARINE:
All during lunch they stayed at a—a fairly *close—distance*. . . .

DOCTOR:
Go on with the vision, Miss Catharine.

CATHARINE [*striding about the table*]:
Oh, I'm going on, nothing could stop it now!!

DOCTOR:
Your Cousin Sebastian was *entertained* by this—*concert?*

CATHARINE:
I think he was *terrified* of it!

DOCTOR:
Why was he terrified of it?

CATHARINE:
I think he recognized some of the musicians, some of the boys, between childhood and—older. . . .

DOCTOR:
What did he do? Did he do anything about it, Miss Catharine? —Did he complain to the manager about it?

CATHARINE:

What manager? *God*? Oh, *no!*—The manager of the fish place on the beach? Haha!—No!—You don't understand my cousin!

DOCTOR:

What do you mean?

CATHARINE:

He!—*accepted!*—*all!*—as—how!—things!—are!—And thought nobody had any right to complain or interfere in any way whatsoever, and even though he knew that what was awful was awful, that what was wrong was wrong, and my Cousin Sebastian was certainly never sure that anything was wrong!—He thought it unfitting to ever take any action about anything whatsoever!—except to go on doing as something in him directed. . . .

DOCTOR:

What did something in him direct him to do?—I mean on this occasion in Cabeza de Lobo.

CATHARINE:

After the salad, before they brought the coffee, he suddenly pushed himself away from the table, and said, "They've got to stop that! Waiter, make them stop that. I'm not a well man, I have a heart condition, it's making me sick!"—This was the first time that Cousin Sebastian had ever attempted to correct a human situation!—I think perhaps that *that* was his—fatal error. . . . It was then that the waiters, all eight or ten of them, charged out of the barbed wire wicket gate and beat the little musicians away with clubs and skillets and anything hard that they could snatch from the kitchen!—Cousin Sebastian left the table. He stalked out of the restaurant after throwing a handful of paper money on the table and he fled from the place. I followed. It was all white outside. White hot, a blazing white hot, hot blazing white, at five o'clock in the afternoon in the city of—Cabeza de Lobo. It looked as if—

DOCTOR:
It looked as if?

CATHARINE:
As if a huge white bone had caught on fire in the sky and blazed so bright it was white and turned the sky and everything under the sky white with it!

DOCTOR:
—White . . .

CATHARINE:
Yes—white . . .

DOCTOR:
You followed your Cousin Sebastian out of the restaurant onto the hot white street?

CATHARINE:
Running up and down hill. . . .

DOCTOR:
You ran up and down hill?

CATHARINE:
No, no! *Didn't*!—move either *way*!—at first, we were—

[*During this recitation there are various sound effects. The percussive sounds described are very softly employed.*]

I rarely made any suggestion but *this* time I *did*. . . .

DOCTOR:
What did you suggest?

CATHARINE:
Cousin Sebastian seemed to be paralyzed near the entrance of the café, so I said, "Let's go." I remember that it was a very wide and steep white street, and I said, "Cousin Sebastian,

420

down that way is the waterfront and we are more likely to find a taxi near there. . . . Or why don't we go back in?—and have them *call* us a taxi! Oh, let's do! Let's do *that,* that's better!" And he said, "*Mad,* are you *mad*? Go back in that filthy place? Never! That gang of kids shouted vile things about me to the waiters!" "Oh," I said, "then let's go down toward the docks, down there at the bottom of the hill, let's not try to climb the hill in this dreadful heat." And Cousin Sebastian shouted, "Please shut up, let me handle this situation, will you? I want to handle this thing." And he started up the steep street with a hand stuck in his jacket where I knew he was having a pain in his chest from his palpitations. . . . But he walked faster and faster, in panic, but the faster he walked the louder and closer it got!

DOCTOR:
What got louder?

CATHARINE:
The music.

DOCTOR:
The music again.

CATHARINE:
The oompa-oompa of the—following band.—They'd somehow gotten through the barbed wire and out on the street, and they were following, following!—up the blazing white street. The band of naked children pursued us up the steep white street in the sun that was like a great white bone of a giant beast that had caught on fire in the sky!—Sebastian started to run and they all screamed at once and seemed to fly in the air, they outran him so quickly. I screamed. I heard Sebastian scream, he screamed just once before this flock of black plucked little birds that pursued him and overtook him halfway up the white hill.

421

DOCTOR:
And you, Miss Catharine, what did *you* do, then?

CATHARINE:
Ran!

DOCTOR:
Ran where?

CATHARINE:
Down! Oh, I ran down, the easier direction to run was down, down, down, down!—The hot, white, blazing street, screaming out "Help" all the way, till—

DOCTOR:
What?

CATHARINE:
—Waiters, police, and others—ran out of buildings and rushed back up the hill with me. When we got back to where my Cousin Sebastian had disappeared in the flock of featherless little black sparrows, he—he was lying naked as they had been naked against a white wall, and this you won't believe, nobody *has* believed it, nobody *could* believe it, nobody, nobody on earth could possibly believe it, and I don't *blame* them!—They had *devoured* parts of him.

[*Mrs. Venable cries out softly.*]

Torn or cut parts of him away with their hands or knives or maybe those jagged tin cans they made music with, they had torn bits of him away and stuffed them into those gobbling fierce little empty black mouths of theirs. There wasn't a sound any more, there was nothing to see but Sebastian, what was left of him, that looked like a big white-paper-wrapped bunch of red roses had been *torn, thrown, crushed!*—against that blazing white wall. . . .

[*Mrs. Venable springs with amazing power from her wheel-*

chair, stumbles erratically but swiftly toward the girl and tries to strike her with her cane. The Doctor snatches it from her and catches her as she is about to fall. She gasps hoarsely several times as he leads her toward the exit.]

MRS. VENABLE [*offstage*]:
Lion's View! State asylum, cut this hideous story out of her brain!

[*Mrs. Holly sobs and crosses to George, who turns away from her, saying:*]

GEORGE:
Mom, I'll quit school, I'll get a job, I'll—

MRS. HOLLY:
Hush son! Doctor, can't you say something?

[*Pause. The Doctor comes downstage. Catharine wanders out into the garden followed by the Sister.*]

DOCTOR [*after a while, reflectively, into space*]:
I think we ought at least to consider the possibility that the girl's story could be true. . . .

THE END

Centerville Library
Washington-Centerville Public Library
DISCARD
Centerville, Ohio